Waving at Strangers:

A Parade of *Inland Valley Daily Bulletin* Columns, 2006-2010

•

David Allen
Inland Valley Daily Bulletin columnist

Waving at Strangers: A parade of Inland Valley Daily Bulletin Columns, 2006-2010 by David Allen
978-1-949790-96-2   Paperback
978-1-949790-97-9   Ebook

The columns in this book first appeared in the *Inland Valley Daily Bulletin* January 2006—December 2010 and are used with permission of the Inland Valley Daily Bulletin. All rights are retained by the Inland Valley Daily Bulletin.

Book design by Mark Givens
Front cover photo by Marc Campos

First Pelekinesis Printing 2024
For information:
Pelekinesis 112 Harvard Ave #65, Claremont, CA 91711 USA

Library of Congress Cataloging-in-Publication Data

Names: Allen, David, 1964- author.
Title: Waving at strangers : a parade of Inland Valley Daily Bulletin columns, 2006-2010 / David Allen, Inland Valley Daily Bulletin columnist.
Description: Claremont : Pelekinesis, 2024. | Summary: "Humorous and local-interest newspaper columns from the Inland Valley Daily Bulletin (Ontario, Calif.) written by David Allen and published from 2006 to 2010. Topics include Shakey's Pizza, public transportation, Tower Records, The O.C., Gumby, Miller's Outpost, being the Grand Marshal of the parade. Cities cited include Rancho Cucamonga, Claremont, Pomona, Montclair, and Ontario"-- Provided by publisher.
Identifiers: LCCN 2024036553 | ISBN 9781949790962 (paperback)
Subjects: LCSH: Inland Empire (Calif.)--History. | Ontario (Calif.)--History.
Classification: LCC F868.I57 A44 2024 | DDC 979.4/99--dc23/eng/20240821
LC record available at https://lccn.loc.gov/2024036553

www.pelekinesis.com

Waving at Strangers

David Allen

Contents

Foreword
    Wendy Leung 13
Introduction
    David Allen 17
Our local icons don't take things for granite
    January 1, 2006 25
Ontario's beauty college was just to dye for
    January 11, 2006 29
End of the line for two much-loved local fixtures
    January 20, 2006 33
Loch Ness monster branches out in Rancho
    April 23, 2006 37
45 years? Shakey's in Montclair must have good mojo
    June 16, 2006 39
Please don't hiss ode to cassettes
    July 2, 2006 43
Invitation from AARP ages him prematurely
    July 16, 2006 47
Drinking increases clarity, or vice versa
    July 19, 2006 51
Race for 11:15 train didn't derail his plans
    September 15, 2006 55
Late-night riders get 15 minutes of fame, er, train
    October 4, 2006 59
Trip to lab turns into a free ride
    October 22, 2006 61
Changed number leaves him hung up
    November 5, 2006 65

Loss of childhood numbers leaves them disconnected
   November 24, 2006 69
Tower Records' demise is this columnist's gain
   December 27, 2006 73
Nudity, guns and hexes: '06 was gold
   December 31, 2006 77

   2006 Items 81

◇

Apparently the I.E. is worthy of literature
   January 14, 2007 95
Rancho Cucamonga sea monster's fate prompts a sinking feeling
   January 17, 2007 99
The end of 'The O.C.' leaves dry eyes in Chino
   February 21, 2007 101
Phone exchanges brought Yukon to Upland
   March 4, 2007 105
Looking back on 10 years of changes
   March 11, 2007 109
Pomona's odd combo makes N.Y. Times news
   April 13, 2007 113
Series cast spell on Potter fan
   July 18, 2007 117
Ontario cemetery holds 51,000 stories
   September 2, 2007 121
Journalist knows, 'They like me!'
   September 23, 2007 125
Phony war hero shoots himself in foot
   October 7, 2007 129

Much-loved movie matinee
	October 14, 2007 133
Ghost clusters? Pomona spirit search is a Fox hunt
	October 31, 2007 137
City's parade grows, and grows older, too
	November 30, 2007 143
Not a gag after all: This columnist leads parade
	December 2, 2007 147
'07's strange news stories
	December 28, 2007 151

	2007 Items 155

◇

Prize-winning clutter
	February 1, 2008 165
Psychic sees all ... maybe
	February 10, 2008 169
Mapping 50 years of change
	February 17, 2008 173
A whale of a tale
	April 6, 2008 177
Regis misses letters
	April 13, 2008 181
RFK's rally was the place to be
	May 18, 2008 185
Another side of Bob Dylan
	May 25, 2008 191
Wealth at his fingertips!
	June 18, 2008 195
It's now lonelier in L.A.
	August 20, 2008 199
'34 drive was quite a journey
	August 31, 2008 203

Cheesy fun at pasta dinner
    September 28, 2008 207
Parade's death leaves confetti on his hands
    November 21, 2008 211
Meter still runs on Waits story
    December 7, 2008 213
Counting down 08's strangest news
    December 28, 2008 217
Stone-cold sobering chatter
    December 31, 2008 221

    2008 items 227

◇

The 144-item menu bowls him over
    January 2, 2009 235
For music fans, Virgin sacrifice was heaven-sent
    January 11, 2009 239
An afternoon at the opera
    March 11, 2009 243
Crowd in Pomona shows a lot of (heart) for Obama
    March 20, 2009 247
Taking measure of the Big Apple
    May 27, 2009 251
Silence wasn't golden for Claremont's champ talker
    July 3, 2009 255
Exploring moon mission excitement
    July 19, 2009 259
'This Film' puts area P.I. under magnifying glass
    August 28, 2009 263
Breaking up is hard to do, even with a magazine
    September 13, 2009 269
Cucamonga justice at $100 a month
    October 18, 2009 273

A night on the (very dull) town in Ontario
    November 1, 2009 277
Kidney stone leads to a display of true grit
    November 11, 2009 281
Parade, and former grand marshal, return
    December 9, 2009 285
Smiles were their umbrellas in parade
    December 16, 2009 287
The year's Top 10 strangest stories
    December 30, 2009 291
    2009 items 295

◇

Gumby creator shaped childhoods
    January 13, 2010 303
Is pageant's return welcome? You be the judge
    January 27, 2010 305
Fresh talk from the strawberry Donut Man
    April 18, 2010 309
Soup Nazi? No, more like Soup Niceguy
    May 12, 2010 315
Positively feverish about getting back to work
    June 18, 2010 321
'Jaws' movie loomed large in 1970s childhoods
    June 20, 2010 325
Mystery woman goes back to the past
    July 7, 2010 331
With bridge gone, one fewer kick on Route 66
    July 28, 2010 335
RC bridge lore: Less than meets the eye
    September 3, 2010 341

One man with two lives and many friends
    August 27, 2010 343
It was headier than dandelion wine
    October 13, 2010 349
Surplus of memories follow passing of Miller's Outpost founder
    October 31, 2010 355
Police say scams against the elderly are age-old
    November 3, 2010 359
Men needing trim won't get Smart
    December 12, 2010 365
At Roberta's, you're always in with the Inn crowd
    December 29, 2010 369
Counting down 2010's strangest news stories
    December 31, 2010 375

  2010 items 379

◇

About David Allen..391

This book is dedicated to newspaper readers new and old.
OK, mostly old.

Foreword

Wendy Leung

Why would statues talk? I don't get it. And even if they could, why would they talk to Jack Benny and William Shakespeare?

Those are the questions you might ask while reading David Allen. The thing is, you don't have to get it to look forward to reading him three times a week.

Who would totally get it anyways? You'd have to be a teetotaling, train-loving history buff who weeps at the sight of a mom-and-pop store closing.

The only prerequisite is an appreciation of the absurd.

Take his piece on the piece of wood. Consider the sheer silliness of the premise, then consider the idea and the execution.

There goes David, driving along Haven Avenue to eat lunch at some diner destined to close, and lo and behold there's a log in a field, and he thinks, "Now that's the kind of fodder that will land me a book deal!"

He pulls over to interview some busy chemists and introduces himself with, "I'm a writer who got into journalism because I wanted to speak truth to power and comfort the afflicted and, say, does that piece of wood over yonder resemble a mythical creature to you?"

Needless to say, he got multiple columns out of it.

It's silly, almost embarrassingly so, and perhaps that's just the kind of thing we needed to wade through the morass of the aughts.

As the Rancho Cucamonga reporter for the *Inland Valley Daily Bulletin* during this time, I had a front row seat to some of these columns. The whack-whack-whack sound of sifting through Virgin Megastore CDs? I heard it. Ordering Mix Bowl's instant coffee? Guilty.

You can't take yourself too seriously in this line of work. Without humor, journalists can get consumed by the heaviness, sadness and extra-ness of news. And the headlines were particularly newsy.

With so many foreclosures and job losses, it felt like we were in the epicenter of the Great Recession. War heroes were coming back from Iraq injured, or worse, in body bags. Michael Jackson and Farrah Fawcett died on the same day.

We didn't know it at the time (or we did but were too heartbroken to admit it) but readers were shifting away from print. New readers were finding David Allen on Facebook or reading him on a first-generation iPhone.

This change, coupled with a halted economy, meant pay cuts, furloughs and layoffs at a time when there was so much news to cover.

For those who remained in the shrinking newsroom, it was still exciting. Editors stood on desks, reporters slammed phones. Pens, paper planes and insults flew through the air. We were muckrakers at the dawn of Twitter. It was magical. Almost as magical as a Euclid Avenue klatch among statues.

Wendy Leung
Inland Valley Daily Bulletin reporter 2005-2012

Introduction

David Allen

Welcome to *Waving at Strangers*, the third chronological collection of my *Inland Valley Daily Bulletin* columns.

First came *Getting Started*, which collected the best from 1997 to 2000, and then *On Track*, which did the same for 2001 to 2005. The book you're holding in your hands rounds up the cream of 2006 to 2010.

That period has already slipped into history, hasn't it? As we put the finishing touches on this book in August 2024, the oldest of these columns is nearly two decades old.

That wasn't how this was supposed to go, but here we are. Let me explain.

After *On Track* was published in 2017, and the promotional events began to abate in 2018, I tasked myself with reading the next five years' worth of columns as time allowed. Along the way I noted which ones had legs, i.e., might be worth reprinting, and which ones had two left feet.

Bear in mind that with me cranking out about 150 columns per year for the newspaper, and five years seeming like a reasonable time period to cover in a book, this meant rereading 750 columns. As 750 columns totaled about 600,000 words, this was the equivalent of reading *Moby-Dick* (209,000 words) three times, only far less rewarding. (My column about reading *Moby-Dick* is reprinted here, by the way.)

Then came the culling. *Waving at Strangers*, like *On Track*, would reprint only 10 percent of all those columns: 15 per year, for 75 columns in all. That would involve a lot of decisions, especially difficult for a wishy-washy person like myself.

It took a year or more, but I managed to read every column from 2006 through 2010 and log the ones that had potential. Winnowing those to a very short list was still ahead of me. It was early in the year, though, and publisher Mark Givens and I planned to go to press that fall.

Unfortunately, the year in question was 2020. Life ground to a halt in mid-March. Thankfully I was still employed, but I was scrambling to fill column space during a shutdown.

In late spring, Mark and I had a conversation about the book. We quickly agreed to let the book go for now. Neither of us felt motivated right then.

Can you blame us? Yes, these books are sold on Amazon. But probably 95 percent of the sales are done by me at events and speaking engagements, in which I hand-sell copies one at a time.

During the pandemic, with no in-person events taking place, we would have put a book out into the world with virtually no means to get it into anyone's hands. What was the point of proceeding under those circumstances? Besides, we had more pressing concerns, such as not dying.

The first half of 2021 wasn't much better. But that fall, we started work on a completely different book.

100 Years of the Los Angeles County Fair, 25 Years of Stories would collect everything I'd written to date about the fair, timed to coincide with its 100th anniversary the following May.

It was a fun project. Conception to production to publication was done at a brisk pace, under six months. It helped that there were few choices to make about the material: We just included everything and it came out to the right length for a book.

To make a music comparison, *100 Years* was akin to a band setting aside a complicated album project and instead recording an entirely different record live in the studio and rush-releasing it, just for the energy and spontaneity.

(To avoid leaving anyone hanging, *100 Years* was my second Pomona book, after *Pomona A to Z*. There, now all four of my previous books have been cited in this introduction. As my offspring, they must all get equal treatment.)

With *100 Years* out in the world, it was time to get back to this next chronological collection.

On Labor Day weekend, 2023, in Moby's Coffee in North Hollywood while housesitting for a friend, I sat down with my thick folder of columns from 2006 to start over.

I had all my notes from five years earlier with a long list of columns from each year for consideration. But it had been so long since I'd read them, my memory had faded. Better to start from scratch, and with my 2023 sensibility, rather than my 2018 sensibility.

So I started reading from January 1, 2006 all over again and taking fresh notes.

A lot had happened to me since 2018, by the way.

The national decline of newspapers had accelerated, with advertising dollars drying up, newsroom staffs shrinking as a consequence and readers giving up (or dying off). This trend didn't spare the *Daily Bulletin*, which covers eastern Los Angeles County and western San Bernardino County, or other newspapers owned by the Southern California News Group.

In July 2019, the *Bulletin* and the *Sun*, which covers San Bernardino County, combined staffs and effectively merged. This meant my columns were now running in a second newspaper, one to the east.

In July 2020, the two papers and their staffs essentially combined with the *Press-Enterprise*, which covers Riverside County. This became a third paper carrying my column in its news section. And a fourth, the *Redlands Daily Facts*, gradually began incorporating my column too.

My columns were now appearing regularly all over the Inland Empire, as well as at times in our three San Gabriel Valley newspapers. I couldn't continue writing exclusively about Rancho Cucamonga, Upland, Pomona and the *Bulletin*'s other cities. I had to get to know San Bernardino, Riverside, Redlands and other communities too.

These changes really upended my whole routine. It was overwhelming. Figuring out how to make it work was also an unexpected midlife challenge, and kind of fun.

Well, that's neither here nor there for a book of columns from 2006 to 2010, but I share the story to explain why 2020 and 2021 were extra stressful, and also to contrast this period with the one you'll be reading about in the coming pages.

By 2006, I'd been a full-time *Bulletin* columnist for five years, and a semi-regular columnist for nine. I was finding my footing, gaining traction and becoming known. My approach was to report most of these columns, going out in the field to find stories – very literally in the case of a log in a weed patch that resembled the Loch Ness Monster.

We still had a relatively large staff of reporters from 2006 to 2010. If I went to a city council or school board meeting, it was a near-certainty that one of my colleagues would be there to do the heavy lifting of reporting the serious news. I could concentrate on the byplay, the wacky stuff, the subtext, the analysis.

I went to a lot of council meetings in this period: regularly in Ontario and Pomona, where I might have had a better attendance record than a few of the elected officials, and frequently in Rancho Cucamonga.

While my usual mode in this period was irreverence, not all my columns were written that way. If a longtime business closed, for instance, I would try to tell that story with tenderness as well as humor. As columnist, I saw my role as bearing witness, as serving as a public memory-keeper.

One column early in this book was a deliberate attempt to expand my range. In writing about Richard's Beauty College, an Ontario institution, I began by quoting from Ernest Hemingway's account of visiting a barber college for a bargain shave by students whose hands could not necessarily be trusted to be steady.

A reporter colleague remarked that that column seemed different to him, in a good way. I was pleased to hear it. After that successful experiment, I felt free to write in a more literary way if I chose, referencing authors or other aspects of culture without feeling the need to apologize for it.

A column in a similar vein was about Bellevue Memorial Cemetery's longtime manager, who was retiring. A writer isn't going to find many subjects larger than death. I was respectful, and a little awed – which made my choice of ending unexpected.

That was the result of a new influence, the late *Los Angeles Times* columnist Jack Smith, whose work I discovered via his collection *Jack Smith's L.A.* and immediately fell in love with. He was a master of, among other things, ending with a line that came out of nowhere and yet seemed inevitable.

I also felt freer to tell a story whatever way seemed best. In writing about the visit by Robert F. Kennedy to Pomona and Ontario 40 years earlier, I was mostly serious and ended on a poignant note. But if a story was light-hearted, like my account of a pasta dinner in Rancho Cucamonga, that's the treatment it got.

Before, I had at times tried too hard to be amusing. Starting in 2006, I set out to expand my range of subjects and to allow for a more varied emotional tone.

One major thing that happened during this period was that I was asked to be grand marshal of the Pomona Christmas Parade.

That invitation led to multiple columns and items, including a capsule history of the parade and a first-person account of riding in it. The next year, the parade was canceled, inspiring another column. The year after that, the parade was resurrected and moved downtown, where it remains today. That sparked a column too.

During this period I had some great colleagues, a wave of young reporters who started in the middle of the decade. We were a tight-knit group. They're mostly out of journalism now, but some of us remain close and know we'll be friends for life.

Wendy Leung leads the pack. She covered Rancho Cucamonga with care and humor. We shared many lunches, dinners and council meetings as well as serving as sounding boards for each other. She's quoted by name in a couple of these columns and about half the references to an unnamed "newsroom colleague" are to her.

Back to Labor Day 2023. Opening the manila folder with my pre-pandemic notes for this book, I was surprised to see, on top, a note on which I'd written the projected title *Waving at Strangers: A Parade of Daily Bulletin Columns, 2006-2010* and "Foreword by Wendy Leung." Apparently that had all come to me in a flash of inspiration in 2019. I'd forgotten the whole thing, but I liked it.

It took almost seven months to reread these five years of columns. Then came the painful process of choosing the columns, plus short items, that would appear here. My guiding principle was to include my absolute favorites, with the remainder made up of columns that seemed of general interest.

Those choices were sometimes by whim. But the idea was to choose a representative range of columns I liked that I hoped you'd like too.

All told, *Waving at Strangers* took a full year to produce, from Labor Day 2023 until roughly Labor Day 2024. Before that were the 12 or 18 months of abortive efforts that began in 2018.

As Huck Finn put it at the end of *The Adventures of Huckleberry Finn*: "…if I'd a knowed what a trouble it was to make a book I wouldn't a tackled it."

This book has been a long time coming, but I'm glad it's here. And now, let me wave farewell and let you get on with the book.

Our local icons don't take things for granite

January 1, 2006

As we awake to a new year, so, perhaps, do the embodiments of our local cities: their statuary. Let's listen in.

GEORGE CHAFFEY: O, what a beautiful moooorning! O, what a beautiful daaaay!

MADONNA OF THE TRAIL: George, could you hold it down? This pioneer woman had a rough night.

GEORGE: You lived it up on New Year's Eve, eh, Maddy?

MADONNA: Hardly. My two children kept me up all night. They won't leave a body alone. Why, I can't get away from them for a second.

GEORGE: No wonder – you're all on the same pedestal.

MADONNA: Isn't it time they moved away from home? Anyway, here's to your first New Year's on Euclid Avenue, George. You look so nice there outside City Hall. My poor tired eyes can just about see you from here at Euclid and Foothill.

GEORGE: It's good to be here, Jay – er, Maddy. I plotted Euclid back in the 1880s, when this land was nothing but dirt. That's why I'm holding these surveying tools, you know.

MADONNA: Quite a job you did, George. Why, I never get

tired of looking at this lovely street. Which is a good thing, since I can't turn my head.

GEORGE: You've been there since 1929, I understand, so you've certainly seen Upland change.

MADONNA: 2006 will be Upland's 100th anniversary as a city. Should be quite a year. La Verne will also turn 100 and Montclair will hit 50. I don't believe either of them has a statue, but La Verne does have a replica of the Liberty Bell.

LIBERTY BELL: Clang clang!

GODDESS POMONA: Is this a private party, or can a poor Roman goddess join in?

MADONNA: Bless my soul, it's Pomona! Happy New Year!

GODDESS: Thank you, dear. Who's your handsome friend?

MADONNA: This is George Chaffey. George, this is Pomona. She's in a glass case in the Pomona Public Library.

GEORGE: Pleased to meet you, ma'am.

GODDESS: Charmed, I'm sure. Here, have a grape from my laurel. I'm the goddess of fruit, you know.

GEORGE: These are quite, um, crunchy.

GODDESS: Like them? They're made of marble.

MADONNA: You must be snug as a bug in a rug inside the library. Land o' goshen, George and I are out here in all kinds of weather. How is Pomona, Pomona?

GODDESS: Oh, we can't complain. It's seen good times and bad since I arrived in 1889 – I was carved in Italy, you know – but 2006 looks to be a good year.

MADONNA: I haven't seen Pomona in years.

GODDESS: You're not a snob, are you, dear?

MADONNA: No, I'm just immobile.

GEORGE: Perhaps I'll, ahem, pay you a visit sometime, Miss Pomona.

GODDESS: Bring your sextant, big boy. Mrr-row.

MADONNA: Ugh. Get a room, you two!

INNKEEPER: There's no room at the inn. I already said so to that young couple: a husband and a pregnant woman on a donkey.

MADONNA: Oh, hello, Innkeeper! I forgot you and your friends were in Ontario this season. How are Euclid's Nativity scenes?

INNKEEPER: Somebody carted off the adult Jesus. We assumed he'd return in three days — sorry, a little Easter humor — but no such luck. Other than that, downtown is sweet paradise. Bear in mind I'm in storage 10 months out of the year.

JACK BENNY: Oh, Don! Oh, Mary! Oh – hi everyone.

GODDESS: Jack! I didn't see you standing there at Epicenter Stadium. What's new in Rancho Cucamonga?

JACK: Homes, homes, everywhere you look. Not that I could afford one. I have to get money from my vault just to buy a hot dog at Victoria Gardens.

GEORGE: I haven't seen your Gardens. How are they irrigated?

JACK: C'mon out, all of you. I'll give you the grand tour, no expense spared. Bring a sack lunch.

GODDESS: Good old Jack Benny, Mr. Generosity.

MADONNA: You're looking well, Jack. In fact, you don't look a day over 39.

JACK: Thank you, ladies. Hey, it's New Year's Day, and I feel like celebrating! How 'bout I play a tune on my violin?

EVERYONE: NO!

LIBERTY: Clang!

Ontario's Beauty College Was Just to Dye For

January 11, 2006

As a young journalist for the *Toronto Star*, Ernest Hemingway wrote a witty feature (reprinted in *By–Line: Ernest Hemingway*) about a visit to a barber college for a cut-rate trim and shave. The future big-game hunter escaped injury, despite visions of doom as a straight razor was drawn toward his neck by an eager amateur.

I often thought of Hemingway's piece when I passed by Richards Beauty College. Housed in a former bank building at Euclid Avenue and B Street in downtown Ontario, the beauty school with its vintage sign and quaint name was a remnant of a bygone era.

The school closed October 29 and moved to Upland under a new name – more on that in a minute – to make way for Ontario's grand downtown makeover. It's a makeover beyond the skills of beauticians-in-training, I'm afraid.

The passing of Richards Beauty College is worth noting in print, especially after I learned its history.

Richards began in 1961 and has had just two owners: founder Richard Gross and, now, his son, Bob Gross.

Two questions come to mind:

- A family named Gross owns a beauty school?
- If the owner was Richard, not Richards, why wasn't there an apostrophe on the signs for Richards Beauty College?

The latter seems to have been an error no one ever got around to correcting; the former is unfortunate, but what can you do?

Richard, who is alive and well, retired and passed the business along to Bob in 1991.

The younger Gross had hoped to stay in downtown Ontario forever, if only for practical reasons. One: After almost 45 years, everyone knew his location. Two: Cheap rent.

"When you're renting a building from your dad, in a building bought in 1961 – you're never going to get that deal again," Gross told me with a chuckle.

Or get a building like that again. The Greek Temple-style building dates to 1923 and housed the Bank of Italy, later absorbed by Bank of America.

Ontario bought the building in June 2003 for $885,000, then leased it back to Gross until he could move. It won't be razed. Hopes are that it can be restored to its original high-ceilinged splendor.

"We want to save it and turn it into a restaurant," Ontario housing director Brent Schultz explained.

Put me down for a reservation, Mr. Schultz.

For his part, Gross is unhappy about his treatment by City Hall, saying his relocation agreement took 18 months to negotiate and didn't cover his moving costs.

Getting permission to occupy his new location – told you I'd come back to that – was also time-consuming. His beauty college is now named Salon Success Academy and it's in the former Edwards Cinema at Foothill Boulevard and Alta Avenue.

It's a bright, airy space with rows of gleaming sinks and manicuring stations.

"We've tried to create a more spa-like atmosphere," school

vice president Susan Turner said as she showed me around just before Christmas. "This is the old concession area."

Prices in some cases are cheaper than concessions. Seniors on a budget especially liked going to Richards.

"They can walk out with a color, style and cut for $24. At a salon, the price is $80 and up," Turner said. "A basic haircut is $6.50."

Bargain hair-cutter Supercuts cut into business at the old location, as did downtown's homeless problem. But Turner, who's been with Richards since 1986, remembers when the line was out the door onto B Street on senior citizen day promotions.

Why, I can almost picture the older, grizzled Hemingway himself in line on B Street, waiting for a shave or fishing for another story. The old man and the sea-nior citizen day.

End of the Line for Two Much-Loved Local Fixtures

January 20, 2006

Everything must go at Baseline Hardware, because Baseline Hardware itself must go, closing next month after 30 years. It's too bad Baseline isn't selling Kleenex – they could make a mint. "We've had a lot of customers cry," owner Dave Kiedrowski told me. "Most of them male," added Kathie Shimansky, his daughter.

A mom-and-pop store, Baseline was owned and operated by a mom (Eva Kiedrowski) and a pop (Dave Kiedrowski), who came to what was then Cucamonga in 1975.

Their store in the Sunrize Center at Base Line and Carnelian was a hit. Two expansions took it from 6,000 square feet to 15,000.

Baseline survived when Coast to Coast, Cucamonga Hardware, Matt's Hardware and Builders Emporium, among others, could not. Blame Home Depot and Lowe's, whose stores are the size of airplane hangars. To the end, the family hoped baby boomers would abandon the cavernous chains for their cozy store, where employees stand ready to advise on electrical and plumbing problems.

"Dad had a motto: People who come in the door have a problem. We're here to solve that problem," Shimansky said.

It was a second career for Kiedrowski, an envelope salesman

whose real love was his do-it-yourself projects at home. So at age 50 he quit to open a hardware store in Norco, relocating to Cucamonga after three years.

He became a community leader, active in Rancho Cucamonga's incorporation, Kiwanis and the Chamber of Commerce, of which he is a past president.

Eva is gone and Kiedrowski, 83, doesn't get around too well. He still comes into the store seven days a week but is confined to the office, where we spoke Wednesday. Spending time on the floor with the customers "was what I lived for," he said with regret.

Because Shimansky is 60 and her daughter has no interest in drill bits, she and her father decided last month to retire and close up shop. Signs went up January 9.

Longtime office manager Anna Strohm joined our chat. She didn't last three questions before burying her face in her hands, crying. (I often have this effect on women.)

"Mixed emotions," she managed to say. "I think the community is losing something."

The final sale – fixtures and all – is expected to last another month. Customers are coming in to pay their respects, and also pick up a bag of nails on the cheap.

"Probably our best-known customer is Sam Maloof," Kiedrowski said. "He was in today, wishing us well."

I hope he brought a hankie.

* * * * *

Molly's Cafe, meanwhile, will close Monday. That's the coffee shop in downtown Ontario being displaced by redevelopment, darn it.

The 230 N. Euclid Avenue location has a long history of feeding Ontario, beginning as a grocery in 1925 and converting to a soda fountain in the 1940s – first Lamb's, then Cooky's.

Cooky sold to Claude Waggoner in 1952, when the place became Wag's, its longest occupant. Originally the counter and soda fountain were on the right, booths were on the left, an open kitchen was in the back and Chaffey High students were everywhere.

Molly's took over the space in 1987. City Hall bought the building last year from the Waggoner heirs, who sold under protest. It's going to be razed for a park.

All told, the place saw some 80 years of food sales. And perhaps the biggest sale of all is Monday.

"Monday, out of appreciation for our customers, 50 percent off any menu item," owner Jay Hong told me. That's not half bad.

I plan to be there myself, raising a chocolate malt in a toast to the end of an era.

Loch Ness Monster Branches Out in Rancho

April 23, 2006

Everyone knows the famous photo of the Loch Ness monster, first published in April 1934 and still the definitive look at the Scottish beastie. Well, the loch has nothing on Rancho Cucamonga, which despite lacking a body of water has its very own sea serpent.

A piece of wood in an open field on Haven Avenue just south of Eighth Street bears a striking resemblance to the Loch Ness monster.

It's even better when the field hasn't been mowed for a while. The creature's neck and head rise from the weeds as if from the sea itself. I've fondly dubbed the creature Nessie, although we might also call him the Log Ness monster. For years I've wondered how he got there.

On Friday, abandoning dignity in an effort to serve you, the reading public, I pulled my car into the nearest business, went inside and asked about that piece of wood next door that looks like the Loch Ness monster.

Thankfully, the nice folks at Degussa Construction Chemicals didn't call security or squirt me with chemicals. Although Degussa doesn't own the field, employees – whew – knew exactly what I was talking about.

"That's what I call it, the Loch Ness monster," plant supervisor Ygnacio Castro told me.

"You look at the photo of the Loch Ness monster in the water with the head and neck coming out," plant manager David Lougheed chimed in, "and (this one) really looks like that."

Castro said his recollection is that the piece of wood has been next door ever since he started at Degussa in 1968.

Isn't that something? Nobody can find the monster in Scotland's Loch Ness, but Rancho Cucamonga's may have been hiding in plain sight for decades.

Lougheed said visitors from Degussa's Cincinnati office always comment on the monstrous piece of wood.

"It is kind of a conversation piece," he said.

The property has changed hands several times over the years, Lougheed said – making it more astounding that the artfully placed branch hasn't been removed.

He doesn't know how it got there. Anybody know the story?

By the way, about that 1934 photo: It was attributed to R.K. Wilson, a surgeon, which gave it a certain credibility.

But in 1993, according to my Internet research, a man named Christian Spurling said on his deathbed that he and two others faked the photo.

Instead of rising many feet high, the monster's head and neck were just a toy submarine's periscope, accented with clay.

I'm pretty sure Rancho Cucamonga's Nessie is a real piece of wood, though.

45 YEARS? SHAKEY'S IN MONTCLAIR MUST HAVE GOOD MOJO

June 16, 2006

With Ontario's A&W Drive-In gone, what's the Inland Valley's longest-surviving chain restaurant? Among the runners-up, as found in old phone directories at the Ontario and Pomona libraries:

- Arby's, 2250 N. Garey, Pomona (since 1970)
- Taco Bell, 850 N. Mountain (1968)
- Wienerschnitzel, 151 N. Mountain, Ontario (1972); 520 E. Mission, Pomona (1968); and 175 W. Foothill, Pomona (1966)
- Denny's, 1409 E. Fourth Street, Ontario (1967)
- McDonald's, 2200 N. Garey, Pomona (1966); 832 N. Mountain, Ontario (1965)
- Sizzler, 5660 Holt, Montclair (1963), the 20th Sizzler in the chain

A silly list? Sure, but better for me to spend two hours in libraries than in pool halls. Oh, and thanks to Jeff Gaul and A&W's Larry Roan for submitting some good guesses.

But what's the valley's oldest chain restaurant?

Shakey's Pizza in Montclair.

The Shakey's at 5639 Holt Boulevard opened in 1961 and is still baking pies 45 years later. (It's across Holt from the 1963 Sizzler and west of Vince's Spaghetti and the former A&W.)

The chain began in 1954 in Sacramento. True fact: Cofounder Sherwood "Shakey" Johnson got his nickname because nerve damage from malaria contracted in World War II gave him the shakes.

In the 1961 Yellow Pages, shortly after its opening, the Montclair Shakey's advertised "Bavarian black beer" and "piano playing and singing Wed. thru Sun. nights."

From a high of 325 U.S. restaurants in 1974, Shakey's is down to 62, a drop blamed on poor management and increased competition. But the Montclair location is hanging in there.

"We're the oldest Shakey's in Southern California," assistant manager Gina Amir told me proudly.

The exterior is largely the same, including the 40-foot "Shakey's Pizza Parlor and Ye Public House" sign, visible from blocks away, and possibly from space.

Other than the original lamps, the interior is unrecognizable if you're an old-time Shakey's customer. The wooden stools, 1920s-style signs and stage where musicians played Dixieland jazz and piano are gone. So are employees' straw hats and the mini-theater where Three Stooges and other comedies played for the kids.

The pizza is pretty much the same, though. And they still have those Mojo potatoes.

One day a Vietnam vet began crying during his Shakey's meal – not usually a good sign. He told Amir that he and his childhood buddies used to eat there and that he was the only one who survived the war. The meal brought back memories.

"The pizza you cooked up for me," he told the staff, "was just like the ones I had as a kid."

Many customers have been eating there for years, if less emotionally. Amir, a gregarious hostess who's worked there 12 years, remembers everybody.

On Monday, only my second visit, I had the Bunch of Lunch buffet before introducing myself. As I paid with exact change, Amir remarked that I'd had exact change the last time. Who knew I was so memorable?

In a further boost to my self-esteem, she also called me both "sweetie pie" and "honeybunch."

Customers invite Amir to weddings and anniversary parties, and I can see why.

"I'm really bad with names, but I remember faces," Amir told me in our post-lunch interview.

Business isn't what it used to be, but there are hardcore fans. Shakey's last month hosted a couple's wedding reception.

"They met here as kids," Amir explained. Guests feasted on the Shakey's Special. The first dance took place near the salad bar.

Two burly blue-collar diners left as Amir and I chatted at the counter.

She called after them: "See you, sweetie pies!"

Please don't hiss ode to cassettes

July 2, 2006

Remember cassette tapes? They seem to be going the way of the telegram. What a rotten thing to see happen to a technological innovation from my own youth.

I used to love cassettes. Not the prerecorded kind, whose only improvement over bulky eight-track tapes was size. I'm talking about blank cassettes.

Before iPods, MP3s, MySpace, playlists and what-have-you, cassettes were the way we shared music with friends. Or forced music on them.

With tapes, we could program music for road trips, win over crushes (or scare them off), and play DJ for ourselves.

But no more. I've got about 100 homemade cassettes piled in a shopping bag. They're headed for the trash.

But first, let me rewind.

I did most of my taping in college, the perfect time to become obsessed with music. Fueling this obsession was one of my senior-year roommates.

Phil Rockrohr not only had all the regular records by our favorite artists, he had the bootlegged concert recording, the 45 with the non-LP B-side and the 12-inch single with the extended mix.

(This is gibberish, like gearheads talking about their cars, but every secret society has its secret language.)

Another taping binge began in the early 1990s, after I embraced the future by buying a CD player. Unable to entirely let go of even spotty LPs, I boiled them down into 60- or 90-minute "best-of" tapes before selling them.

Today, music is still one of my favorite pastimes, but the haze of obsession has burned off like morning smog. When you hit your 40s, keeping track of non-LP B-sides no longer seems like a good use of brain cells. Last year it struck me that my dusty old cassettes were eating up a lot of shelf space. So I spent months playing them all one last time – a swan song for magnetic tape.

It was a rare chance to reconnect with my younger self, and shake my head. There was my three-tape series of '60s Who rarities, painstakingly compiled in chronological order from a half-dozen sources. Every track is now easily available on CD.

If only I'd spent those hours doing something useful, like learning Spanish.

Another tape held two uncommercial John and Yoko albums of the late 1960s, only purchased, with gritted teeth, by Beatle completists. Rather than music, the couple courted each other by recording heartbeats, electronic blips and piercing shrieks. Even Paris Hilton would find John and Yoko self-absorbed.

Some cassettes were fine in theory, like a "best-of" for the Police, but after 20 years to warp and decay, they sound as if they were recorded underwater.

Still, many of my better tapes are keepers. One is a Joan Jett "best-of" made with Rockrohr's assistance that has a better choice of songs than her official greatest hits CD.

(For instance, it has the original version of "Cherry Bomb," when she was with the teen band the Runaways, not her later rerecorded version. Oops, there go more brain cells.)

Obviously, copying music remains popular in the computer era, much to the consternation of the Recording Industry Association of America. But MP3s are intangible. You can't hand them to a woman, your heart pounding, and say with feigned casualness, "Here are some songs you might like."

Sure, you can burn a CD of favorite tracks for a friend, but almost no one does. It doesn't seem to have the same magic as compiling a homemade cassette. Perhaps it's too easy.

Granted, I don't know how to do it. But people tell me it's easy.

Making a cassette was hard work, but rewarding. Many of us loved the ritual: sitting intently by the stereo, cueing up LPs and releasing the "pause" button on the cassette deck.

Songs were taped in real time, and because you could never tell how much time was left on each side, sometimes your tape would shut off in mid-song. This meant you had to rewind a bit and think of a new socko finish for Side One.

Taping would be followed by laboriously writing titles and artists in the tiny ruled lines of the cassette card.

One reason I liked making tapes was dreaming up a dopey title to write on the spine.

A tape of Prince 45s was called "Singles 4 U." The Byrds, perhaps best known for the hit "Turn! Turn! Turn!", were the subject of a compilation I called "Tape! Tape! Tape!"

There was something personal about cassettes. But life is speeding up. Who has time for craftsmanship anymore?

Maybe we can outsource our tape-making to India. Until then, these cassettes of mine are headed for the trash, and we're all moving into the future – on fast-forward.

INVITATION FROM AARP AGES HIM PREMATURELY

July 16, 2006

Well, the dreaded envelope arrived in the mail, the one inviting me to join AARP.

"As a member," the letter from Executive Director William D. Novelli reads, "you'll have the resources and information you need to get the most out of life over 50."

I felt that rush of emotions familiar to those who get the AARP invitation: denial, embarrassment, nervous laughter. But, mostly, confusion.

I'm only 42!

Apparently they're slipping at AARP HQ. These things happen. Especially as we get older.

Once I got past my surprise at my early brush with geezerdom, I had to admit the 22 benefits listed on the back of the letter were pretty enticing.

- "Save at thousands of hotels, motels and resorts worldwide."
- "Save on airfares, cruises, auto rentals, vacation packages."
- "Free rake to shake angrily at neighborhood children."

Kidding.

By nature I'm not a joiner, but signing up for AARP had its advantages. Colleagues urged me to weigh my options.

"Can you get into movies cheap?" arts-lovin' Opinion Page editor Mike Brossart asked me. "Don't turn it down until you see if the Laemmle in Claremont gives a senior discount."

Hey, by the time the Laemmle Theater opens in Claremont, I really will be 50.

So I considered sending in the application as a lark. Could I be accepted by the AARP? The form does ask for my year of birth, and I'm not one to lie.

But my 1964 birth year might not be a dealkiller. I got this far – they even provided me a "member code" in advance – so they're obviously not paying close attention.

An interesting question is whether a 42-year-old could get senior discounts by flashing an authentic AARP card.

My worry is that I could. What if people found me believable as an old man? What an insult. Then again, I could cry about it at 30,000 feet while on a discounted airline flight to Aruba.

As it turns out, this quandary resolved itself through the magic of procrastination. I just dug the application out of my paper pile and found the deadline was last Tuesday.

I er, sort of forgot. Hey, maybe I am over-50 material!

* * * * *

A reader who signed himself or herself Stupid Happy Idiot emailed me the rules for a drinking game to play at home while watching Pomona City Council meetings on TV, which could come in handy if broadcasts resume Monday night.

The rules: Pick a favorite council member, set 'em up and wait for certain behavior patterns to emerge.

Thirsty players should choose a council member toward the bottom of the list. Teetotalers – yours truly is one – can substitute a favorite nonalcoholic beverage.

Take a drink:

1. Anytime Dan Rodriguez speaks about an issue close to his heart.

2. Anytime Steven Banales speaks, period.

3. Anytime George Hunter offers a one-liner for comic relief or says "the bottom line is."

4. Anytime Marco Robles says "at the end of the day" or, while speaking, folds his hands like *The Simpsons*' Montgomery Burns.

5. Anytime Norma Torres sounds like Sally Struthers in a "Save the Children" commercial.

6. Anytime Paula Lantz says the word "clarity," as in, "I need clarity on this."

7. Anytime Elliott Rothman makes a motion. If he makes a motion to approve something "at this particular time," take two drinks. If he makes a motion to approve the consent calendar, take one drink for each item.

Bonus rule for all players: When Rothman makes his obligatory motion to adjourn, everyone takes a drink.

DRINKING INCREASES CLARITY, OR VICE VERSA

July 19, 2006

The Pomona City Council drinking game, rules of which were laid out here on Sunday, seems to have caught on among at least one group: council members themselves.

Moments before the meeting began, Councilman George Hunter advised me that Councilwoman Paula Lantz had already used her favorite word, "clarity" – "but it was in closed session, so it doesn't count."

Under the rules, each "clarity" from the enlightenment-seekin' Lantz – who is prone to saying "I need some clarity on this" – is worth one drink.

Forty minutes into the meeting, Lantz made a request for clarity.

She immediately repeated it.

"I said 'clarity' for Mr. Allen," Lantz added. "I'm going to say it so many times, people won't be able to walk."

Staggering.

(Sadly, Lantz didn't say "clarity" the rest of the evening, making her another politician who can't keep a promise.)

Later, Vice Mayor Elliott Rothman said "clarity," caught my eye and, with a flourish, took a drink of water.

During another item, Hunter began to ask a city planner, "Can I get some clarity," then stopped himself.

"Did I just say that? Does it count if it's me?" he asked.

"Two shots," Councilman Steven Banales interjected, miming a drinking motion.

"I can't think of another word to use," Hunter confessed. "Can I have ... further explanation on this?"

Not everything went as players watching the proceedings on TV might have liked.

While Banales spoke more than usual – at one drink per comment, he gave thirsty viewers a bonus – Marco Robles didn't say "at the end of the day," nor did Hunter opine that "the bottom line is."

Rothman's failure to move the consent calendar or move to adjourn cost his partisans a grand total of 17 drinks.

However, the vice mayor's fans weren't completely shut out.

"Move to open the public hearing ... at this particular time," he said wryly at one point, using a Rothman catchphrase worth one drink.

Frankly, I had gone back and forth on whether to print the drinking game, which was largely the work of a clever, if anonymous, reader. I worried it was in bad taste or that council members would be offended.

I shouldn't have fretted: After all, one thing Pomona council members don't lack is personality. To my delight, most took the ball and ran with it.

Maybe they were flattered that anyone listens to them so closely.

Afterward, Lantz accepted my compliment on her sense of humor. She said it was healthy for council members to have their cliches pointed out to them.

"If we don't have a sense of humor," Lantz told me, "you help give us one."

Thanks for the clari-- I mean, the explanation.

* * * * *

People watching the meeting who hadn't read Sunday's column, of course, must have thought the council was nuts.

(Ditto with people who did read it.)

RACE FOR 11:15 TRAIN DIDN'T DERAIL HIS PLANS

September 15, 2006

I don't need a lot of urging to ride Metrolink. Taking a train into the big city is novel, fun and relaxing.

After promoting the idea here of a late-night train, I naturally had to be on the first 11:15 p.m. Saturday-only train from L.A. to San Bernardino, a service that rolled out last weekend and continues indefinitely.

But is our new late-night train late enough?

To test the train, I decided to see *Curtains*, a well-reviewed musical comedy at the Ahmanson Theatre. Running time was two hours, 35 minutes, which meant the 8 p.m. show would end about 10:35.

Could I make it from the Ahmanson to Union Station in time for the 11:15 train?

If not, I had two backup plans. One, the Route 480 Foothill Transit bus would leave First and Spring streets at 11:49 p.m., with a stop in Claremont. And two, Metrolink spokeswoman Denise Tyrrell had given me her personal number.

"I have a rollaway bed. If you get stranded, I feel responsible for you," Tyrrell told me last month. She also mentioned she's not a night owl. Whether she would answer a call past 11 p.m. on a Saturday night, or simply roll over and finish her dream, was an open question.

I was at the Claremont depot, waiting for the 4:44 p.m.

train west, when Montclair reader Shirley Wofford introduced herself. The 70-year-old was on her way to see *Water and Power* at the Mark Taper Forum, a choice made because the one-act play would let out at 9:40 p.m., in plenty of time to make the train home.

"A person wouldn't be able to go to the Pantages or Dodger Stadium," Wofford, a fan of both theater and baseball, told me. "I do hope they realize in time that 11:15 is not late enough to do a lot of things."

I advised Wofford of my plan to see *Curtains*.

"You're going to have to run like heck," she said.

That's why I wore my sneakers, Shirley.

With a book of Jack Smith columns as my traveling companion, I arrived at Union Station at 5:40 and walked to Philippe for a lamb dip and slice of apple pie. I skipped my usual side of cole slaw. I had to stay nimble.

I descended to the Red Line subway at 6:55, rode to the Civic Center stop and arrived on foot at the Ahmanson at 7:15. To play it safe, I budgeted 30 minutes for the return trip instead of 20, in case I had to wait for the subway or some other hitch developed.

This meant the latest I could leave the Ahmanson was 10:45.

The Music Center atop Bunker Hill was hopping, with a couple of hundred people dining al fresco at the Pinot Grill and couples milling about. Could anyone else here be from the 909 and riding Metrolink, I wondered?

Incidentally, what with the Music Center's 1960s Modernist style, expanses of glass, high columns, one round concrete building and cracked pavement underfoot, it was like being in the Pomona Civic Center. No wonder, as both were designed by architect Welton Becket.

Disappointed at not bumping into Eli Broad, I picked up

my will-call ticket and climbed three flights of stairs to my $40 nosebleed seat in the theater's upper balcony.

That's a lot of stairs. Better leave by 10:40.

The first act of *Curtains* was pretty funny and David Hyde Pierce was a hoot. At the 9:10 intermission, I asked an usher when he expected the show to end – as it's not a movie, there's no guarantee it wouldn't run past 10:35.

"Oh, 10:30, 10:45," he said. "Definitely by 11."

Real helpful, thanks.

On the plus side, I had an aisle seat for a quick exit. After 10 p.m., I began anxiously checking my watch in the dim light from the aisle every few minutes.

Would I be able to stay to the end, or would this be like a Dodger game, where I'd have to leave in the theatrical equivalent of the seventh inning?

At 10:37, the curtain dropped, then rose quickly as the bit players came out first to take their bows. I bolted. Everyone else would have to applaud for me.

I descended the stairs at a trot – in fact, I descended one level too far and had to go back up to plaza level – and exited past startled ushers, then down the outside stairs. Crossing Grand Avenue against the light, I continued down Temple on deserted sidewalks and pivoted onto Hill Street.

Where was the subway station? I momentarily panicked before finding it across the street. Below, I waited five minutes for the next subway, which arrived at 10:50 and deposited me at Union Station at 10:55.

At 10:58, after bumping into Rancho Cucamonga readers Tim and Leslie Sunderland, I settled into a seat – and there were plenty, with only 30 riders – on the waiting train home.

Finally, I could relax. Except for a twinge of guilt.

I guess applauding the bit players wouldn't have hurt me.

Late-Night Riders Get 15 Minutes of Fame, Er, Train

October 4, 2006

Well, Metrolink's Saturday night choo-choo still isn't a midnight train, but it's 15 minutes nearer.

Instead of 11:15 p.m., the last Saturday train headed east will depart Union Station at 11:30 beginning this weekend.

"We're creeping closer to a midnight train," quipped Cheryl Donahue, spokeswoman for San Bernardino Associated Governments.

The agency, which pays for Metrolink service hereabouts, had asked for a midnight train, but Metrolink officials in L.A. said 11:15 was the latest they could run a train.

The service launched September 9. Sometime after that, Metrolink told the agency that an 11:30 departure was possible. The offer was eagerly accepted, Donahue said.

As I wrote here about my September 9 night in L.A., I high-tailed it out of the play *Curtains* at the Ahmanson Theatre at 10:37 p.m. – before the actors took their bows – to make a dash for Union Station to avoid missing the 11:15 p.m. train home.

Did my column about that anxious evening buy the 909 an extra 15 minutes?

Donahue said she doesn't know what prompted Metrolink's offer but that my column was a likely suspect. Either way, she told me, "Next time you go see a play, maybe you won't have to be so fidgety."

Metrolink spokeswoman Denise Tyrrell thought the Associated Governments had initiated the later time. At any rate, Tyrrell told me the extra time will allow passengers "to see a play and make it to the train."

That will be good news for readers Linda Wood and Don Richardson. Each wrote to me last month to say the idea of watching the clock during a play wasn't very appealing, although they were pleased to hear making the 11:15 train after a play was at least possible. No doubt they'll welcome the extra 15 minutes.

Oh, and Metrolink devotee Shirley Wofford – who wants a later train for theater and Dodger outings – said I missed out by not staying at *Curtains* to the end.

Wofford said that when she saw a matinee of *Curtains*, star David Hyde Pierce appeared for his curtain call "in his cowboy apparel on a stick horse."

Niles Crane on a stick horse? That would almost – almost – have been worth missing a train home for.

Trip to lab turns into a free ride

October 22, 2006

On Monday morning I visited a lab to have blood drawn. Things didn't go entirely as planned, in the sense that, after having needles poked in both arms, I blacked out.

In another unexpected development, yours truly was the subject of a 911 call. I left the lab strapped to a gurney.

Paramedics wheeled me out the door for – whee! – an ambulance ride to the hospital.

I don't want to say I needlessly complicate routine tasks, but imagine if the lab had also taken my temperature. I might have wound up being defibrillated.

(Before you panic on my behalf, let me fast-forward to the end: I'm fine. So you can laugh at my tale of personal calamity with a clear conscience.)

I needed blood drawn for an upcoming checkup. Before a blood draw, you're supposed to fast for at least 10 hours, which I did.

Unfortunately, due to a big midafternoon meal Sunday, I didn't have dinner, which meant that when I showed up at the lab in Upland, I hadn't eaten for 18 hours.

The receptionist checked me in and handed me a comment card to mail in later. A comment card at a blood lab? I wondered what I could comment on. The size of the needle?

Needles, and medical procedures in general, make me

nervous, by the way. But I'd had blood drawn at this lab once before, and it went fine.

This time, however, the phlebotomist couldn't get much blood from a vein in my right arm. She said I might be somewhat dehydrated. (Warning sign No. 1.) So she drew blood from my left arm. This went better, but as I held the cotton ball to my arm afterward, I began feeling light-headed. I considered asking if I could lie down.

The next thing I knew, I was coming out of a deep slumber. Several voices were asking if l was OK.

My eyes focused slowly. I was hot, sweaty, groggy and could barely speak.

A paper towel was slid onto the counter atop my copy of that morning's *Daily Bulletin*, which had a big wet stain. Apparently I had drooled all over it.

I was asked my name and birth date. Someone said they'd called 911. I was told I had gone stiff and begun to fall out of my chair when someone caught me. "Have you ever had a seizure before?" one asked.

Hoo boy. I mumbled answers and, seeking a moment's peace, rested my head on the paper towel.

This was going to be a long morning.

Soon paramedics burst in. They asked my name and birth date. (I hope I get birthday presents out of this.)

Still woozy, I was helped up, given an oxygen mask, placed on a gurney and ferried through the lobby past patients waiting to give blood. I can't have been good for business.

In the back of the ambulance, a paramedic inserted an IV to rehydrate me. Great, another needle.

I was feeling a bit better. We bumped along on surface streets to San Antonio Community Hospital. To my regret, we didn't use the siren.

I was checked into the emergency room and given a backless gown. EKG buttons were attached and more questions asked. I was left to get my strength back.

Two patients were brought in and positioned near me in the walkway. A teenager had overdosed. A laborer had fallen off his ladder. All the real beds were full.

"Is this a busy morning?" a man asked. A nurse said, "It's slower than usual."

A doctor checked on me and concluded a combination of needles and hunger had done me in. I said I'd like to eat something, and he ordered me up a hospital lunch.

As I like trying different restaurants, this was a rare treat. The food was fine, but given my drafty gown, I have to say, I didn't care for the dress code.

A couple of people passing my gurney recognized me from my column photo. "Are you here for a cure for writer's block?" one asked.

Once cleared to leave, my IV was taken out and a copious amount of tape yanked from my arm. It was the most painful part of the whole morning.

I went home, freshened up, went to work and, later, to a three-hour Pomona City Council meeting. So maybe my judgment was impaired, but at least I felt fine.

I also stopped by the lab. Knowing my blackout must have alarmed everyone, I felt I should let them know I was fine. They were relieved to hear it.

Still, for the sake of all concerned, it's probably best if I don't fill out their comment card.

Changed number leaves him hung up

November 5, 2006

After 39 years in rural Illinois, my parents got itchy feet. Last week they packed up, watched movers load the van and headed west. Not to Pomona – despite the sales job of my "Pomona A to Z" series – but to the Great Northwest.

By the time you read this, they and their belongings should be in Washington state.

This puts my parents in the same time zone as me for the first time in two decades. Another upside: Eventually we're bound to meet up in Seattle, and by then, maybe the monorail will be working. It was out of commission during my previous vacation there.

I'm happy for my parents. Still, this will take some getting used to.

And the other morning, as I was out for a walk in Claremont, another change involved in my parents' move suddenly occurred to me.

They're not only abandoning my hometown. They're abandoning my hometown phone number.

The power of this realization almost knocked me over. You see, my parents have had the same phone number for virtually my entire life.

It was graceful in its simplicity: 393-6606.

I may be wrong, but I think we got that number when I

was 3, which is when we moved to Olney, Illinois. First my parents rented a duplex on Fair Street. Later they bought a house on East Street. Then they bought a nicer house on Douglas Drive and stayed put. All these moves were within our small town's city limits.

Each time, we kept the same phone number. You remember: 393-6606.

It was the first phone number I ever learned. How many phone numbers do you need when you're a little kid? You're not calling your friends, your dry cleaner, your doctor.

You also don't need to give the number out for job applications, medical forms or video rentals. Basically, you need to know your number in case you need a ride home.

And sometimes I did. Maybe my dad would drive me to a friend's house, say, Mike Wendling's, and later I'd call to be picked up when Mike Wendling and I had had enough of each other.

Once my church youth group went out on a hayride. Have you ever been on a hayride? I have – once.

Way out in the country somewhere, we met at a farm and climbed in the back of a flatbed trailer loaded with bales of hay.

A tractor pulled us at about 2 mph along country roads through a chilly October evening under the stars. The other kids found this a lot of fun. I was bored out of my mind.

Then my allergy to grass kicked in, which in turn got my asthma going, and pretty soon I was wheezing so badly I was barely able to breathe. That wasn't boring.

Our chaperone got the farmer to turn the tractor around. (I imagine the farmer used this as a threat on family vacations: "If you kids don't stop fighting back there, I'll turn this tractor around! I mean it!")

Somehow, in that pre-cell phone era, a message was relayed to the farm. Someone called my parents – that number again: 393-6606 – so they could be there by the time the farmer, who put the pedal to the metal by going 4 mph, got us back.

So the hayride was cut short – although at two hours, it still seemed interminable – and everyone hated me for it. But I was wheezing too much to care. Also, my dad was there, and his car didn't have hay in it, and that was the important thing.

Olney was a remote place, but it was safe. Starting from age 10 or so I could walk from our house to the library, to the movies or to see friends, and no one had any cause to worry.

I left for California after college and only go back for visits. With my parents gone, this pretty much cuts the cord to Olney. I'm not sure White Squirrel Days is enough to lure me back.

Without 393-6606, that cuts the phone cord, too.

As near as I can tell, I've had seven phone numbers since going away to college. My parents' number has been a constant in my life. I know it better than I know my own. Decades of practice, after all.

As a boy, I always looked us up when a new phone directory would arrive. Why, I'm not sure. To a budding writer like myself, maybe having my family's name, address and phone number in a directory distributed all over town was like being published.

We're famous! See, we're in a book!

(A friend asked if I really dial my parents' number. Don't I have my own parents on speed dial? Hey, I don't have anybody on speed dial. I don't know how to work speed dialing. If my phone even has it.)

It'll be a new feeling, looking up my parents' number when

I call them. I doubt I'll ever memorize it.

But that's all right. These are new times. None of my friends know my number. They just enter it into their cell phones, then press a key to dial me. Nobody memorizes numbers anymore.

So even though I can't use 393-6606, that's all right.

Still, I do foresee one possible problem from not instantly knowing my parents' new number.

What if I need a ride?

LOSS OF CHILDHOOD NUMBERS LEAVES THEM DISCONNECTED

November 24, 2006

Losing 393-6606, my childhood phone number, when my parents moved was a recent topic here, and it brought several misty-eyed reminiscences from readers.

Renee Noble said her family had the same number in Phoenix – 957-4283 – from the time party lines were phased out until August 2005, when her mother died.

"It took me three months to realize I should stop the phone service and another month to actually do it. I had received calls at that number most of my life," Noble told me. "After leaving home, I called that number weekly to talk to my parents, and after my father passed away in 1988, my mom.

"The phone people were very nice and told me the day it would be disconnected. I called the number one last time before it was disconnected just to listen to it ring."

When I called 393-6606 one last time, I got the recording saying the number was disconnected and no longer in service. I had to call before putting the number in the newspaper to make sure it was really kaput. But still: Ouch.

Reader Bill Winslow's parents had the same number for 48 years in Arcadia: 355-3254. "It is a number embedded in my mind and heart still to this day," he told me.

His father died 12 years ago but his mother kept the

number. He can still picture her sitting on the end of the family room's green couch, talking on the phone.

"I made it a habit to call on my drive home from work to see how she was or to tell her something great that happened at work or in our family. She was always there to listen," Winslow said.

She died in December 2005. Not long after that, Winslow got some good news and wished he could share it with his mom.

So he called 355-3254 just to get the answering machine. "It was up and running till we had to sell the house for estate taxes and because my sisters still wanted to hear her voice as well," Winslow said.

"Even though she was not there," he said, "I could still hear her voice and it helped."

Let me pause to compose myself.

HONK!

OK (sniff), on to the next letter.

Merritt Humphrey moved to Claremont in 1969 to a rental house with her parents. Then they bought the house next door, but the original phone number moved with them.

The family changed houses twice more within Claremont. The number stayed with them each time.

"My mother has had the same phone number for 38 years," Humphrey said. (As the number is still in service, I won't print it.)

"It was the first phone number I ever memorized. Because I moved back in with my mom 10 years ago with my daughter just before she turned 3, it is also the first phone number she memorized," Humphrey said.

"All of my friends from high school and before know that

number by heart. It's been probably the one constant in all of our lives. Too bad phone numbers can't be retired like football jerseys."

A nice thought.

My brother, Mark, reminded me of a couple of facts involving our old phone number. Our town was so small that for most of our childhoods, we didn't have to dial 393-6606. We could just dial 3-6606 and the call would go through.

That's old school. Or as he puts it: "That's one step closer to grabbing the receiver and asking Mabel for some name, or for a two-digit number."

Our number was also just one digit off from the bowling alley's. This prompted a lot of calls from people asking my dad if they could reserve a lane.

My parents have a new number, and so far I haven't even memorized the area code. But give me time.

As mentioned in that earlier column, what with cell phones and speed dialing, many people don't punch in numbers anymore.

Memorizing numbers is becoming a quaint habit, like programming a VCR or saying "you're welcome."

But here's a comment from reader Bob Almanzar, who's in his 30s.

"It's been a while since I dialed any friend's number from memory," he said, "but for some reason I always go out of my way to dial my parents' number."

In a mixed-up world, seven familiar digits can be oh-so comforting.

Tower Records' Demise is This Columnist's Gain

December 27, 2006

To paraphrase the old Chico Escuela skits from *SNL*: Tower Records' bankruptcy sale has been berry, berry good to me.

Honestly, I do feel bad about Tower closing up shop after four decades. It was a homegrown California chain and its demise doesn't bode well for the future of record stores.

That said, Tower's death throes provided the most fun I've had in weeks.

Unimpressed by Tower's opening salvo of 10 percent off, I held off on going there. Given the chain's notoriously high prices, 10 percent off was *bupkis*.

Then came a newspaper ad on Thanksgiving Day: 40 percent off, starting that very day, with a fifth CD free for every four you bought.

Now we're talkin'. Entranced by the novelty of shopping on a holiday, I headed for West Covina, the easternmost Tower store.

The very best stuff was gone – no Beatles, for instance – so you were unlikely to find what you wanted. But you could find plenty of CDs you'd forgotten you wanted, or never knew you wanted.

I should note that music is an intense interest of mine, that *High Fidelity* is my favorite novel and that my musical tastes are broad.

Probably too broad. Rather than do the smart thing and

specialize, I'm curious about a wide variety of music, past and present. This makes my collection either eclectic or unfocused, take your pick.

In West Covina, I grabbed discs I had been eyeing for weeks, and in some cases years: CDs by Belle and Sebastian, Leonard Cohen, Sonic Youth, Harry Nilsson, Frank Sinatra, the Streets, Sarah Vaughan and They Might Be Giants, among others.

I ended up with 17 discs and three DVDs. According to the receipt, "You saved $189.33 today!"

I saved so much, and so enjoyably, I immediately headed for the Tower in Pasadena. With the help of Otis Redding, the Klezmatics, Pavement, Booker T and the MG's and six other discs, I saved another $86.58.

A couple of days later, I returned to West Covina and giddily snapped up another 16.

Rap was now 70 percent off, so Dizzee Rascal, Ghostface Killah and *Voices From the Frontline* – rap by U.S. soldiers in Iraq, a fascinating concept – went in my basket, alongside Anita O'Day, Radiohead, Gram Parsons, John Coltrane, Procol Harum, Rosemary Clooney and Sufjan Stevens.

From that point, I limited myself to five discs per visit. Unfortunately for my wallet, I visited four more times. These purchases included Lynyrd Skynyrd, Charles Mingus, Neko Case, Bobby Womack and the Flaming Lips. I could open my own record store.

I was like a human vacuum cleaner, sucking up music. Even at that, though, I always left the store wondering why I hadn't gone ahead and bought that Cannonball Adderley or *Rough Guide to Pakistan* disc.

Another one left behind: *Bob Seger's Greatest Hits*. I always picked it up, considered it and ultimately put it back on the rack. Even 60 percent off couldn't offset the embarrassment of buying a Bob Seger record.

Each Tower visit was a bit grimmer.

Ever-larger portions of the store would be partitioned off as the remaining stock was pushed toward the front. Despite the dwindling offerings, end-cap displays revealed that Tower West Covina was, oddly, stocked in depth on Matisyahu.

In those last weeks, I felt like a vulture picking a corpse clean. For a guy who's spent much of his life prowling the aisles of record stores, it was depressing. It seemed like the end of an era.

Record stores, CDs themselves and the idea of a space-hogging collection are becoming *passe*. The continued health of Claremont's excellent Rhino Records aside, our musical future probably consists of buying digitized air from iTunes.

Staggering to the Tower counter with an armload of CDs, I felt like I was stocking up on buggy whips.

Yet Tower's prices were, frankly, exhilarating.

Most CDs were selling for $10, and later for $7 or under. This is what I was paying for LPs back in the 1980s. At that price, why not sample something new?

I took a chance on new bands as a result of Tower emptying its warehouses at fire-sale prices, and no doubt many others did too.

My happiest find so far is the Heartless Bastards, a band with a wonderful name. I expect I'll find more as I make my way through my piles of purchases.

Those purchases have come to an end. I had hoped to hit Pasadena's Tower one last time, but didn't make it back before it closed last week. Which is just as well.

My pile of receipts tell me I "saved" $576.32. If I'd saved any more, something tells me I might be joining Tower in bankruptcy.

Nudity, guns and hexes: '06 was gold

December 31, 2006

Before we bid 2006 adieu, and then give it a swift kick in the pants, let's take a fond look back on the weird year that was. Here are my picks for the Inland Valley's Top 10 Strange Stories.

10. **SLASH ONTARIO**: Ontario International Airport became LA/Ontario International Airport for marketing reasons courtesy of its owner, Los Angeles World Airports. Ontario officials were fine with the new name. They must figure it's better than a hotelier's ill-fated idea a few years ago to name the facility Disney International Airport.

9. **BOBBLE SCHOOL**: In February, RadioShack president and CEO David Edmondson quit after it was learned he had lied on his resume about having two degrees from a Bible college formerly located in San Dimas. It's unknown whether Edmondson has since put the reason for his resignation on his resume.

8. **COURT LEAK**: In the Chino courthouse, jury selection in a drunken driving trial was postponed when a leaky pipe above the jury box dripped water on potential jurors and the prosecutor. They were sent home to dry off. Everyone out of the jury pool!

7. **TAKING LICENSE**: A man who sold illegal driver's licenses, Social Security cards and green cards was pulled over by authorities in Pomona after he was observed selling a card

in public. In a "do as I say, not as I do" twist, when sheriff's deputies asked for his driver's license, he didn't have one.

6. **UPLAND LIBRE**: In quiet Upland, a Cuban exile was found to have stashed nearly 1,400 rifles, machine guns and grenades in every nook and cranny of his house. Some were behind framed paintings, wall thermometers and in a secret compartment behind a bookcase. He said he was helping a paramilitary group planning to overthrow Fidel Castro. Gracious!

5. **NAKED CAME THE STRANGER**: In Claremont, police located a drug-addled nudist in a resident's backyard. He spoke in a mix of English, French and a language police couldn't identify. He also was eating grass. In a victory for lawn order, officers took him into custody.

4. **FLAG FLAP**: In July, 250 miniature American flags were stuck in a Claremont neighborhood's front yards. Each flag had a real-estate agent's business card attached. The homeowners association president confiscated all the flags. Some were mad at him, some at the agent. Happy July Fourth!

3. **STUPID CRIMINAL TRICKS**: In Rancho Cucamonga, a cat burglar abandoned his car – with his wallet inside – near the scene of the crime. In a second stroke of genius, he later went to the sheriff's headquarters in San Bernardino to fill out a stolen vehicle report.

2. **CURSES**! At an Ontario City Council meeting on 6/6/06, a pastor named Sabbath stood during the public comment period and calmly placed a curse on City Manager Greg Devereaux, in front of stunned officials and an audience of Miss Ontario pageant winners. The incident got more news coverage in L.A. than anything else in Ontario in 2006. Devereaux, by the way, survived, although to be safe, employees bought him a voodoo kit.

And the year's top weird story …

1. **GOT THE SHAFT**: What's even better than the Ontario curse? In Montclair, a homeowner hired two men to dig a shaft in his front yard, trusting an internet-purchased "gold detector" that he was going to strike gold. The shaft was 60 feet deep before authorities stepped in. "We just got carried away," the man admitted.

And a good thing he did. If it weren't for people getting carried away, my annual weird-stories roundup would be mighty short.

2006 Items

January 22, 2006

Wandering a byway of Victoria Gardens a while back, I was startled to stumble across what appears to be a classic 1950s police station. It houses a Rancho Cucamonga sheriff's substation but appears to come right out of a Norman Rockwell painting.

The modest building is made of stacked yellow bricks. Venetian blinds shade the front windows. Flanking the entrance are twin globe lamps bearing the word "Police."

The station is so darling, I couldn't imagine why crooks weren't lining up to confess.

The look is in keeping with the rest of the outdoor mall, which evokes various 20th-century styles, as if the 2004-built center were a true, historic downtown.

"I'm from a very small town in the Midwest," said Glenn Miller, the mall's marketing director. "It made me think of a little police station in a small town."

Me too. So last week, having no crimes to confess, I arranged for a tour.

The interior, I'm afraid, is a letdown – industrial and modern. And rather than index cards and typewriters, employees use databases and flat-screen computers. There's an interview room, but no holding cell, which is too bad. I was hoping to see Otis the drunk sprawled on a cot.

"Originally (the interior) was supposed to be more '60s, but it also needed to be more functional than the '60s were," crime prevention officer Sandy Fatland explained.

The station's 11 personnel handle shoplifting, thefts, car

burglaries and the like at Victoria Gardens and two adjacent retail centers.

The lobby has a couple of neat touches. Vintage B&W "Dragnet"-style Sheriff's Department photos fill one wall. On another is a framed copy of a 1953 job posting for a deputy sheriff II. "This exam is open to men only," the posting notes.

Illustrating that times often change for the better, the station is run by Sgt. Kish Doyle, a woman.

February 1, 2006

On the sidewalk outside a Yale Avenue bar and restaurant in the Claremont Village on Saturday night, clusters of people chatted. Nearby, wisps of smoke arose from a trash receptacle into which cigarettes had been tossed. Three nonsmoking bystanders, including yours truly, edged away.

Soon, wisps of smoke became clouds. A public trash can in tony Claremont was about to burst into flames.

Just then a quick-thinking patron drinking on the patio walked over and poured beer from her cup into the trash can. She peered in at the result.

"I need more beer," she reported. She returned to her table, picked up a pitcher and poured a stream onto the smoldering trash, successfully dousing the flame.

Beer. It fights fires.

February 1, 2006

Fontana plans a $200,000 marketing blitz to tout the city's charms. Among the slogans: "Fontana: a Fountain of Opportunities" and "Fontana is for Everyone."

Reader Judi Guizado, a former resident of that windswept burg, offers her own tongue-in-cheek slogan: "Fontana: It Will Blow You Over!"

February 17, 2006

San Dimas High hosted a career day Thursday with speakers from 100 different professions, including yours truly talking about journalism. Students asked good questions. One asked what newspapers I read.

After answering, I tried to make conversation, asking what papers he reads. "I don't read any newspapers," he replied.

As a fellow who has asked countless questions over the years without necessarily caring about the answers, I have to admit he has the makings of a good journalist.

March 10, 2006

No 2005 movie had an Inland Valley reference, as I wrote here the other day? Turns out I missed a big one, as reader Jaime Alvarez alerted me: *Crash*. Yes, the Oscar winner for Best Picture drops a mention of Pomona. No wonder *Crash* beat *Brokeback Mountain*.

After a crucial scene involving off-duty LAPD cop Ryan Phillippe, we hear a DJ on his car radio say: "That was Merle Haggard here on KYHA Reseda, country music here in L.A. It's a cold night and it's getting colder. And we're giving out tickets to the rodeo coming up at the Fairplex in Pomona, so give us a call…"

How about that!

A lot of movies have mentioned our cities over the years, true. But to my knowledge, *Crash* is the first Best Picture winner to do it.

Now that I've said that, of course, some film buff is going to prove me wrong. What are the odds there's a joke about Cucamonga in *Ben-Hur*…?

March 15, 2006

The mural on the west side of Haven Building Materials' tin building in Rancho Cucamonga depicts, from left to right, mountains; an alpine forest; the lowlands; and waves crashing against a beach, all against an azure sky.

The panorama wraps around the south side but trails off unfinished, like Gilbert Stuart's portrait of George Washington. I always meant to ask about this. (The mural, not George Washington.) Unfortunately, the mural has a new, spray-painted addition: "Going Out of Business Sale."

Sue Johnson, who owns Haven with her husband, Bob, told me Tuesday they sold their 4.71 acres to a New York developer for a business park.

"We got a nice price for the land. We were ready to retire anyway," Sue said. They plan to close on Friday.

Located on Haven Avenue at Sixth Street, Haven catered to do-it-yourselfers who wanted decorative brick, rock or stone for landscaping, patios or ponds. The business was founded in 1977 by Joseph and Bobbi Stromme, who sold to the Johnsons in 1995 when Joseph died.

That year, Sue and her cousin, Carol Hughes of Ontario, a real-estate broker, began painting the mural. "We just wanted to dress it up a little bit. They raised us up with forklifts and pallets. I got to do the sky and she did the rest," Sue said. "She's the artist."

The scene served as a backdrop for outdoor sculptures. The south side was to have a lighthouse with a beacon, meant as a landmark to guide motorists.

But Sue had emergency heart surgery and the mural was never finished. Instead there was a gray blotch – eventually blocked by a strategically placed construction bin.

There were other quirky touches to Haven, like a koi pond and a four-hole putting green, complete with sand trap. Almost everything is gone now, as customers buy whatever isn't nailed down, and some that is.

Say, does anybody want a 60-foot-long mural on tin? Consider it a do-it-yourself project. After all, it's unfinished.

March 24, 2006

Kids, sometimes it's OK to talk to strangers. At Monday's Pomona City Council meeting, Vice Mayor Elliott Rothman read a whereas-filled proclamation about Girl Scout Week, then tried to hand the ceremonial document to the two young Scouts with him on the dais.

Both girls looked up at him curiously but kept their hands at their sides.

"Must be the 'Don't take proclamations from strangers' thing," Rothman quipped, handing the document to the Scout leader with them. "Let me try an adult."

March 26, 2006

Inland Valley references on TV are becoming (yawn) routine. Recently viewers of UPN's detective drama *Veronica Mars* heard a teenager worry aloud about being "sent to Chino," while the next night, on NBC's comedy *The Office*, Steve Carell blew a toy train whistle and announced, "Next train to Cucamonga!"

April 16, 2006

Fresh evidence the 909 has arrived: the launch of *Inland Empire Weekly*. The debut issue, released Friday, takes a cheeky, attitude-laced look at the region. Writers mock Riverside County's giant landfill, extol the Rancho Cucamonga punk haven Dr. Strange Records and enjoy, with reservations, Upland's Buffalo Inn ("good times for the downwardly mobile").

As the introductory piece by editor Stacy Davies and contributor Bill Gerdes sympathizes: "Few places on Earth are as misunderstood and misrepresented as the Inland Empire."

True. But is the Inland Empire hip enough to embrace an alternative weekly? My guess is yes, although there may be rough patches at first. For instance, expect the *Weekly* to be inundated with classified ads peddling "pre-owned" meth labs.

Based on its debut, the Corona-based staff knows the region's ins and outs, not to mention its In-N-Outs. While the competition makes me nervous, I'm glad the *Weekly* is here because we'll all benefit.

Not only does the paper promise to be a fun, sassy read, but even if many of you readers never pick it up, its existence will keep me on my toes. See? Everyone's a winner.

April 21, 2006

Decrying the scourge of "degenerative Madisonianism," George Will, the polysyllabic conservative columnist, spoke over the heads of some 200 people Tuesday night at Claremont McKenna College's Athenaeum.

In his remarks on the state of society, Will lamented "the politics of cognitive dissonance" and "nonstop rent-seeking." The latter is a grave concern of mine, especially on the first of the month. But it turns out Will was objecting to what he called "the unrestrained, conscience-free scramble for government benefits," rather than the unrestrained knocking of his landlord.

To drive home his points, Will used such punchy adjectives as "deleterious," "inimical" and "counterintuitive." His audience, including yours truly, chuckled appreciatively at Will's wit. We prayed we did so at the right times. Frankly, it was a little like guessing when to clap at the symphony.

Things got racy, or perhaps not, when Will spoke of the moment in time "when liberalism bifurcated."

Actually, many of his comments were more transparent. Well, unless I'm kidding myself.

Will is aghast at President Bush's big-government expansion of Medicare and the invasion of Iraq. And he's alarmed about the unwillingness of government, and Americans themselves, to make hard choices.

Toward the close, Will was – by his standards – conversational, delivering quips about complex coffee orders and his beloved Chicago Cubs. "On that note," Will said, with a small smile, "I shall subside."

When we realized he meant he was done, we applauded.

August 11, 2006

Knowing me, knowing you, the existence of a doctor's office named ABBA Chiropractic will be of interest. It's on Mountain Avenue in Upland and bears an eye-catching sign that calls to mind the 1970s Swedish supergroup. Is the chiropractor's name Fernando or Chiquitita? Do they treat the back pains of dancing queens?

When I phoned on Wednesday, the receptionist answered simply, "Doctor's office." After confirming this was ABBA Chiropractic, I introduced myself as a humor columnist and asked if she or someone else would mind explaining the name's meaning.

She sighed and said: "Actually, we don't need that. Thank you," and hung up.

I admit I'm disappointed. I'd hoped ABBA Chiropractic would take a chance on me.

September 20, 2006

As I waited for my lunch Tuesday in Rancho Cucamonga, the waitress came over with an update that my food would be out soon. She added: "You ordered the grilled chicken sandwich and fruit, right?"

That was correct, but as I looked around the diner I wondered whose order mine might have been mixed up with. I was the only customer.

September 20, 2006

In Pomona, the drinking game continues to evolve. At the September 11 City Council meeting, Councilman Dan Rodriguez at one point uttered the phrase "at the end of the day," prompting Councilman Marco Robles to say, "Hey, that's my line."

On Monday, it was Councilman George Hunter who stepped on Robles' toes by uttering "at the end of the day." Robles caught my eye, smiled, shrugged and mouthed, "He stole my line."

Viewers at home, you're now advised to drink any time anyone says "at the end of the day."

September 27, 2006

The blues: A week ago, in its first appearance in color, my photo here had a blue tint, prompting one sensitive co-worker to crack that it looked like I'd just been pulled out of the morgue freezer.

So we've switched to a more recent photo. Reviews of my face have not been promising.

"Your new picture in the newspaper looks terrible," a reader called to inform me. "Please go back to your old one. Thank you."

If anyone wants me, I'll either be curled up in a ball under my desk, or back in the freezer.

October 11, 2006

On Friday at a church event in Upland, a senior citizen told me I should get a new photo because I look considerably younger in person. Still flush from this compliment, your columnist spent the next afternoon with members of the Pomona High class of 1956, all of whom are in their late 60s.

One man, informed I write for the newspaper, stunned my 42-year-old self by inquiring: "Are you also in our class?"

Next time you see me in public, I'll either be walking tall in Upland, or in Pomona wearing a bag over my head.

October 20, 2006

It started as word at a Fontana City Council meeting that a teacher and principal at Fontana Middle School would be flipping burgers at McDonald's to raise money for an eighth-grade trip to Washington, D.C. Mayor Mark Nuaimi joked about how many hamburgers he could eat to help out. Taking the bait, Councilwoman Acquanetta Warren said she'd give the class $10 for each burger the mayor could scarf within five minutes.

People in the audience piped up, offering their own pledges of $10, $20 or even $100 for each hamburger Nuaimi could choke down. The per-burger total: $275.

The next day, Nuaimi showed up to the McDonald's event and dug into a plate of single hamburgers, the clock ticking.

"The first two, no problem," algebra/science teacher Daniel Quiroga told me Thursday. After that, Nuaimi took a tip from the world of competitive eating, dipping his burgers into a cup of soda to compress the bun. "The kids were all grossed out," Quiroga said.

But they egged Nuaimi on, chanting "Eat it! Eat it!" as

he doggedly kept chewing. At the 4:40-minute mark, with 20 seconds left, Nuaimi was having trouble swallowing his sixth hamburger. But he sluggishly picked up a seventh.

"He just put the whole burger in his mouth," said an impressed Quiroga. "He took a full minute to begin chewing. He kept showing it to the kids."

I know McDonald's slogan is "we love to see you smile," but not while you're eating, Mr. Mayor.

The class got $450 from Quiroga and Principal Giovanni Annous' three-hour burger-flipping effort and $1,925 from Nuaimi's five-minute stunt. "The kids appreciated it. So did I," Quiroga said. All told, the class has $8,000 and needs another $29,000.

Incidentally, the original $10 challenge to the mayor to eat more McDonald's food was from an unlikely source. Councilwoman Warren is a fitness champion who leads the Healthy Fontana campaign for diet and exercise.

It'll take a lot of exercise to burn off seven McDonald's burgers. Not to mention the soda.

November 1, 2006

Hot Air Dept.: 'Tis the season for gusty Santa Ana winds, which rush through the Cajon Pass, flatten trees in Fontana and Rancho Cucamonga, and heat up fall afternoons. And, for that matter, inspire famous authors. To wit:

"October is the bad month for the wind, the month when breathing is difficult and the hills blaze up spontaneously. There has been no rain since April. Every voice seems a scream. It is the season of suicide and divorce and prickly dread, wherever the wind blows." – Joan Didion, "Some Dreamers of the Golden Dream"

"One night the notorious Santa Ana winds began to blow in from the desert. ... The grevillea twisted, branches broke off, clattering palm fronds were ripped away, trash cans bounced down the street. We were afraid the windows were going to blow in. Finally, when daylight came and the winds calmed, we dragged ourselves out of bed. Everything was covered in dust, and under the closed kitchen window sand was a quarter of an inch deep." – Beverly Cleary, recalling 1930s Ontario in *My Own Two Feet*.

"There was a desert wind blowing that night. It was one of those hot dry Santa Anas that come down through the mountain passes and curl your hair and make your nerves jump and your skin itch. On nights like that every booze party ends in a fight. Meek little wives feel the edge of a carving knife and study their husbands' necks. Anything can happen. You can even get a full glass of beer at a cocktail lounge." – Raymond Chandler, "Red Wind"

By the way, I hope you didn't find this column item long-winded.

December 1, 2006

Called for jury duty at the Pomona courthouse Monday, I went to the Jury Assembly Room. We potential jurors were welcomed with a pep talk by Judge Robert Dukes, who noted the drizzly weather. "Can anyone see out the window if it's raining in the South Bay?" Dukes began. "I want to tell my wife it's coming down in Torrance."

More seriously, Dukes went on to explain why we were called, the importance of the jury system – "it's the only time most of you will become part of one of the three branches of government" – and the 97 percent satisfaction rate of jurors (if not of defendants and lawyers).

He also put in a plug for Pomona, in which his family has lived since 1896. There's plenty to do downtown on our lunch hour, he told us, recommending lunch at 2nd Street Bistro, Lela's, Joey's BBQ or an eatery three blocks south that he cited as his favorite, Mexico Lindo. He also suggested we check out Second Street's art galleries and antique stores.

Isn't that neat? Not only is Dukes a judge, he's a downtown greeter too.

In the courtroom of Judge Charles Horan, 12 people were put in the jury box and quizzed about their background. It was friendly, with a couple of exceptions.

One woman told Horan testily that she had philosophical problems with serving on a jury. Pressed to elaborate, she declared: "I don't believe in the court system."

"It exists. It's here," the judge replied. "Trust me."

Another of the 12 also said he was not fit to serve. Asked why, he spat out: "Because I'm sane!"

"This is quite a day," Horan sighed.

A bit later, the judge, who said he makes an informal survey out of the question, asked the 12 if they had brought reading material and if so, what. In a sobering moment for this writer and lifelong reader, only four of the 12 answered yes.

One had a book. A second had a parenting magazine. A third had a book but hadn't touched it. The fourth? "Just the pamphlet that came with the jury summons," the man said, as everyone laughed.

"You actually read that?" Horan quipped.

I was later chosen for the jury box but was bumped as a juror by the prosecutor, thus completing my service for the year. I'll consider it an early Christmas present.

Incidentally, my own reading material was a vintage crime novel. Next time I'm called for jury service, I'll bring *Moby-Dick* or *Remembrance of Things Past* to really wow the judge.

December 13, 2006

Worrisome economic indicator: On East Holt Avenue in Pomona, the former First Bargain 99 Cents Store is now known as – uh-oh – Everything $2.99 and Up.

December 15, 2006

Eating Chinese recently in Rancho Cucamonga, I got this fortune in my cookie: "You discover treasures where others see nothing unusual." If my column had a motto, that would be it!

APPARENTLY THE I.E. IS WORTHY OF LITERATURE

January 14, 2007

There are no paeans to Montclair, I'm afraid, but *Inlandia: A Literary Journey Through California's Inland Empire* (Heyday Books, $18.95) does explore other parts of our sprawling landscape.

Sure, we can quibble with the dream-like name Inlandia, which as descriptives go is even cornier than Inland Empire.

Still, the book's content is intriguing and unprecedented. Editor Gayle Wattawa collected dozens of stories, essays and poems, some by major literary figures, each one taking the measure of our mildly misunderstood milieu.

A few quotable highlights:

"San Bernardino baked and shimmered in the afternoon heat. The air was hot enough to blister my tongue. I drove through it gasping, stopped long enough to buy a pint of liquor in case I fainted before I got to the mountains, and started up the long grade to Crestline."
— Raymond Chandler, *The Lady in the Lake*

"Past Fontana Drag City and the Fontana Church of the Nazarene and the Pit Stop A Go-Go; past Kaiser Steel, through Cucamonga, out to the Kapu Kai Restaurant-Bar and Coffee Shop, at the corner of Route 66 and Carnelian Avenue. Up Carnelian Avenue from the Kapu Kai, which means 'Forbidden Seas,' the subdivision flags whip in the harsh wind. 'HALF-ACRE RANCHES! SNACK BARS! TRAVERTINE ENTRIES! $95 DOWN.' It is the trail of an intention gone haywire, the flotsam of the New California."

— Joan Didion, "Some Dreamers of the Golden Dream"

"...In Rancho Cucamonga/ burnt offerings/ of native homes/ quickly despair/ into legend/ We all dine on ash/ as California,/ twirls her fires/ layering the sunset/ in a glorious pied sky."

— Rowena Silver, "That Dusky Scent"

"Cruising Base Line, in fact, is rather like watching a Jim Jarmusch movie. The dull moments are always promptly relieved by some new enigma or unexpected absurdity."

— Mike Davis, "The Inland Empire"

And thank goodness they are. Without the 909's enigmas and unexpected absurdities, what would I write about?

If a sequel to *Inlandia* is warranted – suggested title: *The Perris Review* – plenty of other scribes have mentioned the Inland Empire in print, including Jonathan Kellerman, Dean Koontz and Kem Nunn.

They've been quoted here before, but some other authors' works have recently come to my attention.

In Stephen King's *The Green Mile*, a pile of old newspapers is said to be "stacked in a pair of Pomona orange crates," reader Will Plunkett alerts me.

In Michael Connelly's new Harry Bosch crime novel, *Echo Park*, LAPD cops are trying to figure out the birthplace of a murder suspect who claims he was born in L.A., though there's no record of his birth. One cop wonders if the guy "lied about being born here. It's like when you're born out in Riverside, you tell everybody you're from L.A."

Hey, if I were from Riverside, I might tell people I was from L.A., too.

Finally, from Louis L'Amour's *Hondo* (1953), a Western set in Arizona:

"Buffalo looked around slowly. 'Been tryin' to figure out what this place reminds me of, Hondo. It's that ranch of your'n in California. Where we stayed before we went to fight with those people up north. Under a bluff just like this, creek and mesa spreading out …'

"Angie looked up at Hondo. 'You have a place that looks like this?'

"'East of San Dimas.'"

Ahhh, those La Verne cowboys.

Rancho Cucamonga Sea Monster's Fate Prompts a Sinking Feeling

January 17, 2007

Rancho Cucamonga's answer to the Loch Ness monster is – gasp! – gone.

Or at least on its way out.

Our sea serpent, which plied a weedy field on Haven Avenue south of Eighth Street, was a horizontal tree trunk with a neck-like vertical branch. In other words, while not authentic, it was more real than the beastie in Scotland.

When I wrote about her last April, I called the wooden creature Nessie, the Log Ness monster. Employees of neighboring Degussa Construction Chemicals also noted the resemblance to the mythical serpent and said the log had been there since – whoa! – the 1960s.

Despite its terrifying appearance, Nessie's continued presence was actually kind of reassuring.

I say that if a humorous piece of wood can stay in a field in fast-growing Rancho Cucamonga, year after year, with mowers mowing around it, life is OK.

Recently, though, Haven south of Foothill Boulevard has become a hive of activity. Several square blocks, or most of the remaining rural lots, have been cleared in preparation for development. An underpass will be built under the railroad tracks just yards from Nessie.

All this had me worried about Nessie's future. My fears were unfortunately well-founded.

Late last week, I glanced over at the field while driving by. Nessie wasn't in her usual spot.

She was lying on her side near broken concrete and freshly turned dirt, as if ready to be carted off like so much construction debris.

Noooooooo!

She wasn't aware of Nessie, but Maria Perez, associate city engineer for Rancho Cucamonga, told me Tuesday the field will be paved and used as temporary traffic lanes when Haven is closed for construction of the underpass. She said a water district contractor tore up the field.

Don't think me mean-spirited, but I hope when he moved Nessie, he got a splinter.

The end of 'The O.C.' leaves dry eyes in Chino

February 21, 2007

Thursday brings the last episode of Fox's *The O.C.*, the youth soap that put Chino on the map – even if Chino didn't want to be there.

You may recall that the series set in Orange County occasionally depicted Chino as a gritty urban ghetto, much to some residents' consternation.

Thankfully, with *The O.C.* off the air, this cloud will lift. The city's reputation will be restored. Once again, Chino will be known for its signature development: its world-class prisons!

(Which is unfortunate, since Chino is actually a nice place.)

The series' demise has been met by a shrug in Chino, the city that once sent angry letters to the series' producers accusing them of not producing a documentary. They wanted a realistic portrayal of Chino? *The O.C.* wasn't even a realistic portrayal of Orange County.

"I thought it was already dead and buried. This Thursday's the last episode? That's news to me," Chino Mayor Dennis Yates admitted Tuesday.

Chino's younger generation is probably more conflicted. Anyway, after four seasons of occasional prime-time mentions of Chino, Riverside and the like, it seemed to me the passing of *The O.C.* ought to be memorialized in this space.

The premise, as you may recall, is that a Newport Beach family adopts a good-hearted but trouble-prone teenager from Chino. A classic fish-out-of-water saga ensues. Well, if "classic" means "with lots of emo music."

The tone was established in the first episode. Summer, a snobbish Newport girl, learns Ryan's hometown, wrinkles her nose and says: "Chino? Ewww."

This was a joke about Newport arrogance and class divisions, all the more ironic because Orange County is itself a stepchild to Los Angeles. Still, it didn't help that the TV version of Chino usually involved stolen cars and working-class homes with sofas in the front yard.

These Chino scenes, by the way, were really filmed in Sun Valley, Venice, Lawndale, Monterey Park and East L.A., as the online site *seeing-stars.com* puzzled out. In other words, in cities even Chino can be snobbish about.

Will I miss *The O.C.*? Surprisingly, yes. I tuned in expecting to mock it but ended up a fan.

Yes, the plots were ridiculous, but that was the point. Because the show was in on its own joke, the episodes were often hilarious.

For many of us, a highlight was high school outsider Seth Cohen's immersion in pop-culture geekdom, which led to references to cult movies, music and even, obscurely but accurately, comic book writers.

Speaking of *O.C.* dialogue, a few greatest hits:

Anna to Ryan, teasing him about his early mishaps in Newport: "Are you the kid from Chino who steals cars and burns down people's houses?"

Summer: "He comes from a place with knife fights and street racing and sex on the hood of cars."

Marissa: "That's *Fast and the Furious*."

Summer: "It's based on a true story!"

Summer, about a new girl: "She's from Pittsburgh. That's like the 909 of the East."

Sandy Cohen: "It's Ryan's first Seder."

Seth: "How do you know? They have Jews in Chino. Why do you think they want a P.F. Chang?"

Caleb, explaining to his daughter why Ryan wouldn't be interested in seeing a Hollywood Bowl concert with them: "I just figured Ryan wouldn't be a classical music fan."

Lindsey, sarcastically: "Riiight, because they don't have classical music in Chino."

Oh, and one favorite:

Guest star Paris Hilton, upon learning where Summer and her friends are from: "Orange County? Ewww."

Mayor Yates told me he never watched *The O.C.*, and thus never got upset about it, a refreshing attitude.

"One thing about the show, it did give Chino some notoriety – at no cost to us either," Yates volunteered. "You can't get advertising like that for free every day."

No, you (sniff) can't.

RIP, *O.C.*

Phone exchanges brought Yukon to Upland

March 4, 2007

Telephone exchanges are known to many of us today only through old movies. ("Operator, get me Klondike 5-1234!") or the occasional vintage song ("Beechwood 4-5789," "Pennsylvania 6-5000").

An exchange at first was a physical place, an office staffed with switchboard operators connecting callers ("What number, please?"). Names for the exchanges represented local calling areas.

Later, exchanges were simply a word representing the first two digits of a seven-digit phone number. Beechwood 4-5789 would really be 234-5789, for instance.

An exchange made a string of numbers easier to remember, not to mention adding a certain flair.

Exchanges were mentioned here recently courtesy of reader Cecelia Brewart, who offered up several classics from our inland cities. "Maybe your readers can remember the other cities," Brewart suggested.

Did they ever. But first, whatever happened to exchanges?

They remained in use here until 1965, when all phone numbers became seven numerals. "All Number Calling – numerals replace letters," a notice in Ontario's 1965 phone book reads.

Still, some businesses continued to promote their two-letter/five-digit number long after that. Not only were the combinations catchy, but who wants to repaint their delivery van if they can help it?

As for why exchanges were phased out, I blame society's age-old desire to stamp out fun. America also needed more phone numbers, yet some combinations, such as 95, were off-limits because they couldn't be turned into words. Hey, you try starting a word with WXY or JKL.

Now for the local exchanges:

FLeetwood (35) for San Dimas, West Covina, Azusa

LYcoming (59) for La Verne and portions of Pomona and Chino

NAtional (62) for Pomona, Montclair, Claremont and Chino

OVerland (68) for Riverside

REpublic (73) for Norco

PYramid (79) for Mentone

VAlley and TAlbot (82) for Fontana and Colton, respectively

TRiangle (87) for Rialto

TUxedo and TUrner (88) for San Bernardino

YUkon (98) for Ontario, Upland and Cucamonga.

YUkon? Finally, a connection between the Chaffey communities and the frozen tundra.

A tip of the columnist fedora to readers Harriet Hagstrom Butterfield, Julie Geach, Chuck Brasch, Tim Hite, Marian Naito, James Rodriguez, Bob House, Eldon Roberson, Dave Dobbin, Beth Brooks, Barbara Myers, Gene Harvey, Larry and Sherrill Roan, Jay Tissot, Bob Terry, Bill Runyan, Lesley Sherwood James, Nita Ulloa, Shirley Kelley and Kathy Ferguson for the replies.

Clearly there is a lot of interest in the 909 in old phone numbers.

Here's a related note from reader Julie Geach of Pomona:

"My best girlfriend lived in Pomona in 1957, I in Upland. Her prefix was LYcoming, mine YUkon. My father, 'Red' Watson, used to complain, with humor, about the 10 cents for three minutes the phone company charged for our numerous calls."

A website that may be of interest is the Telephone Exchange Name Project. A list of vintage Ma Bell-recommended exchanges on the site would enable most of you to invent an exchange for your own number. For instance, for my work phone, the first two digits of which are 48, exchanges could be HUbbard, HUdson, HUnter, HUntley, HUxley or IVanhoe.

IVanhoe! That's almost as neat as YUkon.

Still, none of these have any Inland Valley flavor, so I experimented with the GHI/TUV offered by my keypad.

Eventually an exchange suggested itself, one with real sentimental value.

Consider my number GUasti 3-9339.

LOOKING BACK ON 10 YEARS OF CHANGES

March 11, 2007

Ten years. It was on March 10, 1997, that yours truly stepped into the *Inland Valley Daily Bulletin* office for his first day of work. I filled out forms in Human Resources and then watched an all-purpose employee safety video starring burly actor Claude Akins, who explained, among other things, how to properly operate a forklift.

No one can say the *Daily Bulletin* doesn't train its workforce. Alas, I haven't had a chance to drive a forklift, but that disappointment aside, my decade in Ontario has been tremendous fun (mostly).

Please indulge me for today's column as I reflect.

I didn't start as a columnist. I arrived here as a news reporter after a decade at papers in Rohnert Park, Petaluma and Victorville.

In my 10 years in Ontario, I've written pretty much every kind of story, from government to crime to features to (really) fashion.

My focus, of course, has become this column, which began in 1997 as an occasional piece, went twice a week in 1998 and became my full-time assignment on – I just looked this up, and what a coincidence – March 11, 2001. Six years!

I could regale you with highlights and lowlights, but instead, let me share something about Thursday night's Charles Phoenix slide show at the Pomona Library.

The room was packed, and afterward, probably 20 people thanked me for alerting them to the event and just for doing what I do. It was a humbling moment, and … just a second.

Honk!

OK (sniff), back to work.

What's really amazing to me is how drastically the Inland Valley has changed since 1997.

Ontario Mills has essentially doubled in size and Victoria Gardens transformed Rancho Cucamonga, making the Inland Empire safe for Crate and Barrel and the Cheesecake Factory.

Fontana got the California Speedway, and what with the city's new high-end homes, Fontana is now envied rather than joked about.

Traffic, however, has gone from bad to awful, offset only somewhat by the addition of the 210 Freeway and more frequent commuter train and bus service.

A lot of mom-and-pop businesses have closed, from hardware stores to restaurants, as giant chains muscle their way in.

And, of course, homes have sprung up everywhere, even in unlikely spots. My favorite is the homes crammed onto a sliver of land along a drainage channel on Rancho Cucamonga's Carnelian Avenue.

Frankly, barring worldwide economic collapse or the Rapture, the next 10 years may prove even wilder.

In Rancho, sleepy Haven Avenue from Foothill Boulevard south is readying for a development explosion, with signs announcing hundreds of homes and businesses coming to virtually every vacant lot.

Developers will also focus on our neglected downtowns. We may not recognize downtown Upland, Ontario and Pomona in 10 years, given ambitious plans in the works to convert parking lots into multi-story housing.

As for Claremont's downtown, I don't recognize it now.

Pomona may see the biggest boom – and not from gunfire. It's the most urbanized city we have, and that makes it ripe for a type of high-rise development out of place anywhere else in the valley.

Even the 400-acre vacant lot across the street from the *Daily Bulletin*'s Ontario office, which we've been staring at helplessly for years, is being sold to developers with the means to do something with it.

Speaking of the *Daily Bulletin*, the news about the newspaper business is gloomy. With younger people treating newsprint like it's toxic, our subscriber rolls are essentially being serialized on the obituary page.

Meanwhile, nobody knows how to make an online newspaper profitable. These are uncertain times, and we could use your support.

Still, while I wouldn't encourage teenagers to pursue journalism as a career path right now, something tells me the *Daily Bulletin*, which will soon celebrate 125 years if you include its numerous predecessors, will survive somehow.

Ten years in one job. For me, it's a milestone and a vote of confidence – who knew I was employable, much less this long? – and the occasion presents a nice vantage point for looking back, and forward too.

What will the future bring for me? I don't know, although I hope to be here chronicling the good, the bad and the ugly of all these changes to our landscape.

But if the columnist gig ever dries up, I'm ready.

Just give me a forklift. And stand clear.

Beep beep beep…

Pomona's Odd Combo Makes N.Y. Times News

April 13, 2007

Pomona was visited recently by the *New York Times*. Was the *Times* interested in urban blight? Gangs? Historic theaters?

No. A *Times* columnist focused on an unprepossessing Pomona restaurant, one whose name comprises two items rarely offered at the same eatery: Donut & Burger.

"Not all the food it serves is circular. You can get fries," observed the *Times*. "You can get fries with your cinnamon roll if you want. Most people, I suppose, order either the doughnut or the burger.

"But I felt I had to order the doughnut and the burger. It was the eponymous thing to do, and I knew I would be doing it only once."

The writer was the exquisitely named Verlyn Klinkenborg. His piece, "Letter From California: A Hidden Populace in a Vacant Lot," appeared on the *Times*' Opinion page March 23. What, you were expecting a Frank Bruni restaurant review?

The hidden populace was in the vacant lot next to Donut & Burger. As Klinkenborg sat in his truck scarfing his doughnut and his burger, he noticed that on the other side of the chain-link fence, ground squirrels were popping out of dirt burrows like prairie dogs in Wyoming.

Somehow, marveled Klinkenborg, these urban squirrels survive despite being hemmed in by an auto parts store, a busy street, an apartment complex's back alley and the parking lot of Donut & Burger. He added: "I wondered if they had been reduced to eating fries."

I emailed Klinkenborg, who replied that he was here as a visiting writer-in-residence at Claremont's Pomona College, his alma mater.

He said Donut & Burger – full name: Sunrize Donut & Burger – is on Towne Avenue at Arrow Highway. Once there, I realized I'd driven past it many times. It just hadn't made an impression.

So much for a job at the *Times*.

On my lunch hour Monday, I drove to the cube-like restaurant, which stood sentry in a cracked asphalt lot. Next door, squirrels emerged from burrows as if on cue and bounded around for my entertainment.

The young woman behind D&B's walk-up window told me with a smile: "Some customers take pictures of the squirrels. Some want to get rid of them."

Tragically, the menu has no burger-doughnut special, so I made my own, ordering the burger-fries-soda combo and adding a chocolate raised doughnut. I ate at an outdoor table by a trash can.

My entire lunch came to a mere $3.80. Weird as it was, it was worth every penny.

Besides its namesake items, D&B sells muffins, teriyaki bowls, bear claws, pastrami, fried rice and croissants. I left a message for the owner, who didn't call, perhaps being too busy learning new recipes.

Although the *New York Times* got me on Donut & Burger, I got them on Pomona's other monument to gastronomic variety: Golden Wok, on Garey Avenue at Artesia Street.

"Since the piece came out, any number of people have told me about the one at Garey," Klinkenborg said via email, sounding chastened.

Golden Wok sells doughnuts and burgers, plus 15 Chinese entrees, fish and chips, fruit smoothies and – why not? – Louisiana fried chicken. But there are no squirrels next door.

Be warned, the extreme swing of choices makes reading the menu board an almost paralyzing experience. The sense of culinary dislocation didn't end there.

When I ordered the fried chicken, the woman behind the counter asked solemnly: "French fries or fried rice?"

Manager Alan Chow told me the new owners, who bought the former Mandarin Express and Burger six months ago, added the fried chicken franchise while upgrading the Chinese food.

Bakers come in at 10 p.m. to make the doughnuts, muffins and croissants. Three shifts in the kitchen deal with everything else; they serve food 24 hours.

You could spend your day at Golden Wok, or at Donut & Burger, eating a different cuisine at each time of day. They're like all-in-one food courts.

Will Golden Wok add any more items – say, quesadillas and spaghetti?

"One of the customers did propose pizza," Chow said with a laugh. "I don't know. If we added anything, we'd have to take something off. We're at the max now."

Maybe so, but I wouldn't be surprised if a sushi bar were installed by the bakery case.

No survey of Pomona dining oddities would be complete without mentioning the L.A. County Fair. The fair last fall debuted a chicken sandwich served on, instead of a bun, a halved doughnut – and topped with Swiss cheese and honey.

Thriving next to an auto parts store is one thing. But even Pomona's squirrels might not be hardy enough to survive a Krispy Kreme Chicken Sandwich.

Series cast spell on Potter fan

July 18, 2007

Shayna Ingram was finishing seventh grade at Alta Loma Junior High when her teacher, Mrs. Walker, began reading aloud to the class, a chapter a day, from a then-obscure book, *Harry Potter and the Sorcerer's Stone*.

Entrancing? No.

"I thought it was really stupid," Ingram recalled this week. Not only did she find the book confusing, she resented being all of 13 years old and yet read to as if she were a child.

Worse yet, Mrs. Walker got only halfway through the book by the end of the school year. Fuming about being left hanging, even on a book she despised, Ingram bought a copy.

Maybe this was part of her teacher's evil plan, because Ingram went bonkers for the book. She loved the vivid characters – Harry was her own age – and the plot twists. She quickly read the second book, which was newly published, then searched the internet for more information.

This was 1999, and hard as it may be to believe today, the internet had almost nothing on Harry Potter. And so the Rancho Cucamonga girl who was years away from a driver's license launched *harrypotterrealm.com*, one of the first Potter sites.

Diligent readers may recall that I interviewed Ingram in 2003, before the release of the fifth Potter book, when her site was getting 6,000 visitors a day.

Her site hasn't been updated in quite some time because of other priorities. But Ingram, now 21 and a junior at UC Santa Barbara, is still a hardcore Potter fan. Eight years of magical thinking? Joan Didion only got one.

As Ingram told me when we met Monday at a Rancho Cucamonga coffee bar, she's eagerly, and nervously, anticipating the seventh and final book, *Harry Potter and the Deathly Hallows*.

"At least we'll have closure," she said solemnly.

Ingram will be at Barnes and Noble in Rancho Cucamonga at midnight Friday for the book's release, dressed as character Luna Lovegood and praying the book's surprises aren't ruined before she can finish reading its 784 pages – which she hopes to do within 24 hours.

"England will have the book eight hours in advance, so it'll be all over the internet what happens," Ingram told me worriedly. She's heard rumors that spoilsports will show up at the midnight book-release parties and shout out plot points.

"I'm going to wear earplugs," she vowed.

Personally, as a slow reader, I'm resigned to having the ending spoiled before I can get there. The big surprise (I won't say what it is) of Book 6 was ruined for me by two separate newspaper articles. At the time I hadn't even read Book 5.

Ingram, who was midway through a fast re-read of the six books when we got together, hopes to finish Book 6 by Friday night. We sat down to hash out some theories.

Although the character Professor Snape did a very bad thing in Book 6 and everyone hates him, I'm convinced he's a double agent who is pretending to be bad to help the good guys. Ingram agrees.

"You can't always believe what Harry and the students

think," she said sagely. "I really think Snape will be the one who can help Harry defeat Voldemort."

Author J.K. Rowling has said two major characters will die. My guess is Snape and Voldemort, not Harry or his friends. Ingram said my theory is "totally valid," which was nice to hear, but she thinks the goners are Voldemort and – gasp – Harry himself.

"I really like Snape, so I hope he doesn't die, but I think Harry's going to die no matter what," Ingram said grimly. "I don't really have a hopeful outlook on his survival."

He's suffered so much, and will have to sacrifice so much more, that by the end of Book 7 Harry will be beyond saving, she explained. Cheerful, eh?

But I'm not surprised she envisions a miserable ending. Her favorite character is the tortured Snape, an ambiguous figure who delights in making Harry's life miserable. He's played in the movies by Alan Rickman, who is disdain personified.

"He's so cool. I love Snape. He's so angsty," Ingram confided. "I've always liked him. I thought he was a misunderstood character."

Incidentally, her favorite *Lost* character is the hated, embittered Sawyer, so I'm sensing a pattern.

As for Book 7, explaining the setup is impossible, so I won't try. For fans, then, here is one paragraph, undiluted, of Ingram's predictions, based on dangling loose ends, close study and wishful thinking:

The house elves and Lupin may play crucial roles, Draco Malfoy will be redeemed, Wormtail's debt to Harry from Book 3 will be repaid, the "R.A.B." who stole the horcrux is Sirius' brother and Harry – this one floored me – may constitute a horcrux himself!

Can I say "horcrux" in a family newspaper?

In case her devotion to the boy magician has made her seem myopic, let me add that Ingram is a smart and seemingly well-rounded person.

She studied abroad in England last year and is majoring in English and international relations. (The Potter books inspired both interests.) She also likes the novels of Don DeLillo and Milan Kundera and the plays of Henrik Ibsen.

She even has a boyfriend. I didn't ask if he's angsty.

Through her website, "I made a lot of good friends from all over the world," Ingram said. "So, yeah, Harry Potter's been good for me."

Too bad he may bite the big wand.

ONTARIO CEMETERY HOLDS 51,000 STORIES

September 2, 2007

I was taking a trip to the cemetery – under my own steam, thankfully – for what might sound like a hopeless mission: an interview.

Yes, dead men tell no tales, but I had been promised a live one. Bud Christian had retired after 18 years of running Bellevue Memorial Park in Ontario, and Gino Filippi, the cemetery board member who introduced us, assured me Christian was a fascinating character.

Although he retired effective July 31, Christian agreed to come out of retirement long enough to show me where the bodies are buried. Talk about a journalist's dream.

Bellevue, on West G Street, was founded in 1892. It's the final resting place for much of the West End.

"When I came to Ontario in 1957, the population of Ontario was about 28,000 and Upland was 12,000," Christian notes. "We're at 51,000 interments now."

He's a trim, sharply dressed man with a head of white hair, a sedate if twinkling manner and a concern for the departed. The grounds are well tended, even in sections that get few visitors.

"If we don't look out for and speak up for the dead, who will? That's our charge in life," he says of cemetery employees.

We start our tour in Bellevue's oldest section, toward Mountain Avenue. It looks like the Gothic cemetery of our imagination, full of upright tombstones, family crypts and atmosphere. Modern sections have flat markers and resemble a park.

"We don't have any celebrities," Christian had told me earlier, "just people who have added to the fabric of our community."

At a curb alongside a winding road lie the Harwood clan. "That man was born in 1837 ... 1830 ... 1836," Christian reads from the series of markers.

One of the most impressive monuments is a statue of a female angel, head bowed. It's photographed often. Less classically, a waist-high stone a few paces away is topped by a sphere the size of a bowling ball.

"A reporter at your paper once called me about a woman who thought the sphere had a powerful aura," Christian says dryly.

A family crypt holds the Lucases, an old farming family who died off in the first half of the 20th century. "Podrasnik," a large marker reads. He was one of the valley's last Civil War veterans.

No one escapes death.

"There's some of the Drapers, the mortuary family," Christian points out. Millikens, Latimers, Atwoods and Chaffeys are all here.

Hiram Edgar Phelps has a vertical stone that resembles a chess piece. A short resume takes up two sides. An attorney, he lived from 1838 to 1896 and was a private in the 97th New York Cavalry, fighting in five Civil War battles, including Appomattox.

"He was in those last battles as they chased Lee, and caught up with him," says Christian, a Civil War buff.

He leads me to a favorite grave, a flat marker for Ruth Danforth. Kneeling, he brushes the freshly mown grass from the modest stone.

Danforth lived from 1825 to 1911 and was an Army nurse from 1861 to 1865, the entire length of the Civil War.

"She would've been 36 years old or so when she started service," Christian muses. "The wounds she saw must have been horrible."

He had told me about her earlier in the Bellevue office, saying if he could talk to anyone buried there, she'd be the one.

Someone like Phelps is an exception. With most stones, details of the life lived are scant.

"When I wander around out here, I think, 'There's got to be more to this life than this date, a dash and another date,'" Christian says earnestly. "I think the dash is what counts."

Few people visit the older part of the cemetery. Generations have passed since the deaths memorialized there.

Loved ones typically come to a gravesite regularly for three years before visits become sparser, Christian explains.

A section for veterans sees activity more frequently, especially on military holidays. Eight hundred veterans are buried at Bellevue, from the Civil War, Spanish-American War, the two World Wars, Korea and Vietnam.

"We now have an Iraq war casualty. We also have a Medal of Honor recipient. That goes back to the Philippine insurrection," Christian says.

Leonard Davis Jr. died in Vietnam on November 20, 1969. Four days later, his father, Leonard Davis Sr., who had served in World War I, followed him.

"I talked to him about his son," Christian says. The elder Davis died of a heart attack from grief. Father and son are buried side by side.

Christian is 72 and the dash representing his own life can't be filled in adequately here. Prior to Bellevue, he spent 32 years at Ontario's Draper Mortuary. He lives in Lake Arrowhead with his wife.

In his 50 years in the funeral industry, he's seen many changes in the way we send off our loved ones, from acceptance of cremation to increasingly personal and even multimedia funeral services, of which he approves.

Yet one thing that hasn't changed much, he says, is our discomfort with the topic of death, from which most of us run but none of us can hide.

Christian gestures in two directions. His parents are buried there. His in-laws are over there.

"I've got a spot," he says brightly.

We go to the Sunset Mausoleum, his last big project, dedicated in 2005.

In the chapel, light pours in through a large stained glass window. Organ music plays, but no one is there playing it. The effect is reverent but unsettling. The Great Beyond has never seemed quite so near.

The mausoleum has 900 crypts for bodies and 800 niches for "cremains," as ashes are called.

In the Vineyard Room, a cozy nook with a mosaic of a grape cluster in the floor, Christian taps on a glass niche at chest level.

"I'm going to be right here," he says.

He seems serene about the whole thing, either because a lifetime of dealing with death has made the reality of his own life cycle natural to him, or because he'll be quite a ways from his mother-in-law.

Journalist knows, 'They like me!'

September 23, 2007

A message was left on my voicemail the other day by Karen Davis, who identified herself as chairwoman of the Pomona Jaycees' Christmas Parade.

The parade, one of Pomona's biggest events and a tradition since the 1950s, this year takes place on December 1, starting at 10 a.m.

Davis had an unexpected request.

"We would like to invite you to be this year's grand marshal," she said.

Those Jaycees – what a bunch of kidders!

But it turns out the Junior Chamber of Commerce, chartered in 1936 and one of Pomona's oldest organizations, is serious. They want me – me! – to ride in a convertible and wave to the crowds as the parade travels East Holt Avenue.

When I called her back, Davis not only repeated the invitation, she insisted I was her first choice.

A real estate broker who moved here only this year, from Atlanta, Davis joined the Jaycees and volunteered to helm the parade. I got the impression she may be regretting that, and it's only September.

Why me? She said she likes my work, especially my Pomona coverage, saying it keeps her "up to date" on local news. I'm wondering if she gets her national news from Jon Stewart.

When she proposed my name, the parade committee, she said, agreed enthusiastically.

"Everybody I polled is excited about it," she said.

Of course, you know how polls are – they never ask you.

Anyway, after checking my calendar to confirm I wasn't leading any other parades that morning, I accepted.

Other cities are scrambling to respond to this bombshell. Main Street Upland announced last week that its December 1 Christmas Parade has been rescheduled to start at 5 p.m. It's obvious, if only to me, that Upland is afraid to go head to head with a David Allen-marshaled parade. Booyah!

Seriously, I couldn't be more pleased about being grand marshal of a parade. How could I not be honored?

Choosing me is not only totally unexpected, it's completely ridiculous. I am so there.

C'mon, a journalist as the star of a parade?

While we're at it, let's put a lawyer, a tax collector, a repo man, a used-car salesman and a child-welfare investigator in the car too. The driver, for the good of humanity, would send that car over a cliff. And next year he would be grand marshal.

But that's flattering myself. Realistically, very few people on the parade route will know who they're waving at. I say this from experience.

A few months ago, I spoke to a service club in Ontario. Of the 18 people there, 16 claimed they read this newspaper regularly. Of those 16, only four had any idea who I am or what I do. The other 12 had no clue.

Presumably they subscribe to a daily newspaper because they collect rubber bands.

Then there are all the people who don't read the *Daily Bulletin*. I began picturing hundreds, if not thousands, of people along the parade route watching the man in the car and saying: "Hmm. David Allen? Must be a male model."

But then something occurred to me: So what? Does anyone at a parade ever know who they're waving at? It's just some dope in a convertible.

"Look, it's an assemblyman! ... What's an assemblyman?"

I asked a Jaycees official about previous grand marshals. He said last year's was "the lady from Pomona Valley Hospital," whose name he couldn't remember.

So perhaps when you're grand marshal in Pomona, that takes the pressure off.

For me, though, this is a huge thrill. (That's the anticipation; I expect the actual experience, like most experiences, will be a letdown.)

In complete seriousness: One reason I'm flattered is that, as must be obvious, I have a lot of affection for Pomona, the underdog city. I just love that place. So, being asked to lead a parade in Pomona is doubly sweet.

To paraphrase Sally Field: "They like me! They really like me! And let's face it, if mothers ruled the world, there wouldn't be any (expletive) wars in the first place."

Friday, more than a week after our first conversation, I checked back with Davis to make sure I hadn't been bounced. She assured me I'm still the grand marshal.

So did Hector Rodriguez, the Jaycees' president.

"When she approached me with the idea, I was just ecstatic. 'He's the man,'" Rodriguez claimed to have said.

Rodriguez, by the way, is a Pomona police sergeant. He supervises the gang and vice units, the neighborhood enforcement team and the SWAT team.

With those credentials, he should be well-equipped to protect me from rotten tomatoes and heads of lettuce.

So that settles that. Everyone says I'm the grand marshal, and at this point I'm lulled into believing them.

The Jaycees are probably waiting until I show up December 1 to take me aside and tell me they were kidding. I hope they break it to me gently, because I'm kinda looking forward to the whole thing.

Phony war hero shoots himself in foot

October 7, 2007

Xavier Alvarez, you may recall, is the self-proclaimed military war hero from Pomona who's in hot water just because he wasn't in the military, wasn't in a war and wasn't a hero. Picky, picky.

The FBI says it has Alvarez on tape claiming to possess a Congressional Medal of Honor. It's a crime to pretend to have a military medal or decoration and a bigger crime to say you have a Congressional Medal of Honor.

Alvarez faces a misdemeanor charge punishable by a year in the federal pokey. In other words, this is worse than falsely claiming you're an Anna Nicole baby-daddy.

Nevertheless, the walrus-mustached Alvarez was cheerful when we spoke Friday – but more on that in a minute.

As you may have read on our front page, in pieces by my colleague Fred Ortega of the *San Gabriel Valley Tribune*, several witnesses say Alvarez told them far-fetched tales of single-handed heroism in Vietnam or, alternately, in the Iranian hostage crisis. He came across like a combination of Rambo, Airwolf and Scheherazade.

Alvarez was elected last November to represent Pomona on the Three Valleys Municipal Water District board of directors. He made his Medal of Honor claim at a July 23 public meeting, which was taped, the FBI says, although the agency declined to release a transcript.

Alvarez admitted to Ortega that he was never in the military and said everyone was confused about the rest.

"When you show up at these meetings, they introduce you," Alvarez said. "Sometimes they want you to say what you have done for the community. I must have been taken out of context."

Curious what that context could have been, I went to the Three Valleys office in Claremont last week and listened to the tape.

The July 23 meeting actually involved the Walnut Valley Municipal Water District, but Alvarez and several other Three Valleys members were in the audience.

After the Pledge of Allegiance, Mike Holmes, Walnut Valley's general manager, introduces the guests.

"Mr. Alvarez, why don't you stand up? I don't think you've been to one of our meetings before," Holmes says.

"You want me to say something about myself?" Alvarez responds.

The answer is affirmative, so Alvarez begins:

"I'm a retired Marine, for 25 years. I just retired in the year, uh, 2001. Back in 1987 I was awarded a Congressional Medal of Honor. I got wounded many times, at the same time." He chuckles.

"I'm still around. When I came out, I went to school, graduated from Cal Poly, got my engineering degree. I got a notion to run for this position, 'cause I'm the type of person who gets tired of seeing people warming the bench, so it was time to make a removal.

"Now that you see me, I will continue to do the same thing I've been doing for the last eight months."

One hesitates to ask what that would be.

It looks to me like the FBI has its smoking gun. And since he's not a war hero, this could be the closest Alvarez has ever come to a smoking gun.

I phoned him to get his side of things. This wasn't easy, because Alvarez didn't seem entirely sure what his side of things was.

First he blamed people for "improvising stories" about him and political enemies for targeting him. He repeated his claim that he's a member of the American Legion, then said he's a past member.

He said the Legion renewal paperwork came with a feel-good certificate with a phony title.

"I have a certificate here that says I'm a Congressional Medal of Honor holder. Maybe he didn't understand it," said Alvarez, who seemed to think the confusion lay in a one-on-one conversation at the July 23 meeting.

"Everything they say, it must be taken out of contents. They make me look like some Bazooka Joe wannabe," Alvarez complained.

Either he meant G.I. Joe, or he aspires to appear in bubble gum wrappers.

Anyway, I explained that the tape was of comments made in front of a roomful of people. I read his words back to him. There was a pause.

"Yeah, I remember saying that," Alvarez said quietly. Then an explanation tumbled out in a rush.

"I was trying to say, I was just nervous, saying anything. There's no truth to that. What harm did that do to them?"

He told me he invents stories, usually to kid people or to brush them off.

He said that was the case with Melissa Campbell, who tipped off the FBI after she met him at an Edison retreat last summer and concluded he was a phony.

According to the story she told the *Tribune*'s Frank Girardot, Alvarez claimed in her presence to have won the Medal of Honor for service in the 1979 Iranian hostage crisis.

He rescued the American ambassador to Iran, then went back to grab the American flag, except he was shot in the back.

Alvarez told me that he did say those things, but only to get rid of her because she was annoying.

"I told her these stories to brush her off and make her think I'm a psycho from the mental ward with Rambo stories," Alvarez explained.

Ah. It's all clear now.

Incidentally, you'll be thrilled to know that Alvarez will collect $200 from Three Valleys for attending the July 23 meeting, as well as mileage to drive there.

Alvarez, who unseated incumbent Luis Juarez by a margin of just 50 votes, has no experience with water. But as a Three Valleys director, he gets $200 per meeting, for up to 10 meetings per month.

He also gets free medical, dental and vision coverage, which is lucky for him. Since he was (ahem) "wounded many times," he must need a lot of doctoring.

Alvarez pledges to be more careful about what he says in the future.

That's smart, although it may be too late to suit the FBI – or authentic military veterans, for that matter.

If the feds really want to stick it to Alvarez, I suggest they go after him for a more obvious crime, one of fashion.

C'mon, wearing that enormous mustache has got to be a felony.

Much-loved movie matinee

October 14, 2007

When I was a lad in Olney, Illinois, our local movie theater had summertime kiddie matinees, but there wasn't much to them other than annual screenings of James Garner's *Support Your Local Sheriff*.

This makes me envy children in 1960s Upland. The Grove Theater had the Pal Club, and based on what people have told me, screenings were jam-packed with jollity.

It was, reader Dave Linck recalls, "a kid-oriented Saturday afternoon that featured a movie, cartoons, shorts and an intermission with pie-eating contests and local bands."

Linck, a movie publicist who lives in Rancho Cucamonga, sent me a warm, detailed recollection of the long-running matinee program. So let's kick back for today and recall a simpler time of childhood summers and moviegoing.

Children lined up at noon along the east side of the Grove, "the air filled with the curious aromas wafting from the neighboring chicken-feed factory," Linck recounts.

A "Coming Attractions" window showed what would be playing next week, offering something to debate, speculate about or deride while waiting in line.

At the door, the pint-sized patrons got a red-and-white grab bag filled with loose candies, toys and, for the lucky, a free movie pass or two.

The theater manager, known to the kids as Pal Chief Bob – "I don't think we even thought he had a last name," Linck admitted – ran the event in his well-tailored suit while brandishing a microphone.

Linck saw a few stink bombs, including *Zebra in the Kitchen*, *Way...Way Out* and – love the title – *The Littlest Hobo*. But he remembers a lot of great ones.

Favorites included the Ray Harryhausen gems *Jason and the Argonauts* and *The Seventh Voyage of Sinbad*, which remain touchstones for him. His Hollywood career may owe something to those formative experiences in Upland.

I also heard about the Pal Club from another perspective.

Gene Harvey managed the Grove from 1968 into the late 1970s, taking over from Pal Chief Bob. (Whose real name was Bob Bell, by the way.)

Pal Chief Gene told me the Pal Club screenings were tremendous fun, for him as well as for the kids.

Merchants donated prizes like bicycles, toys and board games to be given away during intermission. Harvey might start a "yelling contest," asking the boys or the girls, or one half of the room or the other, to prove they could yell louder.

"If you can imagine 730 kids, ages 6 to 12, screaming ...." Harvey said, smiling at the memory.

Admission cost 50 cents, or 35 cents with a Pal Club card. The card was worth having.

"We had a typewriter set up in the lobby to type their name and birthday on the card. On their birthday they got in free. Same with every fourth visit," Harvey explained. "Anytime they got in free, they could bring a pal in free."

Ah. So that's why it was the Pal Club.

But what the Grove gaveth, the Grove could taketh away.

"If anyone misbehaved and we had to call their parents, they'd get their Pal Club card taken away," Harvey said. O, the indignity.

The audience was populated almost exclusively by young children. "Teens and adults couldn't come in unless they were accompanied by a child 6 to 12," Harvey said.

The Pal Club shows ran from noon to 4 p.m. No one could leave early, making the shows "effective baby-sitting," Harvey said. He added: "Now we have Chuck E. Cheese for that."

At 4 p.m., so many parents arrived to pick up those 730 children that whistle-blowing police officers would direct traffic on foot.

Pal Club shows ended in the late 1970s. Harvey said the matinees remained popular but that Mann Theaters, which owned the Grove, desired uniformity at its theaters and couldn't be bothered to do unique programming.

What with chain ownership of theaters, the demise of single-screen movie houses and the decline of G-rated movies, kiddie matinees faded away everywhere.

Kind of a shame. Although maybe there's a silver lining for today's youngsters.

At least they don't have to sit through a movie titled *The Littlest Hobo*.

GHOST CLUSTERS? POMONA SPIRIT SEARCH IS A FOX HUNT

October 31, 2007

Is the Fox Theater haunted, and if so, who ya gonna call? In this case, it was the band of Azusa-based ghost hunters who placed the call. They heard that a movie location manager, who was scouting the long-closed Pomona theater, saw a face in a bathroom mirror that – uh-oh – wasn't hers.

The ghost hunters then called Jerry Tessier, who is in escrow to buy the downtown movie house. Tessier one night let them into the theater, which dates to 1931 and is dusty with disuse, and they were so impressed they've been back on three other occasions.

No ghost sightings as yet, but their audio recorders pick up sounds inaudible to the naked ear, heard only when the recordings are dumped into a computer and analyzed with ghost-hunting software.

"So far it's just been a lot of voices. A little girl. A voice said one of our investigators' names. A lot of whispering," Troy Tackett, founder of the West Coast Paranormal Research Society, told me by phone last month.

He continued: "One recording says 'Get out.' One says 'No, thank you.'"

Well, the latter ghost is at least polite, and as for the former, Tessier, the developer, speculates that maybe that ghost is actually playful. To demonstrate, he pushed my shoulder with his palm while saying in mock-surprise, "Get out!," like Elaine shoving Jerry on *Seinfeld*.

Always on the lookout for marketing gimmicks, Tessier added that if enough evidence is gathered, a "haunted Fox" tour could be mounted someday.

Unable to wait, I arranged to tag along on the society's next ghost hunt.

Thus, on October 6 at 9 p.m., I parked across from the Fox and crossed Third Street. A police car passed by and stopped.

"Do you have authorization to be here?" the officer asked me sternly.

"Um ... yes?" I responded.

"Just messing with you. They told me you were coming," the officer said, laughing, and drove on.

Whew. I knocked on the door and was allowed in by Troy Tackett. The Fox's lobby was ablaze from construction lights. A half-dozen ghost hunters were setting up equipment.

We signed liability waivers provided by Tessier's company: "I have voluntarily chosen to enter the Fox Theater ... for the sole purpose of filming, photography and other paranormal investigations."

I introduced myself to the crew: Johnathon Rosales, Athena Del Rosario, Liz Ramirez, Especial Campbell, Keisha Rachal and the co-leader, Ryan Mangini. They range in age from their 20s to their 40s and most are friends or neighbors of each other.

They have jobs in computers, property management, paralegal research, filmmaking and carpentry. Some were on their first investigation, some were veterans.

The group's philosophy is to debunk ghost reports, and they try to remain objective, attributing some foggy photo images, for instance, to the copious dust inside the theater.

"You always want to try to disprove it," Ryan told me. If the group jumps to a supernatural conclusion for something natural, its reputation will suffer, he explained.

One night in the Fox, they heard faint piano music that seemed to be coming from the stage. Rather than wet their pants, they went out a side door into the alley and learned that a loft-dweller next door "was playing piano at 2 a.m. with his window open," Ryan said.

"We don't want to say this place is haunted," he said, "unless we have multiple pieces of evidence."

Objectivity doesn't come naturally. Each ghost hunter, even the first-timers, told me he or she has had some contact with the supernatural.

"Have you been on many ghost hunts before?" Liz asked me earnestly. When I replied that this was my first, she asked, in surprise: "Really?"

"It's not really what I do," I admitted.

The ghost hunters were armed with the tools of their trade: infrared cameras, electromagnetic-field readers, digital thermometers, audio recorders, penlights and walkie-talkies.

Also, crucially, matching T-shirts.

"Every single time we've come here we've gotten evidence. There's something going on," Ryan insisted. "I don't want to say it's haunted yet. The Holy Grail would be a full-blown apparition."

I liked Ryan, an outgoing man with the manner of a camp counselor. I would never have pegged him as the group's demonologist. He has that coveted position because he once, as a Mormon missionary, witnessed an exorcism, which he says changed his life.

At 10:40 p.m., we split into two groups. I went with Troy and Athena up the grand staircase to the mezzanine.

The lobby lights were turned off, plunging the theater into darkness, the better to hunt haunts with.

Troy led the way with his penlight, and we followed. I clicked my penlight on only when necessary, mostly for jotting notes. Aiming the tiny light, I felt like Carl Kolchak, the monster-chasing reporter on TV's old *Kolchak: The Night Stalker*.

In the projection booth, Troy began asking questions of any spirits who might be about: "Can you tell me your name? Are you bound to this room?"

On a previous visit, he had asked for a sign. A metal vent propped up in a window sill had fallen, spooking everyone. Nothing appeared to be happening tonight, though.

"It seems a little dead right now," Troy observed.

Dead?

Audio recorders were set up in various rooms, as were video cameras, which fed to a monitor in the lobby. Athena carried a camera and shot still images, three in a row, of any room we visited, to document any activity.

We prowled through the upstairs bathrooms and the manager's office. The only activity was a very large roach skittering across the carpet in the penlight's beam.

Troy put an audio recorder in the women's bathroom at Athena's suggestion.

"People generally talk in the women's room," she noted.

At midnight, we walked through the cavernous auditorium and upstairs into the dressing rooms, the organ pipe room and back down to the broad stage.

Troy shouted questions. "Is anyone here?" he asked. "Can you tell me what year it is?"

I hoped the ghost knows what year it is. Especially if it writes a lot of checks.

Ryan called Troy on the walkie-talkie, swearing that while in the lobby watching a video feed, he saw a giant shadow striding across the stage. This would have been just a few feet to our left, and we missed the whole thing.

At 1:45 a.m. I went to the balcony with Liz, Especial and Keisha. The Fox balcony, in two tiers, has as many seats as most modern theaters, rows stretching toward the ceiling, far beyond the range of our penlights.

The only light was what leaked in through the projection booth windows. One ghost hunter shot photos every now and then, her camera flash exploding in the inky blackness.

"What is your name?" one of the women shouted.

Silence.

"Are you a boy?"

Silence.

"What did you say your name was?"

We didn't catch a name this time either.

"We have a special guest with us," Liz announced. "He'd like to write a story about you."

More silence. Maybe the ghost wanted to go off the record.

I left shortly afterward. After five hours inside the Fox, I had witnessed no full-blown apparitions and, in fact, nothing out of the ordinary (other than questions shouted at the air).

Although the night seemed uneventful, the group's later analysis of the audio recordings did turn up ghostly whispers.

Audible are such disparate remarks as "who am I?," "kill you," "help me" and, chillingly, "hey."

Oh, and if there was anything particularly odd on tape at 1:10 a.m., that might have been me.

It is recorded in my notebook that at that moment, as I climbed the stairs to the Fox stage, I hit my forehead on a metal rod in the dark and whispered "ouch."

City's Parade Grows, and Grows Older, Too

November 30, 2007

Saturday I'll be tooling down Pomona's Holt Avenue, waving to the throngs as grand marshal of the Christmas Parade, trailed by marching bands, the Pomona City Council and that nobody, Santa.

I have to hand it to the Pomona Jaycees. Me, ceremonial leader of a city parade? That's funnier than most of my columns.

The parade begins at 10 a.m. at the Ebell Club, which is on Holt just east of Towne. From there we'll slowly proceed east along Holt for a mile. I believe this route was chosen to show off Pomona's world-class array of muffler shops.

The Jaycees are still insisting I'm their guy. I phoned parade chairwoman Karen Crye on Wednesday to ask if they'd found a better grand marshal. She replied: "There is no better grand marshal." Isn't that sweet?

The Jaycees tout this as their 56th annual Christmas Parade. Of course I wanted to know some parade lore. But the Jaycees don't seem to have records of the parade's history, or a list of previous grand marshals.

"Did I mention we're a volunteer organization?" Crye said with a chuckle.

She asked around for me and was told that among previous grand marshals are actors Chuck Connors of *The Rifleman* and Ed Nelson of *Peyton Place*, boxers Shane Mosley and Alberto Davila, cowboy actor and trick roper Montie Montana, and Sally Cortez, wife of the late mayor.

Curious to know more, I journeyed to the Pomona Public Library this week to pore over microfilm of the *Pomona Progress-Bulletin* for select years of the parade's heyday.

Grand marshals have included a 4-year-old boy, Donny Verassi, who was a recent Casa Colina patient (the 1957 parade), California Angels pitcher Bill Singer of Diamond Bar (1973), L.A. County District Attorney Evelle Younger (1966), *Here's Lucy* actor Gale Gordon (1970) and locals whose distinction was unexplained (Steve Dunne in 1962, L.H. Gann in 1952).

Oh, and in 1976 the grand marshal was Donald Duck. These are big, webbed footprints to follow in, folks.

Many years the parade included celebrities who were not the grand marshal, according to *Prog* reports. That would include 1957, when Jon Provost ("son of Mr. and Mrs. B.A. Provost, 1195 N. Washington Ave."), who had just been named as the new kid on TV's *Lassie*, rode on a firetruck.

(Fun trivia: 1957's Sputnik-inspired parade theme was "Christmas in Outer Space." Santa rode on a rocket.)

In 1973, two *Brady Bunch* stars, Ann B. Davis (Alice) and Greg Williams (Greg Brady), rode as division marshals. I've been told by an eyewitness that Davis wore her character's housekeeping smock.

The parade for years took place in the evening, and the route was usually along Second Street downtown, until the 1970s, when downtown was dying and Holt from Hamilton to Palomares was substituted.

How did the parade begin, and when?

If this is the 56th annual, that would mean 1952. Yet a

Jaycees official told the *Prog* in 1952 that that year's Christmas parade would be "the largest in its history."

Hmm.

Further digging showed the 1952 parade was actually the fifth. The first was in 1948. Let me set the scene.

Beginning circa 1928, downtown merchants sponsored an event known as the Christmas Preview. By 1948, this meant that street decorations were lighted for the first time that night, and crowds showed up by the thousands to see Christmas merchandise unveiled in window displays at stores like John P. Evans, Hiatt's, Ewart's and the Orange Belt Emporium.

You might be intrigued to learn that 1948's Christmas Preview took place Nov. 23 – two days before Thanksgiving. And you thought an early start to Christmas was something new.

Unlike 1947, when stores were closed during the Christmas Preview, the 1948 Preview was bigger and better. Stores were open for business until 9 p.m. and a street dance (whoa!) and quiz show, both sponsored by the Jaycees, lasted until midnight.

Also new that year: Four marching bands parading from four directions converged at Second and Garey, then separated for individual outdoor concerts on Second, all under the auspices of the Jaycees.

This must have been a hit, because in 1949, the four bands became part of a full-fledged parade on Second from Rebecca to Elm, led by grand marshal Spade Cooley, the king of Western swing music. Cooley's band performed afterward at a dance at the Rainbow Gardens.

In 1950, the *Prog* described the parade as the third annual by the Jaycees.

Yet somewhere along the way somebody slipped up on the math, because 1970's parade, really the 23rd annual, was billed as the 18th, and nobody ever caught the error.

The Christmas Preview was quite an occasion. Parade counts are probably inflated, but in 1957, for instance, 40,000 people were said to have been downtown. In 1952, the post-Preview dance at the Armory drew 1,000 people.

Well, I'm sure Saturday's parade will be nice too. In fact, despite what the Jaycees have been telling people, by my count the 2007 parade is actually the 60th.

Sixty years? That's a milestone and I'm honored to be part of it. Celebrate by joining us, won't you?

Not a gag after all: This columnist leads parade

December 2, 2007

I had assumed my perch in a 1957 Ford Thunderbird convertible, feet on the seat, bottom on a blanket draped onto the car's back, moments from the start of Saturday's Pomona Christmas Parade.

Councilman Steve Atchley came over to introduce me to his daughter Sophia and point out an uncomfortable fact. "There's still time to replace you," Atchley said.

I knew it, and I'd been waiting for it to happen all morning.

My fear was, someone from the Pomona Jaycees would walk up, introduce me to the real grand marshal and thank me for playing along with the gag. I would say I knew it all along, we'd share a hearty laugh and then I'd retire to a quiet corner to weep.

But no, there I was, sitting in a classic car with signs reading "Grand Marshal David Allen" on each door, as driver Bill Newton pulled onto Holt Avenue.

"We're not worthy!" yelled Vice Mayor George Hunter, genuflecting from a street corner.

I'm not worthy either, but somehow I was in the parade anyway.

I took the role seriously. This would be most people's only look at a real live newspaperman. And since most people's image of us is from black and white movies, I didn't want to disappoint anyone.

So I dressed the stereotype.

On Friday I spent $45 on a fedora at Replay Vintage Clothes in Claremont and stuck a homemade card reading "Press" in the band.

My outfit also included a skinny tie, purchased at the Goodwill Store in Pomona for $1.99, and a vintage camera slung over my shoulder.

Not bad. All I was missing was a pack of Chesterfields, a flask of cheap booze and a Racing Form and I could have stepped out of a 1940s newsroom.

You heard me, dollface.

Still, my expectations were low. To most people I would be just a dope in a convertible, and I was right. All along the route, people looked at me in bafflement.

I looked back sympathetically.

But I did the best I could, making sure to smile and wave at little children, most of whom waved back happily. Perhaps being waved at by a grand marshal would set them off on the right course in life.

As we passed the judging area, the announcers read from a biography I'd submitted:

"David is a resident of Claremont, which he chose because it makes Pomona his next-door neighbor. He'll be over to borrow your lawn mower soon."

As I noted here Friday, the route seemed to have been chosen to showcase Pomona's muffler shops. We also passed the 99 Cents Store, outlet shops, liquor stores, the Pala Motel, tire shops, Vietnamese and Mexican restaurants and the Everything $2.99 and Up store.

Some blocks had people sitting in lawn chairs, while some were virtually depopulated.

There were fun surprises. Numerous people shouted my name or yelled "we love your columns."

One couple held campaign-type signs on sticks reading "David Allen for Mayor of Pomona." That was hilarious.

"No rotten produce, David!" one woman yelled, showing her empty hands.

As we passed a motorcycle officer stationed at an intersection along one gritty stretch, he got on his intercom to say two words: "Muffler shop."

Speaking of Holt Avenue, its ladies of the evening were nowhere to be seen. Maybe they were at the rear of the parade with Santa, asking him to declare them naughty *and* nice.

Just one person approached my car. It was a nice fella carrying Friday's *Bulletin*, folded to show my column. David Ybarra handed it to me with a pen and asked me to sign it. I bet he does this with all the grand marshals.

We got to East End Avenue in a half hour. It was over much too soon. Newton, my driver, took me back to the Ebell Club, where we'd started.

A former *Progress-Bulletin* paperboy, Newton saw the Donahoo's Chicken rooster being lowered into place circa 1966. I should've been driving him.

So how did my grand marshalship go? Well, there was no gunfire, I didn't fall out of the convertible and nobody carjacked us, so by those measures it was a great success.

I ran into Karen Crye, the parade chairwoman, and asked if the parade was still being billed as the 56th annual. No, she said, she'd instructed the announcers to call it the 60th, after my research showed the parade was older than anyone remembered.

Nice to know I left my mark. Thanks for the memories, Pomona.

'07'S STRANGE NEWS STORIES

December 28, 2007

Before bidding farewell to 2007, let's take a fond look at the Inland Valley's 10 strangest news stories of the year while smiling and backing away from them slowly:

10. **PO' SPELLING**: Nurses at Pomona Valley Hospital Medical Center picketed for a new contract in September by holding signs reading "Pomoma Registered Nurses on Strike." Yes, "Pomoma." Is that sick, or sic? Nurses accepted a new contract last week before a threatened 10-day strike, either because the terms were to their liking or they couldn't afford new signs.

9. **A VILLAGE VENTURE**: Surveillance cameras were set up outside Three French Hens, a Claremont boutique, after a boxed chandelier was stolen in broad daylight from a stash temporarily stored outside. Two decoy chandeliers were stolen on successive weekends but the thief was caught on tape. Pushing his luck, the Whittier man returned for a fourth weekend and was arrested.

8. **CELEBRITY GOES BAD**: After a report of gunfire, Pomona police found a gang member walking innocently near the scene with an oversized Garfield plush toy. He dropped the toy and officers heard a "clunk." Inside Garfield's stuffing: a loaded pistol. Perhaps in response, the *Daily Bulletin* later dropped *Garfield* from the comics pages.

7. **MOD SQUAD**: State Senator Gloria Negrete McLeod of

Chino and two fellow Democrats were locked out of their Capitol offices for a day by Senate Majority Leader Don Perata. Why? For the sin of supporting a (gasp) moderate voting bloc. No wonder nothing gets done in Sacramento.

6. **THIS DIAMOND RING**: Baseball fans Robert Alderete and Liza Frias were wed in front of friends and family on the baseball diamond at Ontario's Jay Littleton Ballpark. "I first knew we had chemistry when we were playing catch and she made my glove pop," Alderete confided.

5. **LIKE CLOCKWORK**: For at least six straight Wednesdays, narcotics investigators made a major find of live marijuana plants growing in suburban homes in Chino Hills, Diamond Bar, Phelan or Rowland Heights. It could only have been stranger if each pot bust occurred at 4:20. (That's drug lingo for the time to light up.)

4. **UP ON THE ROOF**: A flying instructor and two students took off from Van Nuys Airport and were nearing Upland's Cable Airport when their Piper Seneca lost power. They landed atop a homeowner's garage after clipping two homes and a tree. No one was injured seriously. That's some flyin'.

3. **SHAKE A LEG**: A man slipped a chain around a 1,500-pound automated teller machine inside a Pomona supermarket and tried to haul it away with his pickup truck. His attempt to run from the cops failed when his prosthetic leg fell off.

2. **RAMBO**: Xavier Alvarez of Pomona said at a public meeting that he had served in the Marines for 25 years and had a Medal of Honor. Neither was true. The Three Valleys Municipal Water District director is now in hot water with the feds for making a false claim about a medal for valor. Notably, Alvarez is the first person in the nation to be prosecuted under the 2006 law. Finally, a real achievement he can

boast about.

And the Inland Valley's strangest news story of 2007:

1. **GRACIOUS**: In Upland, a Claremont man held up an adult bookstore for cash and hailed a taxi. Police stopped the taxi and the driver escaped. The suspect then drove off in the stolen taxi with police in pursuit. They stopped him on the 210 Freeway and took him into custody after he reached for his waistband. He didn't have a handgun there, just a phallic sex toy, which a police sergeant said the man kept "tethered to his belt loop for whatever reason." City of Gracious Living, meet the City of Trees and Ph.Ds.

2007 Items

January 12, 2007

Fontana has launched a weight-loss contest for City Hall employees under the punning name Fontana's Biggest Loser. The man and woman who lose the biggest percentage of their starting weight will claim victory and a cash prize. (Using the cash to splurge on a big dinner out is probably a bad idea.)

Best of luck to the 91 contestants, who will have the free aid of nutritionists and trainers during the eight-week contest, which ends March 7.

I imagine the contest will close on an affirming note, with the announcer telling all the runner-ups: "True, this contest can have only one biggest loser. Yet, in a way, you're all losers."

February 2, 2007

Not long after my November columns on long-lived phone numbers, I came across a news item about the 1970s punk band the Stooges, which is reuniting after 30 years.

Bitten by the nostalgia bug, leader Iggy Pop took a chance and tried phoning bandmates Ron and Scott Asheton at the last number he had for them. Luckily for Stooges fans, the Asheton brothers were able to pick up the phone. Why? Because they hadn't changed phone numbers in 30 years.

On a related note: "I wish you would ask your readers

who had their number the longest," writes reader Cecelia Brewart.

"I remember when phone numbers had prefixes. Rialto was Triangle (87), San Bernardino was Turner (88), Upland/Ontario was Yukon (98) and Colton was Talbot (82)," she says. "Maybe your readers can remember the other cities."

March 7, 2007

Perhaps you saw the brief item in this newspaper's Crime and Public Safety section last week about the arrest of "David Allen, 27, of Rancho Cucamonga."

Authorities say that David Allen, a parolee and Pomona gang member, was in possession of cocaine, marijuana, weapons and about $15,000 in cash.

My newsroom colleagues, as you'd expect, have been ribbing me about "my" arrest ever since. To their credit, only one has asked me for cocaine.

Reader Ed Hanney phoned me. "I just wanted to find out if you're out of jail," he deadpanned. Disappointingly, he didn't offer to post bail.

At first I was tempted to complain about this other David Allen dragging down my good name. But, putting myself in his shoes, I began wondering if he might not be equally dismayed.

After all, he too has to share his name with a person of low repute: a member of the (shudder) media.

March 14, 2007

Zodiac, a drama now in theaters about the real-life 1970s serial killer, takes audiences on a virtual tour of California, including the Inland Empire:

After learning that a reporter colleague is following a tip to Riverside, a *San Francisco Chronicle* cartoonist asks curiously: "Where is Riverside?"

A San Francisco police inspector says regarding suspect Leigh Arthur Allen: "The first contact with Allen was in Pomona. They brushed him off."

A climactic scene takes place in 1991 at Ontario Airport.

That scene, by the way, was filmed at the old Ontario terminals, which are often used for film and TV shoots requiring an airport setting. But this could be the first time LA-ONT plays itself on the big screen instead of some other airport.

Another trivia note: A scene set at the KGO-TV studio in San Francisco was filmed at Mt. San Antonio College in Walnut.

And that's everything from A to Z about *Zodiac*.

March 30, 2007

Steve Lustro was startled to see what his meal receipt from Chino's El Gran Burrito gave as the restaurant's Chino Hills-adjacent address: "Chino Hell."

"Does this mean Chino Hills has given Chino an inferiority complex?" wonders Lustro. Perish the thought. But I am wondering if the road to Chino Hell is paved with good intentions.

April 1, 2007

Relating to the topic here of telephone exchanges, Jim Frost of Etiwanda loaned me a reproduction of the 1933 Ontario-Upland phone book, which weighed in at a mere 56 pages.

The listings include such oddities as Joya Mutual Water Company's number, Upln-8700-R-2. Attorney E.H. Jolliffe, an early adopter who must have had the first phone in Ontario, claimed the number Onto-1.

Frost directed my attention to the Information Pages at the front, specifically, the section headed "Using the Telephone."

Showing how unfamiliar the average person of the era was

with telephones, the section offers tips on how to pronounce phone numbers – speak two of them, pause, then say the other two – and what a busy signal means.

More handy advice: "How to Speak."

The explanation: "Speak slowly and clearly in an ordinary tone of voice directly into the telephone with the lips just clearing the mouthpiece."

Can you hear me now?

May 25, 2007

Commenting about the Base Line/Baseline spellings that change from city to city, Tami Schumacher writes with a totally unexpected twist. Her father, she says, used to own a business at Foothill and Indian Hill boulevards in Claremont.

"One day a gentleman came in and asked where the street 'Bass-a-leen' was. He pronounced it like Vaseline," Schumacher relates.

"My dad said he had to think a minute and then realized what street the man was talking about. So everyone gets confused about that street, avenue, rt, whatever."

I'm now mulling whether to refer to Base Line as Bass-a-leen – or the Vaseline as Vase Line.

May 30, 2007

Mentioned here was the person who once asked a Claremont storekeeper for the location of "Bass-a-leen," which turned out to be an exotic pronunciation of Baseline.

That reminded Marian O'Dell of a long-ago encounter at Upland High School with a student aide. O'Dell asked for the location of a Chino school where her son's baseball team would be playing an away game.

"The girl looked up the address and told me it was past what sounded like 'Peep-a-leen-a' Avenue. I asked her to repeat it several times and then gave up.

"I was horrified when she spelled it out and it turned out to be Pipeline Avenue," O'Dell said. "And this was from a senior in high school!"

Perhaps not the smartest kid to emerge from the educational pipeline (pronounce that however you like).

June 10, 2007

Block That Metaphor!: Speaking at last week's Rancho Cucamonga council meeting about the city's high development standards, a Planning Commission member said of city planners: "A lot of what you see is because they go through those blueprints and hold people's feet to the fire with a fine-, fine-toothed comb."

July 13, 2007

From the *Upland News* in 1968, this eye-catching headline: "Bonnie and Clyde Liked Their Milk."

Bill Burns of Ontario told the paper that when he was a 20-year-old in Missouri in the early 1930s, the gangsters' hideout was on his route for milk delivery.

Were Bonnie and Clyde hoping to disguise themselves with milk mustaches?

Burns delivered milk to them for several weeks until they abandoned their hideout. It was only later that he learned who they were. He offered the *News* no description of Clyde Barrow but a memorable one of Bonnie Parker.

"Bonnie was seldom seen, but when she was, she always had a stogie in her mouth, wore a man's dirty felt hat and a holster with gun," Burns said. "She was short and, I thought, homely. She wore grimy blouses and long, ugly skirts."

Just like Faye Dunaway!

September 14, 2007

In Claremont, police are on the lookout for a cookout.

A gang of "barbecuing thieves," as the *Claremont Courier*'s police blotter dubbed them, robbed a local market, sprinting out the door with carne asada, chicken and a 10-pound bag of charcoal.

What, no potato salad?

October 21, 2007

Nobel laureate Orhan Pamuk spoke Thursday evening at Claremont McKenna's Athenaeum. "To write well," the novelist said at one point, "is to have the reader say, 'I was going to say the same thing myself but I thought it was too childish.'"

Next time you're tempted to dismiss my own writing as childish, please stop to consider that this could be part of my Nobel strategy.

October 28, 2007

Name Game: The headquarters of the West Valley Mosquito and Vector Control District is in Ontario – on Locust Street.

November 7, 2007

Attentive readers of the *Daily Bulletin* may have noticed in recent days that the paper seems whiter and the colors are sharper. It's true, and it's not a fluke.

This newspaper is now being printed on the modern presses of *The Sun*, our sister paper in San Bernardino, rather than on the older presses here in Ontario. The Ontario presses, which date to our days as the *Daily Report*, have been shut down, probably for good.

While the out-of-town printing offers a better product for you readers, who will no longer have to contend with smeared ink and off-register photos, in some ways it's a bittersweet milestone.

Personally, there's a certain romance to working in a newspaper office where the presses are thrumming.

And historically speaking, this is the first time since September 12, 1910, the launch date of the *Ontario Republican* (later the *Daily Report*), that no daily newspaper has been printed in Ontario.

"Stop the presses," indeed.

November 25, 2007

Did you see *Kitchen Nightmares* on Fox last Wednesday? The reality series certainly lived up to its title as it went behind the scenes at Lela's, a troubled restaurant in Pomona that had asked Gordon Ramsay, the show's celebrity chef, to come to the rescue. Among the revelations:

Despite touting itself as fine dining, Lela's served a lot of frozen or canned items, its mashed potatoes were powdered and a lot of items on the menu were unavailable when diners asked.

The chef and a waitress had potty-mouthed shouting matches in the kitchen audible in the dining room.

In a blindfold taste test, the executive chef couldn't tell chicken from beef.

The "freezer" was 51 degrees.

The light-fingered prep cook, nicknamed "Buzzard," was caught on camera smuggling out a complete meal and two bottles of wine.

Reacting to the overly ambitious menu and the incompetent kitchen, Ramsay made the place over as casual dining with a "famous" burger and a Pomona salad.

On the night of the relaunch in February, the place was packed, but the chaos in the kitchen meant lousy service. Mayor Norma Torres, who was considered a VIP, was kept waiting, and servers wandered the dining room with plates of food, asking customers randomly if the entree was for them.

The owner, who was a sincere person, had never run a restaurant. Based on the TV evidence, she was in over her head. The makeover didn't take, and Lela's closed around July. It was sad to watch on camera: The owner, who had raided her retirement funds to open Lela's, was deeply in debt.

Despite alternately laughing and cringing for an hour, I didn't think Pomona itself came off badly on the show. And it was fun to see Second Street storefronts, Savoie Hair Designs and various Pomona residents on camera.

Among them: Xavier Alvarez, standing in line at Lela's for a table. I hope he wasn't given a military discount.

December 5, 2007

At Monday's Pomona City Council meeting, during council member comments, Vice Mayor George Hunter thanked police and volunteers for making Holiday Lane events a success on Saturday. He also began to remark on the Christmas Parade.

"We're fortunate to have the grand marshal sitting here in the back row," Hunter quipped. A few smiling heads turned.

"Enough about him," Mayor Norma Torres blurted out. After a momentary, awkward pause, the conversation shifted.

Well, you know what they say: Fame is fleeting.

December 14, 2007

The Ontario Reign is the name of the hockey team set to debut in late 2008. An Ontario-based hockey team, eh? It's high time the city's Canadian name worked to its advantage.

An affiliate of the L.A. Kings, the Reign – a play on this "empire" we're supposedly dwelling in – will compete against hockey teams from the dusty burgs of Fresno, Bakersfield, Stockton and Las Vegas.

Given Canada's dominance in hockey, the name Ontario Reign might give the team a psychological edge. And if opposing teams mistakenly fly to Toronto for games, Ontario might win a few victories by forfeit. Score!

December 21, 2007

Mystery solved: Introducing himself to me at Monday's Pomona council meeting, Ron Estrada said he and his wife, Tamra Yoder, were the ones waving the silly campaign-style signs at the Christmas Parade touting me for mayor.

Estrada handed me my very own copy of the sign. It'll be a nice keepsake. As for being mayor, forget it, and not just because I live in the wrong city. Frankly, even as grand marshal I was in over my head.

Prize-winning Clutter

February 1, 2008

My desk is fairly well organized, what with my annual ritual of cleaning it each January, but keeping on top of things is a never-ending task.

Messy desks are common, of course. But as in any field of human endeavor, there are those whose achievements in the realm of toxic work spaces are so impressive, they render the rest of us, with our mere scattering of paperwork, humbled and diminished.

John Jacobs is just such a titan.

Jacobs, 46, the co-owner of a La Verne bathroom business, has a work space that is prize-winningly bad. He recently won a national contest by an office supply maker to determine "America's ugliest office."

I dropped by Grecian Marble-Onyx on Wednesday to congratulate him.

(I'd have been by earlier, but his December 15 note had been lost on my desk.)

"This is it right here," Jacobs said, showing me his desk. At least, there were hints of a desk underneath all the paper.

The battered old wooden desk has seemingly no usable work area. Every inch is covered by piles of paper and debris.

An attempt at order was made at one point with a seven-shelf organizer. What's in it? Jacobs isn't sure.

"It's supposed to be an 'in' and 'out' thing. It's more of an 'in,' not an 'out,'" Jacobs admitted.

What's in his desk? He opened drawers for me. One was a tsunami of hundreds of business cards handed to him by visitors and tossed in haphazardly.

"Half of these guys are probably not in business anymore," Jacobs said.

Stapled to the wall above his desk are Christmas cards from 2007. And earlier. Way earlier. Some date to the 1990s. Also, the 1980s.

Perhaps Jacobs is too sentimental. Many of the cards are preprinted messages from suppliers. A few customer testimonials are mixed in.

"It's nice to have them up where customers can see them," Jacobs remarked. "But I don't know if anybody can see them."

Stapled to the wall to the right are faded business licenses, one per year, dating to Grecian Marble-Onyx's start in 1979.

"It's sort of a history of La Verne business licenses," Jacobs quipped.

The desk is technically that of George Jacobs, who is John Jacobs' father and the business's other owner, but father and son share the desk.

Asked if he inherited his organizational skills from his father, Jacobs chuckled and said that's true. The elder Jacobs, who was there when I entered, had slipped away. Either that, or he was under a pile of paper.

A second desk is immediately behind the prize-winning desk. It's topped by a foot-high mound of paper. Even the chair is piled high.

Jacobs described that space as "kind of a catchall" of half-read newspapers, unpaid bills and expired fast-food coupons.

He added: "We can find things. It's here. It's just pinning it down to an exact location. When you don't throw anything away, you know it's here, you just have to pinpoint it."

We talked about the contest. ACCO Brands sponsored it. Jacobs' wife, Susan, saw it online. She entered using a photo taken by their daughter, Jessica. The 16-year-old had documented her father's work space to laugh at it with her friends.

Their contest entry was one of 10 semifinalists and received the top number of votes online.

"I talked to the guy who handled the contest. We won overwhelmingly," Jacobs said.

Jacobs won airfare and lodging for a six-day trip to Maui, which he plans to take this spring with Susan and Jessica, and $1,690.97 in office supplies from ACCO.

What supplies, exactly? Jacobs has a list.

"I had it printed out and... oh, if I can find it," Jacobs said, shuffling through the pile on the second desk. "Oh, here it is," he said, handing me the list.

That took five seconds. Maybe he really does know where everything is.

The biggest part of the package is a $639.99 "jam-free" shredder, which he's looking forward to giving a workout.

I must point out that the shop area of his business, where he and his father make countertops in cultured marble and onyx, is very neat.

The shop is where the bulk of the work is done. The creative end is their focus.

"We do a better job of making people's bathrooms look good than we do making our work space look good," Jacobs said.

Cleaning the place up will probably take three solid days, he estimates. Since they're benefiting from the contest, his wife and daughter will pitch in.

I envy their Hawaiian vacation, but not the job of cleaning up 29 years of clutter.

Jacobs and I shook hands and said our farewells.

Out of sympathy for the task ahead of him, I decided not to hand him my business card. It would be just one more piece of paper.

Psychic sees all ... maybe

February 10, 2008

There's a house with a psychic reader on Indian Hill Boulevard in Pomona, next to a drive-through dairy and across the street from my favorite Thai restaurant.

I see the house with its large sign and stone lions probably once a week and, never having visited a psychic, always wonder what goes on within.

So when an interview opportunity arose with Laura Ronzo, the psychic reader herself, I decided to communicate with her telephonically.

We spoke twice to schedule a meeting. Intriguingly, each time we spoke she thought it was a different day of the week than it was.

Brilliant as she may be at "past" and "future," perhaps "present" is her Achilles' heel.

Keeping our appointment, I went to the house at 11 a.m. last Monday and rang the bell.

I'm not sure what I was expecting – a wizened Eastern European in a head scarf? – but Ronzo was smartly dressed in a gray turtleneck, gray skirt and a wide black belt.

A cheerful, energetic woman with her hair cut in a stylish bob, she would fit in at any business. At least ones that weren't dependent on her being 100 percent sure what day of the week it is.

Likewise, her living room gives no indication Ronzo is a psychic. No seance table, no beads, no black cats. Just tasteful decor in tan and gold – Ronzo told me she also does interior decorating – as well as a large portrait of Elizabeth Taylor. Ronzo said it was a gift for some advice she gave Taylor on her perfume line.

I had been unsure how early in the morning to phone a psychic, thinking her shift might begin at midnight. But Ronzo again defied my expectations.

Opening the drapes, Ronzo explained: "I'm a morning person. I always have to have it real bright."

She started by giving me a reading. I'll come back to that. First let's learn more about her.

Ronzo is a practicing Catholic and a daily Bible reader.

"I'm a spiritualist, not an occultist," she explained. "My goal is to make a difference in people's lives."

Yes, even psychics want to make a difference. She helps with marital and relationship problems and with people who need direction. She calls it spiritual counseling.

"I also have many products," Ronzo said, listing books, candles, oils and crystals.

Those are sold mostly from a psychic healing center she opened recently on Garey Avenue across from – she said it's coincidental – another healing center: the hospital.

Originally practicing in Beverly Hills, Ronzo and her husband, a luxury car dealer, relocated here circa 1980 to be closer to his ailing mother. A rental property they owned on Indian Hill Boulevard became her home and headquarters.

You may have seen Ronzo's tent at the L.A. County Fair. Since the early 1980s she's done readings for fairgoers. (Easy fair prediction: weight gain.)

Her gift manifested itself as a girl. She knew if people

would become ill, knew who was cheating on whom in high school. Other students were afraid of her.

"There was a blessing and a curse growing up with this," Ronzo said. "It's a gift I never wanted."

Ronzo has read for actor Anthony Quinn and the singer Shakira.

"I read for Reagan several times," Ronzo said. "I read for Dukakis when he was running and I told him he would lose. He didn't like that very much."

Of course, the only special ability it took to know Dukakis would lose was brain activity. A better test will come in November: Ronzo predicts that Hillary Clinton will become president, possibly with Obama as vice president, and the health of McCain's wife "will hold him back" from an all-out campaign.

As for my reading, she put a pillow between us on the sofa and placed my hands on top of it.

My palms have more lines than hers, and she's older, she observed. This means I've had a lot of past lives. Most of them female.

"You're a man's man," she said, "but you have a female heart."

Her hands firmly on my wrists, staring into my eyes almost hypnotically, she disclosed what she saw about my personality and life. Among the highlights: I'm an analytical loner, a male figure in my life has let me down and my life is in a rut.

Also, worryingly, my third eye is blocked. But 2008 will be better for me, and I will make "significantly more money this year and be promoted," she said.

When I told her more money is unlikely given the state of the newspaper industry, Ronzo insisted it would happen, possibly from "a change in your newspaper company."

We should be so lucky.

(When I later informed my editor about the big raise he's going to give me, he laughed. I think he's the male figure who let me down.)

It was a disconcerting experience, having a perfect stranger claim to be divining my secrets. Especially with that penetrating gaze. And she remained confident of insights that didn't ring true to me.

What is psychic ability, anyway? Is it mystical and very real, or is it mostly close observation and a sympathetic understanding of human nature?

Reading done, Ronzo asked: "How accurate was I? On a scale of 1 to 10."

Tough to say, as some of her statements were about future events. Of the remainder, I weighed the accurate from the inaccurate.

"A 6 or a 7," I said after a moment's thought. That sounded impressive to me but not so hot to Ronzo.

"That's strange," she said. "I'm usually 98, 99 percent."

Either she knows me better than I know myself, or I am, very literally, unpredictable.

MAPPING 50 YEARS OF CHANGE

February 17, 2008

An Ontario home now on the market has a unique feature for any house-huntin' history buffs: a den with a wall entirely papered over in SoCal topographic maps, circa the 1950s.

Carefully taped together, the maps form one large image, some 15 feet long and 6 feet high, showing an enormous area bordered by Anaheim, Pasadena, Yucaipa and Perris, as they existed a half-century ago.

At this point I'm calling it the Great Wall of Ontario. Too bad it's not a few miles south, so we could call it the Great Wall of Chino, but we can't have everything.

Real-estate agent John Boal, a man steeped in local history, invited me to 325 E. Rosewood Court for a visit because he thought I should see this for myself.

I'd like to congratulate the interior decorators but, alas, they're gone.

The 1928 home belonged to the late Tom and Elinor Stallard. He was a Chaffey High math teacher. She was a school psychologist and teacher.

He died in 1995 and she followed him in 2006. Their house is on the market for $399,000. I think the maps are thrown in free.

Boal and I took a squint at them. They predate Rancho Cucamonga, which is represented by Alta Loma, Cucamonga, Etiwanda, Grapeland and Rochester.

Each community was tiny, the proverbial wide spot in the road, like Petticoat Junction, Mayberry and Hooterville. Except now they have a Bass Pro Shops.

There was no Diamond Bar or Chino Hills. The future Montclair was known as Narod. South of Fontana was Declezville.

Name changes aren't reserved for cities. Upland's Cable Airport was called Cable-Claremont Airport. Fontana had two airports: Miro-Fontana and Gilfillan.

Holt Avenue in Pomona became Valley Boulevard to the east and then A Street through Ontario, while Mission Boulevard was called 5th Street in Pomona.

A vanished institution named Upland College was at Arrow Route and San Antonio Avenue. An area between Upland and Claremont was described as College Heights.

A portion of Claremont near Harrison Avenue that may be today's Pilgrim Place, a retirement home for religious professionals, was designated on the map, in plain-spoken fashion, as the Old Folks Home.

Isn't that great? I picture elderly people on its porch in rocking chairs, drinking lemonade, as a banjo plucks out Stephen Foster tunes.

Most of the Inland Empire was undeveloped. Vast acreages are marked with dots that Boal surmises represented citrus groves and grapes. Train lines and oil tanks are noted. So is the Pacific Electric trolley line.

In this panoramic view plastered upon a wall for study and reference, cities were anomalies, few in number, their borders small patches of bright yellow afloat in an ocean of pale green representing everything else.

On these maps, Ontario began at the 10 Freeway, which was either new or in its planning stages, and continued south just past Mission Boulevard. Pomona's southern border was at Philadelphia Street, with Phillips Ranch not even a gleam in a speculator's eye.

Chino, meanwhile, was a tight square: 1st to 15th streets, Riverside Drive to Chino Avenue. An able-bodied person could walk from one end of Chino to the other in an hour.

"I've never seen anything like this in my life," Boal said of the map collage.

Whoever buys the house, he lamented, probably won't see the value in keeping the unusual wallpaper.

Especially if the buyer is Martha Stewart.

The Stallards obtained the decor from the U.S. Geological Survey in 1965, according to their daughter, Susan. (Maybe Crate and Barrel was closed that day.)

"It has been a point of interest to visitors to our home for decades," she said by email.

As for me, certainly I know the broad outlines of how the inland region has, for good or bad, changed from rural to suburban. For us latecomers, who are responsible for and beneficiaries of the change, it's hard to picture what the area was like before.

When old-timers sweep an arm and say "all this used to be groves," you can gaze in that direction sympathetically, but mentally erasing the Taco Bells, subdivisions and power lines takes more imagination than most of us can muster.

Old aerial photos capture a broader view, depicting acres of agriculture, not rooftops. They make the changes more vivid.

With their omniscient view, these vintage maps are even more powerful. They offer the perspective of God gazing down upon a vanishing Eden.

True, some elements of the old days remain unscathed. For eight decades, the little Rosewood Court house has stood near the 1894-founded Graber Olive House.

Still, I suspect few people here at the time of these 1950s maps could have envisioned the Inland Valley of 2008.

For one thing, who'd have dreamed that even in a housing slump, a modest house would cost $399,000?

A WHALE OF A TALE

April 6, 2008

You wanted to lose weight or spend more time with your family. Did you?

My personal New Year's resolution was weirder but perhaps no less fantastic: to read *Moby-Dick*, all 577 oversized pages of it.

It wasn't like I had to hunt for a copy. One had been sitting on my bookshelf since 1998. I was an English major, but I'm much better at buying books than at reading them.

What finally prompted me to read it was a friend telling me he'd just seen the 1956 movie version. He mentioned having read the book in high school, too.

Apparently a lot of California high school students have to read *Moby-Dick*, which blows my mind. In my high school in Illinois, our towering achievement was *Lord of the Flies*. California students read more in one semester than we read in all of high school.

Shamed at never having read the book, seen the movie or even skimmed the Classics Illustrated version, I decided to tackle *Moby-Dick*.

Granted, the tackling was done in slow motion. I started the book on January 1 and read a little every single day – usually very little. The point was to inch closer to the end and not lose heart.

Call me incrementalist.

"Call me Ishmael," of course, is the famous first line. From there, Herman Melville's sentences get a lot longer. In the most egregious instance, one endless sentence barreled on through 11 semicolons.

So reading the novel was no breeze. And it's hefty as a brick. Melville keeps dropping the plot to write chapter after chapter about whales and the work of dismantling one. The title creature doesn't really show up until the last 30 pages.

Incidentally, it's not clear why the title has a hyphen when the whale is known as Moby Dick.

Thing is, though, I loved *Moby-Dick*. Exasperating as the book could be at times, the writing is lyrical, the tone reflective. A few sample lines:

"Top-heavy was the ship as a dinnerless student with all Aristotle in his head."

Ahab, depressed: "But do I look very old, so very, very old, Starbuck? I feel deadly faint, bowed, and humped, as though I were Adam, staggering beneath the piled centuries since Paradise."

Moby, breaching: "So suddenly seen in the blue plain of the sea, and relieved against the still bluer margin of the sky, the spray that he raised ... glittered and glared like a glacier."

There are hundreds of lines like these, startling in their beauty or their humor. Melville touches on history, science, sociology, philosophy and religion as he inflates what could have been a simple adventure story with myth and significance.

My favorite chapter may be the one devoted to a whale's forehead, in which Melville rhapsodizes about its absence of a nose. This didn't advance the plot, but it was an amazing read.

Is there a local angle? Well, my edition was designed by Andrew Hoyem, who turns out to be a Pomona College graduate. Also, as a whale boat sets off from the Pequod, its men are "seated like Ontario Indians."

OK, that's Ontario, Canada, but that's where our Ontario got its name, you know!

Melville spent a year and a half writing *Moby-Dick*, beginning it when he was just 31. Meanwhile, midway through February, closing in on age 44, I was at the novel's halfway point.

It felt so good to have half the epic behind me and half still lying ahead that I allowed myself to drift lazily, as if becalmed at sea, reading four pages per day for two weeks.

Soon enough, favorable chapters arrived and off I went, the wind again filling my sails.

Much of my reading was done in Claremont's Coffee Bean and Tea Leaf during chill evenings over a cup of hot tea.

There I could sit at a table and concentrate for a rare hour, which with Melville's dense prose might be good enough to get me through 30 pages.

The sole distraction was the chatter of people who go to coffeehouses with friends, spouses or dates, not difficult 19th century novels. The superficial fools.

At last, on Easter afternoon, I went to Coffee Bean to read the final 20 pages.

That day the temperature was well into the 80s. I got a cold drink and finished the book outside in the Village Expansion courtyard, warmed by the setting sun.

It was a bit sobering to realize that in the time it took me to read *Moby-Dick*, the seasons had turned.

Still, this was one of my life's most rewarding reading experiences. Aglow with achievement, I can now return Melville's masterpiece to my shelves.

It will stand near my unread copy of *Ulysses*.

Regis misses letters

April 13, 2008

Andy Rooney, the *60 Minutes* curmudgeon, also writes a syndicated newspaper column. A recent one began:

"Because I'm uncertain about whether 'Ontario, CA' is in California or Canada, I don't know where David Grossberg lives, but he has written me a good letter about handwriting."

Not the Ontario thing again. Anyway, Rooney noted that Grossberg's missive decried "the disappearance of the thoughtful, handwritten letter."

Rooney, ever the contrarian, wrote that he prefers typed letters and email: "I get a lot of handwritten letters that are hard to read and most of them aren't worth the trouble if I spend the time deciphering them."

Grossberg, an insurance agent, didn't single Rooney out.

In December, he began mailing form letters to middle-aged and senior celebrities in various fields – sent to their homes, the better to ensure a personal response – asking for their thoughts about handwritten letters.

He's heard back from people as diverse as Janet Reno, Rex Reed, Phyllis Diller and Noam Chomsky. Hugh Downs sent a two-page response.

"Turns out I hit a much bigger nerve than I thought," Grossberg, 42, told me last week in his B Street office.

"Those of us who are pre-keyboard, it really sets people off like a volcano."

A Cal State Fullerton communications graduate, Grossberg is researching an article for *Autograph*, a magazine for autograph collectors like himself.

He's sold them several pieces, including, in 2005, a real page-turner about quill pens.

In the 19th century, Grossberg told me, Americans fretted that the typewriter and telegraph were changing how people communicated.

He thinks something has been lost with email too: the touch of pen to paper, the chance to sleep on a rash letter before mailing it and the emotional pull of, say, decades-old letters from a parent.

"Alex Trebek said as long as fountain pens are around, the handwritten note will survive, which I think is a bit simplistic," Grossberg told me. Ouch.

Then again, his own handwriting is so poor – "I'm legibly challenged," he joked – that his letter to celebrities was typed.

Whether they replied in typing or longhand, many agreed with his premise.

Lee Iacocca said his daughter saved letters he wrote to her when she was away at college. Jack Kemp said he wrote a long letter to a grandchild about life when he was her age and the concept of handwriting was so alien, her mother had to read it to her.

Thomas Kinkade, meanwhile, had just received a handwritten letter from a relative about personal problems and it had moved the painter and his wife to tears.

"I think the mere physicality of the letter was an inspiration – the thought that one could touch the page where so much emotion was transferred," Kinkade wrote.

Some offered the sort of responses you might expect from people in their 60s, 70s and 80s.

Regis Philbin, in longhand, said he doesn't like "the abrupt e-mail jargon." Martin Sheen wrote that he doesn't own a computer and doesn't even like to talk on the phone because he can't see the other person. (He ended with a cheerful "Peace in '08!")

Paul Volcker, the former Federal Reserve chief, lamented by hand that "handwritten communication is dieing." He might benefit from a computer's spellcheck.

Like Rooney, though, several celebs aren't losing sleep over the shift away from handwriting.

Jane Russell, who said she tries to be forward-looking, replied: "... This will probably be the last letter I shall ever write. It's emails for me from now on."

Hugh Downs said emails are more efficient because the writer may dispense with greetings and elaborate signoffs.

Helen Gurley Brown, typing her letter on a manual typewriter, wrote: "I think a letter recipient would rather read the typed letter (easily and comfortably) than sludge through my handwriting."

A half-dozen people responded by phone – obviously Sheen wasn't one of them – including Jay Leno and Fess Parker.

"You're in the middle of insurance business and Davy Crockett calls," Grossberg marveled.

While I was reading the letters in his outer office, Grossberg took a call, came over, tapped my arm and jotted a note excitedly: "Jacqueline Bisset."

She was just back from Europe, read his letter and wondered if she still had time to write him back. He assured her she did.

The logical question, once the thrill of a Jacqueline Bisset phone call wears off, is who in the world would care what she thinks about handwriting. Unless she's writing about her wet T-shirt scene in *The Deep*.

That's true of a lot of the correspondence, which is earnest but rarely insightful, other than offering the insight that famous people can be pretty ordinary.

The time I spent deciphering Monty Hall's penmanship – his favorite letters are the ones that say "I love you, Grandpa" – is time I will never get back.

Of course, there's a reason Grossberg polled famous people rather than random old people: He's writing for a magazine named *Autograph*.

Speaking of which, one can't help but be impressed at how Grossberg managed to expand his autograph collection in the guise of research.

I wonder what the last letter Jane Russell will ever write will be worth someday?

RFK'S RALLY WAS THE PLACE TO BE

May 18, 2008

Forty years ago Tuesday, Robert F. Kennedy came to Ontario and Pomona.

Kennedy hit both cities on May 20, 1968, part of a frenetic day of campaigning in Southern California before the state's June 4 Democratic primary.

"Kennedy Due Here Monday," the Saturday edition of the *Pomona Progress-Bulletin* reported on Page One.

Kennedy would speak at Robbie's, a banquet hall on East Second Street, for which tickets would be sold in advance for $2.50. (If you're chuckling about the low price, note that Kennedy's luncheon topic was inflation.)

May 20 began with Kennedy and his entourage leaving L.A.'s Ambassador Hotel, where they were staying, to make campaign stops in Alhambra, San Gabriel and Duarte.

Around noon, his motorcade of two convertibles, two motorcycle officers and two busloads of journalists exited the 10 Freeway at Garey Avenue and headed south.

At Second Street, they turned left to travel the four blocks to Robbie's.

As the *Progress-Bulletin* described the scene: "A crowd of 3,500 greeted the presidential hopeful in a frenzied appearance on the Pomona Mall."

Illuminating one source of Kennedy's appeal, a poignant

photo caption read: "Senator Robert F. Kennedy gazes briefly at a Pomona man Monday who shouted, arm outstretched, 'I knew your brother! We talked once!'"

Bob Terry was there.

Terry, then 14, was an eighth-grader at Fremont Junior High. He and his classmate Lou Maestas cut class and walked to the downtown pedestrian mall to see Kennedy, guessing correctly that it was the place to be that day.

When Kennedy's convertible rounded the corner from Garey, Terry and Maestas ran alongside. They paced his car for two blocks as Kennedy shook or touched hands with people in the crowd.

"I got to shake his hand twice," Terry told me proudly. "Lou got to shake his hand once. ... Not a lot of things I remember from 40 years ago, but that one I'll never forget."

The *Prog* painted a vivid description.

"Kennedy appeared weary as he rode into Pomona but he smiled steadily and leaned down to shake hands with his admirers who followed his slowly moving convertible along the Mall. He was in his shirt sleeves, sunburned, the familiar shaggy haircut windblown.

"An aide held the New York senator about the waist to keep him from being pulled from the car. Several people tried to snatch his tie pin. Parents held their infants up to see Kennedy over the crowd."

Not everyone was on board: One or two signs for Democratic rival Eugene McCarthy were spotted.

Kennedy changed shirts, put on a jacket and, refreshed, spoke to a luncheon crowd of 400, many of them Pomona Valley movers and shakers.

His speech, most of which was printed in the *Prog*, was boilerplate stuff. But the New Yorker did make a local joke.

"I understand this is a nonpartisan lunch, so I'll just say *if* I was running for office, and *if* I won the California primary, then I'd be able to come back to the Los Angeles County Fair in September. That's actually why I'm running for president."

At about 1:30 p.m., after the luncheon, Kennedy's motorcade headed back up Garey to the 10 and east to Ontario. His guest for the ride: Ontario Mayor Howard Snider.

"The driver and Kennedy were in the front seat and I was in the back with his dog," Snider, now 79, told me with a chuckle last week.

Because it was an open car, and he had a dog to contend with, Snider couldn't really have a conversation with the candidate. But it was a memorable ride.

Other motorists on the freeway spotted Kennedy.

"People would honk their horn. They would see who it was and beep their horn," Snider said.

At Vineyard Avenue, the motorcade headed south to Ontario International Airport.

Some 1,500 people were waiting.

"As Kennedy's convertible swung into the driveway in front of the terminal," the *Ontario Daily Report* wrote, "the crowd cheered and pushed in to greet him."

Many held pro-Kennedy banners. A few had posters for McCarthy and Richard Nixon. One jokester waved a sign reading "Mrs. Kennedy for Secretary of Labor," referring to her and her husband's 10 children.

A description in the *Report* was picturesque and, viewed in retrospect, eerie.

"...his jacket was missing, his hair was disheveled, his bright blue shirt was hanging from his trousers and his arms appeared scratched and red from the clutching grasps of the crowds.

"But the senator appeared cool and calm at all times, even when what was believed to be a firecracker exploded when he arrived at the airport. It sounded similar to a gunshot."

Kennedy gave a five-minute speech outside the terminal. He was against taxes, welfare, Vietnam and a guaranteed annual wage.

"Will you support me in my campaign?" Kennedy concluded.

"Yes!" the crowd shouted. (Except for the Nixon supporters.)

Soon he was inside. Snider, a Republican, said Kennedy posed for pictures with him and other dignitaries. A *Daily Report* photo showed Kennedy walking along the passenger concourse to a waiting plane as more hands reached out for him.

And that was all.

Kennedy flew to San Diego, made four appearances there that afternoon, then landed at Long Beach before a motorcade took him through L.A. suburbs, including Monterey Park.

An Associated Press story in the *Prog* about the evening of May 20 described the throngs around his motorcade as "the wildest scene in nine weeks of campaigning."

Kennedy was held about the waist by his security guard as he stood on the hood of the convertible, shaking hands. The clutching crowd grabbed – why not? – his shoes. An aide had to lend Kennedy his own shoes to be presentable for a speech at a synagogue.

The *Prog's* headline: "People Tear Off Kennedy's Shoes in L.A."

Fourteen days later, on the night of June 4, Kennedy won the California primary. But shortly after midnight, during a victory party at the Ambassador Hotel, gunman Sirhan Sirhan mortally wounded him.

He died the next day, June 6, 1968.

Bob Terry recalls how school let out when President Kennedy was killed in 1963, but Terry was young enough that the event didn't mean much to him.

Robert Kennedy's death was different for Terry and his pal Maestas.

"There we were, tough little eighth-graders," said Terry, now a 54-year-old salesman in Rancho Cucamonga, "but when we heard he was killed, me and him were just in tears. We couldn't let anybody else see us.

"We felt so special that we got to shake his hand."

Another Side of Bob Dylan

May 25, 2008

He's a sophisticated songwriter and a Pulitzer Prize winner, true. But on his XM Radio show, *Theme Time Radio Hour*, Bob Dylan's between-song comments reveal not only a man with an encyclopedic knowledge of music, but a man with a weakness for silly humor.

How silly? Keep reading, because I transcribed Dylan's quips from his show's first season and am presenting the best – or worst? – below.

And happy birthday to Dylan, who turned 67 on Saturday. Some of his jokes are even older than that. Personally, I think they're a scream, but even if most of you disagree, I expect Ontario politicians Paul Leon and Gary Ovitt will be repeating them for years.

"I got a friend who's learning to become a ballerina. She's improving by leaps and bounds."

"Getting married's a lot like getting into a tub of hot water. After you get used to it, it ain't so hot."

"I once had a cross-eyed teacher who couldn't control his pupils."

"You know, I sleep at the edge of the bed. It doesn't take long for me to drop off."

"Two dogs talking. One says to the other: 'You're crazy. You ought to go see a psychiatrist.' The other dog says: 'I'd love to, but I'm not allowed on the couch.'"

"I was having dinner with our announcer, Pierre Mancini. The only difference between Pierre Mancini and a canoe is that sometimes a canoe will tip."

"Take our engineer, Tex Carbone. He's so laid back it takes him two hours to watch *60 Minutes*. I'm the complete opposite. I can make Minute Rice in 30 seconds."

"I just came back from a pleasure trip. Took my mother-in-law to the airport."

"What do you do if you miss your mother-in-law? Reload, and try again."

"All musicians get girls, but a guitarist always has his pick."

"What's the difference between a drummer and a savings bond? Eventually, a savings bond will mature and earn money."

"They got a new 'dial-a-prayer' for atheists. You call it, and nobody answers."

"A lot of people don't celebrate Christmas. Like my buddy Dexter Quinn. He's an atheist. You know what his favorite Christmas movie is? *Coincidence on 34th Street*."

"If diamonds are a girl's best friend, why do so many girls get mad when you want to go to the ballpark? You tell me."

"I gave a bald-headed friend of mine a comb. You know what he said to me? 'I'll never part with it.'"

"My friend's wife is a really bad cook. I broke a tooth on her coffee."

"I was at a restaurant. I said to the waiter, 'There's a needle in my soup.' He said, 'I'm very sorry. It's a typographical error. It's supposed to be a noodle.'"

"A cat has nine lives, but a bullfrog croaks every day."

"If you think the sun is too hot, just remember, you don't have to shovel it."

"In Sweden, they have a system of higher taxes, but welfare for everyone. They call it the Swedish model. Well, I could go for a Swedish model right about now."

"Here's a tip on how you can save your money. Use somebody else's."

"He opened a restaurant on the moon. It had great food, people say, but no atmosphere."

"My friend was happily married for 10 years. Too bad he was married for 30."

"Every day in the United States, 200 new jail cells are constructed. I hope we can keep up!"

"A giraffe can go a long time without water. But he wants to see a menu right away."

"I was having dinner the other day when the waiter came over. I said to him, 'There's a fly in my soup.' And he said, 'That's very possible. The cook used to be a tailor.'"

"Married men don't live longer. It just seems longer."

Today's column, by the way, was the usual length. It just seemed longer.

WEALTH AT HIS FINGERTIPS!

June 18, 2008

In noting here recently that my email address had changed, I said that spammers, unlike you regular readers, never seemed to have a problem reaching me at my old d_allen account (which expires today).

Well, spammers seem to have an even easier time of it without the tricky underscore in my address. My new inbox has been flooded with unsolicited offers of immense wealth and notices of foreign lotteries I've won.

Nothing, though, about male enhancement. I suppose there's no improving on perfection.

Ejner Andersen, country unspecified, claims to have been referred to me during his exhaustive search "for a reliable person (he) could do business with."

My sterling reputation precedes me all over the world.

It seems that Mr. Andersen's late boss Richard Williams wanted to leave $10.5 million to his family. Tragically, however, the same November 11, 2006, automobile crash that killed Williams also claimed every last member of his family.

Must have been a large car.

In any event, Mr. Andersen would like to submit my name as the next of kin and split the proceeds, which is awfully decent of him, given that he could submit his wife's name and take the whole thing.

Strangely enough, Gert Gilbertson also contacted me regarding his ex-boss Richard Williams and his oil money. Except in this email, Williams had $13 million – $2.5 million more than in Andersen's email – and he died on December 11, 2006, one month later. Obviously, it was a profitable month.

Rather than come between Mr. Andersen and Mr. Gilbertson, I'm going to sit this one out.

And why not? Numerous bank employees worldwide are anxious to cut me in on some action.

Patrick K.W. Chan said he is head of an unnamed Hong Kong bank. "I have an obscured business suggestion for you," Chan wrote.

Wanting something a bit less obscure, I read a note from Brian Drick, who would like me to "invest and manage" an account of "vast wealth."

"I was bron in Cananda as a citizen. I stay in, Belgium," wrote Drick, rather unpersuasively.

Jason Kane, "a banker by profession with Rand Merchant Bank (RMB) South Africa," wrote several times to offer me 40 percent of $15.5 million.

Anthony Aka of the International Commercial Bank wants to give me 30 percent of $3.5 million. He began deferentially:

"Pardon me for not having the pleasure of knowing your mindset before making you this offer and it is utterly confidential and genuine by virtue of its nature."

Sorry, but knowing my mindset is a pleasure that will be denied you. Especially with your lowball offer of 30 percent.

A woman named Wan Yonghong of Standard Chartered Bank, country unknown, wants to share $23 million with me, a secret deposit by yet another deceased client.

Refreshingly, she addresses the ethics matter head-on.

"What I wish to relate to you will smack of unethical practice but I want you to understand something," she wrote. "It is only an outsider to the banking world who finds the internal politics of the banking world aberrational."

I feel better already.

Foreign women want to hand me money too. For example, there's Mrs. Jennifer Peters, who describes herself as "a dying woman who has decided to donate what I have to you/church."

Me-slash-church?

She'd like to send me $2.5 million "for the good work of humanity and also to help the motherless and less privilege and also for the assistance of the widows."

How about unwed mothers – could I work with them? Sorry, that's an old Steve Martin joke.

Rich widows are dying all over. Mrs. Maria Elena Fernandez wrote from "Philippine" about her late husband's money. She's going to be late herself from the sound of things.

"Recently, my Doctor told me that i have serious sickness which is cancer problem," she wrote. "The one that disturbs me most is the high blood pressure sickness."

Gasp. Not the high blood pressure sickness!

Not to say all these offers aren't attractive, but I've also been on a lucky streak with foreign lotteries.

By my count, 26 lotteries tell me I've won amounts from $500,000 to $2.5 million, as well as various amounts in pounds and euros.

With this sort of wealth flowing my way, I don't know why I didn't change email addresses years ago.

It's now lonelier in L.A.

August 20, 2008

I'm going to do something rare today by writing about a competitor, and I don't mean an Olympian. A competing journalist.

Steve Harvey wrote "Only in LA." for the *Los Angeles Times* for the past 20 years, a humor column full of tidbits contributed by readers. I was both a reader and a contributor.

Harvey, I'm sorry to say, was among the casualties of the *Times*' recent staff cuts. Thus, no more "Only in L.A." in the newspaper, although it's been promised that Harvey will contribute occasionally.

For his readers, though, it's going to be lonely in L.A.

His column was a collection of SoCal oddities, such as a computerized contest letter that promised its recipient, "You'll be turning quite a few heads on the streets of Los Angeles as you roar down P.O. Box 3543 in your new Corvette."

There was a lot of wordplay like that in the column: misspelled for-sale ads (a "naughty pine" dresser), fractured English on restaurant menus ("sweat and sour pork"), ads seeking "conscious" employees.

Here's one that appears in a "Best of Only in L.A." tribute at *latimes.com*, a golden wedding anniversary notice that read: "Celebrating 50 Years of Marriage, 46 Years of Friendship, a World of Love."

"Were the 46 years at the beginning or at the end?" Harvey cracked.

"Only in L.A." was consistently amusing, and sometimes laugh-out-loud funny. This despite the handicap of quoting occasionally from my work.

Harvey picked up many items from me, with full credit, over the years. In fact, I just counted, and he did so even more than I'd realized: 82 times.

That's 82 mentions of the *Inland Valley Daily Bulletin* in the *L.A. Times*. I should be getting a kickback from our marketing department.

A sample, from January 18, 2003:

"Just say neigh! An Ontario mansion became a brothel recently for a scene in the unreleased racehorse film *Seabiscuit*. Columnist David Allen reported: 'Tobey Maguire, Jeff Bridges and Chris Cooper were here for two days for the brothel scene. My fingers are crossed that Seabiscuit wasn't involved. It's so hard to find heroes in the world of sports anymore.'"

Steve Harvey obviously appreciated my work. Either that, or he took pity on me as another columnist with two first names.

He also gave me grand-sounding job titles to match up with items he was using, dubbing me "wiseguy columnist," "the Monitor of Montclair" and, my favorite, "the conscience of Ontario." That was after I pointed out that the city's then-new logo of a rising sun was almost identical to the one on Folger's Coffee.

Some of you two-newspaper families noticed these appearances. People would bring it up to me in person, or even clip a pertinent "Only in L.A" and mail it to me, wondering if I'd seen my name.

That was unnecessary, of course, but very sweet. I had the feeling you were proud of me.

What you didn't know was that Harvey wasn't finding my columns blindly. Unwilling to trust to chance, I was emailing them to him.

I first contacted him in 1996 when I was a columnist for the *Daily Press* in Victorville. Harvey had a silly contest in one of his columns and I sent in an entry, plus, by way of introduction, a short note and one of my columns.

He didn't use my entry, but imagine my surprise when he plucked an item from that column for print. Who knew the Times would be interested in Hesperia humor?

When a *Best of Only in L.A.* book was published, I drove to Long Beach for his book signing. He inscribed my book as follows: "For David, a columnist after my own heart (but hopefully not after my job). Best wishes otherwise, Steve Harvey."

We struck up a loose friendship and I traveled to L.A., or to Long Beach, where he lives, for lunch about once a year after that – which I plan to continue doing.

Harvey is a low-key guy, very soft-spoken, modest, always quick to disparage himself. We would swap stories of filling space on deadline, or recount with a sigh the slights from readers or editors.

I don't know how much Harvey got out of these lunches, but they were always instructive for me. He's an old-school journalist. He knows the old *Times* hangouts. He knew Jack Smith, my columnist hero.

More importantly, despite the disparity in the size of our respective readerships, Harvey never looked down on me. He treated me as an equal, just another ink-stained wretch hacking out a column. That was well worth the price of a

Metrolink ticket.

From his example, I also picked up writing tips. One is that a lot of things are only half-funny in and of themselves. It's how you set them up or respond to them that puts them over the top. He elevated that to an art – see the golden anniversary item above.

In other words, he got 82 items from me, but I got a lot from him in return, including occasional notes of praise or encouragement. He also urged me a few years ago to add him as a reference on my resume.

Speaking of which, Steve, I'll need a current phone number. Thanks. Not that I'm looking, mind you, but anything can happen, as he found out himself.

As has been reported on *laobserved.com*, Harvey was among the recent wave of layoffs at the *Times*. He heard the news while at a Cal Poly San Luis Obispo workshop, where he was training high school journalists.

Ironic, no? This may have been more real-world journalism experience than students were expecting.

Harvey, who was nearing retirement age, was philosophical about the blow. His farewell email to colleagues read in full: "At least now I'll have time to polish up my audition for *Dancing With the Stars*. Best to all, Steve Harvey."

'34 DRIVE WAS QUITE A JOURNEY

August 31, 2008

Arlene Wildman noticed my column in the paper one morning and phoned with an idea.

"You should write a second column in which seniors contribute stories from their lives," she said. "You could call it 'Now and Then.'"

A fine idea – for someone else. Unless there's a way to add 40 hours to my work-week, such as through cloning.

But Wildman, who was born in 1915, told me a pretty interesting story about how she came to live in Pomona: She drove there from Iowa. In 1934. By herself.

Impressed by her resourcefulness, I drove to Pomona from Ontario for a visit.

Wildman lives alone in a Ganesha Hills home since her husband of seven decades died a few years ago.

"His name was Wildman, but he wasn't a wild man," she quipped. "He didn't drink, he didn't do anything like that. But I indoctrinated him into being a dancer."

She married Keith Wildman when she was 18. He was a meatcutter in small-town Iowa and times were hard in the Depression.

Her mother, meanwhile, had left Iowa for Pomona with her second husband. At Pomona's Fifth Avenue Market one day, the owner confided to her that he needed a meatcutter.

She dispatched word to her son-in-law and soon Keith was on the train to Pomona.

Arlene stayed behind to settle their affairs in Malcolm, Iowa. This involved selling some of their possessions and figuring out a way to haul the rest to California.

She had a Model A Ford and removed the back seat to make room for a cedar chest full of linens and dishes, a wedding present from her mother.

To carry less-precious items, her grandfather built a trailer on a Ford chassis for her to haul. This practical but unlovely trailer was covered with tar paper in case of rain.

Sounds like a good candidate for *Pimp My Ride*.

One September morning, 1934, she set out.

"I stopped at a Conoco station and got a map," Wildman said. She studied it carefully and decided to take what she recalls only as the northern route.

Traveling to California took six days.

"The only accommodations were broken-down motels. Farmers would fix their chicken coops for a bed and you could rent one for $2 a night," she said.

One evening, when she had parked by the side of the road to admire a view, her car wouldn't start. A passing cowboy in a Buick pushed her car into town, where a repair cost 50 cents.

That was as troublesome as the drive went.

Her final night was spent in the dusty outpost of Las Vegas. She left at dawn and arrived in Pomona around noon, chugging to the tiny house her mother rented on Gordon Street behind the Methodist Church.

"I actually fell on the ground and kissed it," Wildman said. "I was so grateful and tired."

Obviously that's far from the end of Arlene Wildman's story.

There were more hard times. One day she stood in the market eyeing a 5-cent can of food she couldn't afford, and cried.

But hers was a happy marriage, with two children and a rented ranch in Chino, where, she said proudly, "I worked like two men and a horse."

After that came a return to Pomona in the 1950s to the house she still calls home, years of activity with the Ebell Club and the hospital, a large garden in her yard that still has peaches, persimmons, grapes, pears and cactus.

I might also note that the china hauled in that homemade trailer not only survived the trip but last year was passed on, intact, to a granddaughter.

But let's end with what happened shortly after Wildman arrived in Pomona that September day in 1934.

Her family told her the fair was on.

"I'd never been to a fair," Wildman said. She didn't even know what one was. So they went.

She remembers tents set up in a field and the Agricultural Building full of fruit that was exotic to her: not only oranges but seedless grapes. She was transfixed.

"It was the biggest thrill of my life. I thought, this is Utopia. I'm going to stay.

"And that was over 70 years ago."

If she's regretted her decision, it's only been now and then.

CHEESY FUN AT PASTA DINNER

September 28, 2008

Rancho Cucamonga's Sons of Italy Lodge touted its first pasta dinner at a recent City Council meeting, leading to some joshing by council members about whether the lodge planned an authentic experience or a meal out of a can.

"I assure you, this is a real Italian pasta dinner," speaker Frank Annunziato proclaimed confidently.

The tongue-in-cheek dialogue was repeated here along with Annunziato's phone number for tickets. Soon he sent me a letter thanking me for my "beautiful" column. He said 40 people had contacted him.

That news was all I really needed to feel good, but he also included a complimentary meal ticket and promised, "you will have a 'real Italian pasta dinner.'"

Thus, I showed up last weekend at Lions Center West, ticket in hand. What can I say, it was a slow Saturday night for me.

Lodge member Sam Spagnolo, a councilman and Italian American, was greeting everyone at the door. He was happy to see me. He shuttled me into line, where lodge member Lucille Seibel got me a plate.

"You look just like your photo!" she said cheerfully. I told her I was sorry to hear that.

The chef, Sartaj Singh, scooped me up a plate of penne pasta and two meatballs. Deciding that wasn't enough, the newspaper reader asked for my plate back and gave me two extra meatballs.

His generosity quickly proved controversial among the city's movers and shakers.

"You got four meatballs? I only got two," Mayor Don Kurth noted enviously as I passed by with my plate.

"I could give you one and then we'd be even," I offered.

Helen Ammannito, a lodge member and newspaper reader, invited me to sit at her table with her and her daughter, Flora Magnon.

I took a seat and dug in. Councilman Rex Gutierrez, who was sitting across the table, looked at my plate.

"I only got two meatballs!" Gutierrez said.

This time I didn't offer to share. My mouth was full.

(Gutierrez didn't really begrudge me the extra meatballs, confiding to our RC Now blog: "It looked like he needed it, he looked kinda frail. He could use some meat on his bones.")

Ammannito was so looking forward to the 5 p.m. dinner that she showed up at 4:30. I couldn't finish my pasta – must have been all those meatballs – but she insisted on my getting a cannoli for dessert.

OK. After I'd redeemed my ticket for a cannoli and polished it off, Ammannito volunteered to get me a second cannoli for the road and stood up.

Before I realized what she was doing, the 95-year-old bent over to pick up a stray cannoli ticket from the floor. She redeemed it and carefully wrapped the cannoli for me in two paper trays and a napkin.

Her sense of balance is exceeded only by her kindness.

Playing no favorites, she asked Gutierrez if he'd had a cannoli. "I did," he said as he stood up to leave. "I'm going to look for extra tickets."

He was kidding, but it wouldn't have surprised me. He recently achieved notoriety for plucking an unused $25 gift certificate from Sisley Italian Kitchen out of an illegal dump site and using it to treat City Manager Jack Lam to lunch.

To my left, a senior named Marie Wright thought she recognized me but couldn't believe she was sitting with a *Daily Bulletin* columnist.

"You're joking!" she exclaimed. When I assured her it really was me, she said delightedly: "This is darling!"

Why isn't the Ontario City Council ever this pleased to see me?

Lodge member Ted Seibel introduced himself as I shoveled my leftover pasta, including the fourth meatball, into a takeout container.

They'd sold more than 400 tickets and had almost 80 walk-ins, making the "first annual" dinner a big hit. The proceeds will go to various good causes, including the blood disorder thalassemia.

Is he an officer?

"I'm the president," Seibel said, "and I'm not even Italian. I'm Polish! My wife is Italian, that's how I got into the club."

Ah, that would be Lucille. Small world.

The Italians are plenty smart, Ted Seibel informed me, "because they got this Polack to do all their dirty work."

Well, Annunziato did tell the City Council that you don't have to be Italian to join the Sons of Italy.

Speaking of multiculturalism, Singh, the cook, is from India. But he went to college in Italy. Reflecting his diverse background, Singh owns two restaurants in Rancho Cucamonga, one Indian, one Italian.

So was this a real Italian pasta dinner? Even though it was

cooked by an Indian?

   I'd say so. And to the councilmen, let me add: That's-a spicy meat-a-ball. All four of 'em.

Parade's death leaves confetti on his hands

November 21, 2008

Did I (ulp) kill the Pomona Christmas parade?

Sorry to say, the 2008 parade, scheduled for December 6, has been canceled. City Hall withdrew its financial support and the event collapsed.

OK, so the demise of a 60-year tradition is a budget thing.

Still, given my role as the 2007 parade's grand marshal, in which I dressed as a 1940s newspaperman and led the parade in a convertible, I can't help but wonder if I should have done more somehow.

Did I not wave vigorously enough?

The Christmas parade, sponsored by Pomona Jaycees, has gone on every year since 1948. The club pays some $3,000 to City Hall for permits and other fees.

Traffic control, blockades, portable toilets and other costs, which total about $10,000, mostly for police overtime, have been borne by city departments.

But not this year. The parade was quietly de-funded amid belt-tightening for the 2008-2009 city budget approved in June.

City officials, however, waited until October to break the news to the Jaycees. Their message, according to parade Chairwoman Karen Crye-Davis: "If you want a parade, you've got to come up with $10,000." Tough news for a low-budget service club less than two months before the parade. "I don't know when they decided they didn't have the money, but we don't have time to raise that amount," Crye-Davis told me.

As a result, the 61st parade was canceled and all participants were notified not to show up. "There's no physical way to pull it off at this point," Crye-Davis said.

I wonder who broke the news to Santa.

Pomona won't have a lack of public cheer: The annual Holiday Lane event will take place December 6, courtesy of nearly $40,000 in city funds, City Manager Linda Lowry told me.

With a year off, Lowry said, perhaps the parade can be reorganized and brought back in 2009.

Larry Egan, head of the downtown business improvement district, wants the parade back on Second Street, its home until the 1970s.

Fine by me. The modern route, which sends a feel-good parade east on Holt Avenue past muffler shops, tire stores, doughnut stands, empty lots and discount stores, doesn't exactly show off Pomona at its finest.

Some blocks last year were almost barren of people. Even when the sidewalks were crowded, Holt is so broad that a parade down the middle seemed far away.

Closer quarters, such as downtown, might help. The recent Founders Day Parade in Rancho Cucamonga gained energy by winding through the comparatively narrow streets of Victoria Gardens.

Wherever the parade winds up, I hope it's not the scrapheap.

Unless the parade returns in 2009, "you'll go down in history as the last grand marshal," Crye-Davis told me.

That's not how I want history to remember me!

METER STILL RUNS ON WAITS STORY

December 7, 2008

Happy birthday to the gravel-voiced singer-songwriter Tom Waits, perhaps best known for writing "Jersey Girl" (made famous by Bruce Springsteen), "Ol' 55" (the Eagles) and "Downtown Train" (Rod Stewart).

Waits, who turns 59 today, may be the most famous artist who hails from Pomona.

Or does he?

Well, he does, although Waits' sometimes-fanciful statements on his birth have him born in a taxicab in a hospital parking lot in, depending on the version, Pomona, Whittier or L.A.

For instance, here's a comment he made between songs at a 1976 concert in New Jersey:

"I was born at a very young age in the backseat of a Yellow Cab in the Murphy Hospital parking lot in Whittier, California.

"It's not easy for a young boy growing up in Whittier. I had to make decisions very early. First thing I did was pay, like, $1.85 on the meter.

"As soon as I got out of the cab I went out looking for a job. The only job I could get was as labor organizer in a maternity ward for a while. I got laid off. Got a little disenchanted with labor."

Ha ha. That comment and others to follow were retrieved a

year ago from an entertaining Waits timeline found online; the site, alas, is no longer active.

Here's a second version of the birth story, from a 1976 interview in Ohio: "Well, I was born at a very young age and I was born in the backseat of a Yellow Cab at Murphy Hospital parking lot in Pomona, California."

And a third version, from a 1976 interview in England:

"I was born in L.A. at a very young age. I was born in the backseat of a Yellow Cab in Murphy Hospital parking lot. I had to pay $1.85 on the meter to move. I didn't have my trousers on yet and I left my money in my other pants."

More seriously, Waits continued:

"I lived around L.A. and moved around L.A. My dad's a Spanish teacher, so we lived in Whittier, Pomona, La Verne, North Hollywood, Silver Lake, metropolitan areas surrounding Los Angeles."

That part seems to be true. His dad, Jesse Frank Waits, was a Spanish teacher. His mother, Alma, was a teacher too.

Waits grew up mostly in Whittier but did spend some time in La Verne. Here's what he said in a 1983 interview published in England's *New Musical Express*:

"My grandmother lived by an orange grove and I remember sleeping at her house and hearing the Southern Pacific go by. This was in La Verne, California. My father moved from Texas to La Verne and he worked in the orange groves there. I also have a memory of wild gourds that grew by the railroad tracks, and putting pennies on the tracks."

But where was he born?

In Waits' telling, Murphy Hospital really gets around: Whittier, L.A., Pomona. Murphy was actually a Whittier hospital.

But it's not where Waits was born.

This birth notice appeared in the December 9 and December 14, 1949 editions of the *Pomona Progress-Bulletin*, as follows:

"To Mr. and Mrs. J. Frank Waits, 318 N. Pickering street, Whittier, a son, Thomas Alan, 7 pounds and 10 ounces, born December 7 at Park Avenue hospital."

Park Avenue Hospital, now an empty lot, was located at Park Avenue and Jefferson Street.

I have no way of knowing if Waits was truly born in a taxicab, but I suspect not. That strikes me as the sort of story that would have made the *Progress-Bulletin*, but a page-by-page search of the December 7 to December 9 papers turned up no such novelty item.

But it could be true, or somewhat true. Unexpected labor could be why a couple from Whittier would end up at a Pomona hospital. One can imagine a dash via car or cab from that relative's house in La Verne, with the baby arriving before the vehicle did.

In any event, while the hospital is gone, there's still a Yellow Cab franchise in Pomona.

Take a cab in Waits' honor today.

COUNTING DOWN 08'S STRANGEST NEWS

December 28, 2008

Assuming nothing else weird happens in the next four days, here are my choices for the Inland Valley's Top 10 strangest news events of 2008:

10. **MYSTERIOUS WAYS**: In an unusual case of road rage, a former chaplain at the sheriff's Chino Hills station was sentenced in August to one year in jail after cursing at another driver, pulling a handgun and firing at him. So much for turning the other cheek.

9. **ONTARIO, EH?**: After a man was nabbed in Arizona, authorities suspected he was in the country illegally from Canada. In a novel twist, the man from Sudbury, Ontario, tried to claim it was all a mistake: He was from Ontario, California, and his mother was from Sudbury, Massachusetts. He was convicted after a birth certificate, passport and passport application showed otherwise.

8. **NAME GAME**: In the Ontario-Montclair School District, school board member Paul Avila blew up at a middle school event in May, leaving employees in tears, because his name was left off the program. He later issued unconvincing denials, declaring at one point: "Whether my name was on the program is irrelevant and I deserved to be on that program." If it's any consolation, his name is in my Top 10 list and it deserves to be on that Top 10 list.

7. **PUSHING IT**: In April, a woman in a Claremont restaurant refused to pay her bill, threw objects and verbally abused customers. Police responded and asked the woman to pay her bill. "I'm a woman Marine," she replied. "I don't take orders, I give them. Drop down and give me 50." Officers declined, but they did arrest her for public intoxication.

6. **IN THE JAILHOUSE NOW**: A retired Pomona police sergeant, 61, was arrested in October in connection with a series of bank robberies in Escondido, Glendora and Rancho Cucamonga. Perhaps he got bored sitting around the house and thought he'd try a new line of work.

5. **CHARO IN POMONA**: The original famous-for-being-famous performer drove out from Beverly Hills to Western University of Health Sciences in December so that Pomona veterinarians could examine her rescue animal, a 250-pound bull named Manolo, for a heart murmur. At this point, words fail. (He was fine, by the way.) A slightly more euphonious story would have seen Charo visit Chino, but that's just being greedy.

4. **DEPLANE! DEPLANE!**: In December, passengers were kept on board a plane at L.A/Ontario International Airport for nine hours because of confusion over protocol. The airport and the airline, TACA, blamed each other. To make amends for the ordeal, I think the airline should pay passengers a $15 fee for giving them emotional baggage.

3. **HEAD CASE**: A crystal skull on loan to a New Age shop in Claremont was reported missing by its owner, who believed the skull originated hundreds or thousands of years ago and had healing powers. The reported theft in April coincided with publicity for the fourth Indiana Jones movie. To my knowledge, Claremont suffered no stolen fedoras.

2. **CURRENCY WE DON'T BELIEVE IN**: In October, a Republican women's club in Upland got attention of the unwelcome kind after its newsletter included a photo of Barack Obama on a food stamp surrounded by stereotypical African American food: fried chicken, watermelon, ribs and Kool-Aid. If this creaky attempt at humor was any indication of how "with it" Republicans were in 2008, it's no wonder they lost.

And the No. 1 strange story of the year:

1. **TURKEY DAY**: At Claremont's Condit Elementary School, a Thanksgiving celebration of diversity, tolerance and mutual respect prompted protests that drew national ridicule. Some parents said the kindergarten feast between "Pilgrims" and "Indians" glossed over the uglier parts of America's colonization. To which everyone else said: Of course it does! It's kindergarten!

The flap did make some of us rethink our assumptions. For instance, I now worry that the ABCs gloss over the more controversial letters of the alphabet.

STONE-COLD SOBERING CHATTER

December 31, 2008

Once again our new year is seen in by a series of unique city representatives: their statuary. Let's listen in.

MADONNA OF THE TRAIL: Happy New Year's Eve, Mr. Chaffey! Are you ready for 2009?

GEORGE CHAFFEY: Hello, Madonna. Yes, I'm looking forward to the new year. As the fellow who envisioned Euclid Avenue and put in the region's first electric lights, I always did enjoy looking forward.

MADONNA: Do you have a special reason for looking forward now, George?

GEORGE: Yes. As a statue, I can't turn my head. They tell me Upland City Hall is right behind me, but who knows?

MADONNA: Oh, George, you always cheer me up. These are such dreary times. Reminds me of the Depression. I've been here at Euclid and Foothill since 1929, you know.

GEORGE: Is the economy affecting you, too, Maddy?

MADONNA: And how. My two children here were talking about getting their own pedestal somewhere, but now it looks like I'm stuck to them another 80 years.

JEDEDIAH SMITH: Of all the gol-durn messes, this economy is it.

MADONNA: Why, I never!

JEDEDIAH: Pardon mah language, ma'am. Ah didn't realize there was womenfolk present. Ah'm just a rough ol' trapper and explorer memorialized outside Mud Springs City Hall.

MADONNA: Mud Springs?

GEORGE: He means San Dimas. That's been the name since 1887, but Jed saw the place while roaming the West in 1826. Looks as though you stuck around, eh, Jed?

JEDEDIAH: Ah like the pie at Roady's.

LIBERTY BELL: Clang!

GEORGE: Why it's our old friend, La Verne's replica of the Liberty Bell! How are things in La Verne?

LIBERTY: Clang clang clang!

GEORGE: What's that you say, Libby? Timmy's in the well again?

MADONNA: I believe what he said was he's sad Jon Blickenstaff is retiring as mayor.

GEORGE *(musing)*: Maybe Jon Blickenstaff is in the well again.

LIBERTY: Clang!!

GEORGE: Just pulling your clapper, Liberty.

WILLIAM SHAKESPEARE: Enter, stage right.

GEORGE: I don't believe I've made your acquaintance, sir.

SHAKESPEARE: 'Twas a time when every schoolboy made my acquaintance. I am the bard of Stratford-on-Avon, now transplanted to Rancho-on-Cucamonga.

GEORGE: William Shakespeare? By thunder, man, this is an honor. But what are you doing in Rancho Cucamonga, outside the Cultural Center? Is this a gag?

SHAKESPEARE: Some have gagged, true. But 'tis a nice bench 'pon which I sit, and a shady spot. Yet ask a ballplayer if 'tis an honor to be benched.

JACK BENNY: You and your puns. Hi, Will. Hi, George. Hi, Madonna. Hi, Jed. Gosh, it's great to have the gang together.

MADONNA: Oh, Jack, you and Mr. Shakespeare are just a few yards apart, aren't you? He's outside the Cultural Center and you're inside, ever since they moved you from the Epicenter. You two entertainers must have hit it off famously.

SHAKESPEARE: Alas, poor Benny. I know him well.

JACK: Will is such a kidder. We have a lot in common. After all, I was in a movie with Carole Lombard titled *To Be or Not to Be*.

GEORGE: How are things in Rancho Cucamonga, Jack?

JACK: They've been better. Oh, maybe I'm just getting old. Suddenly I'm feeling every one of my 39 years.

GEORGE: Er, quite.

GODDESS POMONA: Greetings, all!

MADONNA: Land o' goshen, it's the Goddess! How are things in Pomona?

GODDESS: Don't ask. But my perch in the Public Library seems secure. And the Fox Theater is reopening in March, which ought to be the social event of the year.

SHAKESPEARE: What's this about a theater? Oh, how I

would love to trod the boards of the Globe again.

GEORGE: It looks like we have another visitor. This one's from the West Valley Courthouse in Rancho Cucamonga. Hello!

OFFICER DOWN: *(silence)*

GEORGE: Rather a quiet type, isn't he?

JACK: Well, you can't expect him to say much. He *is* Officer Down.

(Moment of reflection by all.)

GEORGE: What an assemblage! Officer Down, the Goddess Pomona, Madonna of the Trail, Liberty Bell, Jedediah Smith, Jack Benny and William Shakespeare.

HORSE: Neeeeigh!

RAM: Baaaah!

BEAR: Rooooar!

GEORGE: Why, look, it's Claremont's horse, that new figure on Indian Hill Boulevard! And the ram who pokes his head from the fountain on Rancho Cucamonga's Haven Avenue! And the bear in front of Rancho's Sycamore Inn! Welcome!

MADONNA: What's it like in that pool of water this time of year, Mr. Ram?

RAM: Brrrrr!

JACK: Say, everyone, what are you doing tonight for New Year's Eve? You should come up to my place. I'll be staying in. Of course, in this alcove, I'm always in. Anyway, it'll be a potluck, and BYOB, but I'll provide the napkins.

MADONNA: You're generous to a fault, Mr. Benny.

JEDEDIAH: Ah'd be pleased to escort you, Miss Madonna.

MADONNA: Why, Mr. Smith! I hadn't planned on going anywhere. Especially since I'm a statue. But why not? I'm tired of the bright lights of Euclid Avenue. Let's see, I'll need a new bonnet. Hope you won't mind if I bring the young'uns. It's so hard to get a sitter.

JACK: This will be a real wing-ding! Are you in, Will?

SHAKESPEARE *(softly)*: To party or not to party, that is the question.

JACK: Sounds like he's on the fence. Or the bench. How about you, Liberty Bell?

LIBERTY: Clang clang!

GEORGE: I'm so pleased the Liberty Bell will attend our New Year's Eve party.

GODDESS: Why is that, George?

GEORGE *(triumphantly)*: He can help us ring in the new year!

SHAKESPEARE: Bravo! A marvelous pun!

EVERYONE ELSE: Grooooan.

RAM: Baaaah.

2008 ITEMS

January 2, 2008

As I write this on New Year's Eve, I'm back from a few days of showing my parents around the valley and L.A.

Their flight arrived at LA/ONT at 6:40 p.m. Christmas Day and they had alerted me they would want to go out to eat. This was going to be a problem because virtually no restaurants were open other than Denny's.

Granted, Christmas dinner at Denny's would have made a fascinating anthropological field study. But as culinary luck would have it, I discovered that the Benihana chain of Japanese teppan restaurants, including the Ontario location near the airport, is open on Christmas.

I wasn't sure how my parents would feel about something so exotic. But when I mentioned Benihana, my mom said, "Isn't that the place where they ate on *The Office* and Dwight had to sit on the far end of the table?"

So we had a Benihana Christmas, as did dozens of other people – the restaurant was nearly full. Who knew?

Denny's no doubt did all right as the restaurant of last resort for a Christmas dinner. But unless a Denny's server makes a steaming volcano out of onions and water at your table, I think Benihana has them beat.

January 20, 2008

In the Rancho Cucamonga council chambers Wednesday, before council members arrived at the dais, two high school students at the meeting for class credit chatted in the back row:

Boy: "Are there going to be really important people sitting up there?"

Girl: "Not really-really important. Just, like, the mayor of Rancho Cucamonga and stuff."

January 30, 2008

Driving Sunday on the 210 Freeway through Fontana, Governor Arnold Schwarzenegger and his family pulled off at Sierra Lakes. Reason: a Starbucks fix.

Maria Shriver and the couple's children went in first, followed a few minutes later by Schwarzenegger himself and his security detail.

As a small crowd gathered, California's first family ordered. The Starbucks staff was respectful. They refrained from asking for autographs or taking photos. And they tried, not altogether successfully, to keep their cool.

"They were kind of in awe. It *was* the governor," manager Scott Holdson told me Tuesday.

It's the first celebrity sighting at that Starbucks location, which opened last summer. But don't expect to see a Governator Special on the menu. That's because employees were so nervous, they aren't sure what Schwarzenegger and Shriver ordered.

"Everybody has said something a little different," Hodson, who wasn't on duty Sunday, reported with a chuckle.

"I talked to everybody, and nobody could agree on what they all got. I said, 'Guys, you couldn't write it down?'"

February 22, 2008

Several high school students attended Tuesday's Ontario council meeting for class credit. I stood near one teenage boy in the back of the room – it was standing room only –

and looked over his shoulder at what he was writing, assuming it was about the meeting.

"I want 'happy time' sex," he had written. "I suffocate when your (sic) not around. Kiss me like you'll never see me again."

His meeting notes were certainly more interesting than mine.

February 27, 2008

I understand that a race at the Auto Club Speedway last weekend was set to include a car sponsored by San Bernardino County's government. Question: To truly represent the 909, was this car up on blocks?

February 27, 2008

Mat Holton is the (unusually spelled) name of the new superintendent of the Chaffey Joint Union High School District. On this auspicious occasion, only one greeting is appropriate:

Welcome, Mat.

March 26, 2008

Eating lunch at San Biagio's Pizza in Upland on Tuesday, I heard, but couldn't see, a couple at the counter announce they had read about the place in the newspaper. (That would be a column of mine from December.)

Trying to elicit a compliment on my behalf, counterman Bobby Coleman asked them, loud enough that I could hear: "Do you read all of David Allen's work?"

An awkward pause followed as the couple tried to place my name.

"No," the woman said at last, "I don't really pay that

much attention to what he writes."

That comment was (sob!) loud enough for me to hear, too.

March 28, 2008

On Sunday, I leaned several thin, oblong boxes outside my front door in preparation for taking them to the recycling container.

A wasp soon found them of great interest, buzzing around and weighing the possibilities. It alighted against the window behind the boxes and remained there quietly for some time.

I carefully removed the boxes, exposing the wasp. Undeterred, and perhaps suffering a loss of perspective on the changed circumstances, the wasp began building a nest, inches from my front door.

This was serious. Retrieving a can of wasp spray, I stepped outside again at a suitable distance and gave the wasp a squirt. It flopped to the stoop, recovered and flew off.

The next morning, I wiped away the tiny bit of equity the wasp had abandoned. Just another foreclosure.

April 9, 2008

Courtesy of Cal Poly Pomona, Robert Mugabe, everyone's favorite Zimbabwean president-for-life, came close to also being Dr. Mugabe.

In 1998, before the deal unraveled, the university planned to confer an honorary doctorate on Mugabe, who in return would have delivered a commencement speech to graduating business students.

How, er, inspirational.

"Chase your dreams," Mugabe might have exhorted graduates. "If necessary, use dogs and water cannons."

So how did Cal Poly almost land a global pariah as commencement speaker?

Mugabe, among his other important dictator duties, was chancellor of the University of Zimbabwe, with which Cal Poly Pomona had exchanged professors. Somehow the idea of a visit by Mugabe was broached and eagerly accepted by dazzled administrators.

Good thing Cal Poly didn't have an "in" at Pyongyang University, or we'd be in a nuclear standoff with Dr. Kim Jong-il. (His degree would likely be in cosmetology.)

Thankfully, Mugabe's visit fell through. Faculty, staff and students questioned his human rights record and said a degree would confer legitimacy on him. Then the Academic Senate voted to pass a resolution condemning the honorary degree. Mugabe must still be kicking himself that he didn't rig the vote.

"The whole issue became moot when Mugabe decided not to come to Cal Poly Pomona and Cal Poly decided not to grant him an honorary degree," university spokeswoman Uyen Mai told me Monday.

In a way, that's too bad. If Mugabe had a doctorate in business, maybe Zimbabwe wouldn't be suffering 80 percent unemployment and 100,000 percent inflation.

April 20, 2008

Second-oldest?: At last week's Ontario council meeting, during discussion of a new inspection fee on apartments, City Attorney John Brown launched into an explanation that began: "Being a landlord is an honorable profession that has existed for a very long time."

He paused. "I'm going to resist any other analogies."

July 13, 2008

Which Way L.A.?: Writing about Moe, the chimp who escaped in Devore, the *Washington Post* offered this bit of geography: "He's been out there, somewhere, in the rugged, brushy, snaky foothills of the San Bernardino Mountains west of Los Angeles since last Friday when he escaped from his cage.

No wonder nobody can find Moe – they've been looking for mountains west of Los Angeles.

October 3, 2008

Another low-speed pursuit: This will be one of the more unusual police traffic stops you'll have heard about. In Claremont recently, a 19-year-old was flagged down by police at 3:40 a.m. while skateboarding.

According to the *Claremont Courier*'s police blotter, the skateboarder "initially did not comply with police officers' demands to pull over. Instead, he waved at them from his skateboard."

The effrontery. But he eventually stopped. Officers smelled alcohol and detected slurred speech and watery eyes. He was arrested for public intoxication.

As a citizen of Claremont, I'm relieved this pursuit ended before police had to lay down the spike strips.

November 9, 2008

On my way out of Ontario City Hall after Tuesday's council meeting, fellow Illini alumnus Ken Jeske, the public works director, stopped me for a joke of alarming physicality.

Clamping his open palm to the top of my head, the jovial Jeske said: "You know what this is?"

I didn't.

"A brainsucker!" Jeske said. "You know what it's doing?"

No.

"Starving!"

Pretty funny, Ken.

I wonder: Does this sort of thing happen to George Will?

November 12, 2008

Michael Crichton's death last week at age 66 reminded me that one of his novels included a scene involving the Inland Valley. No, not *Jurassic Park*. *Airframe*, from 1996, puts aerospace quality-assurance vice president Casey Singleton on the trail of an airline accident's cause.

In one crucial scene, Singleton is in a Compton warehouse, examining documentation about every part of the aircraft, when she finds what she's looking for. Crichton writes: "She was staring at a photocopy of a sheet of paper from Hoffman Metal Works in Montclair, California."

Bom-bom-bom-bom!

Singleton learns the "slats locking pin" had "come direct from a reputable supplier" – hooray for fictional Hoffman Metal Works in Montclair, California! – but that the pin found on the crashed plane was, suspiciously, bad.

Reader Berny Alexander said, when sending me a copy of the relevant page: "First time I have seen Montclair in a novel." More evidence that Crichton, a writer, doctor, traveler, inventor and movie director, really was a pioneer.

November 26, 2008

PFF Bank and Trust was seized by the feds on Friday after losing $289.5 million so far this year. Branches will continue under the auspices of US Bancorp.

It's unclear if the PFF name will go away, but the bank as we know it appears to be defunct. And therein may lie a cautionary tale for Pomona businesses with itchy feet.

Founded in Pomona in 1892, the savings and loan became a bank in 1996 and shortened its moniker to PFF, taking the Pomona out of its name. After 114 years in Pomona, PFF made the snub official in 2006 by pulling up stakes and relocating its corporate offices to Rancho Cucamonga.

Brighter days were predicted. Now, PFF is out of business and gobbled up. Its share price this week fell to 1 cent.

Let this be a lesson: The Goddess of Pomona will not be mocked.

To be fair, PFF was following our lead. This Ontario-based newspaper is the result of a late-1980s merger of the *Pomona Progress-Bulletin* and the *Ontario Daily Report*.

Technically speaking, then, we're only half the newspaper we used to be. Perhaps in the Goddess' eyes, that's punishment enough.

THE 144-ITEM MENU BOWLS HIM OVER

January 2, 2009

I took the Mix Bowl challenge – and won.

It's not a formal challenge. But the menu at Mix Bowl Cafe, a Thai restaurant in Pomona, is long, and each item is numbered, from No. 1, grilled meatballs, to No. 118, mixed fruit.

When new items are added, the numbers aren't shifted, which would upset the routine for the servers and cooks. Instead, those additions are given a letter. For instance, No. 12, seafood soup, is followed by 12A, rice soup, and 12B, joke, which is a kind of porridge.

(If you spill the latter on your sleeve, the joke is on you. But I digress.)

All told, then, Mix Bowl has 144 items. The sight of all these numbers is catnip to compulsives like yours truly.

And so I embarked on a quest to try every item.

This wasn't my intention at first. My friend Naomi loves Mix Bowl and invited me there a few times in 2004 when she was living in Claremont.

When she would suggest we order, say, Nos. 2A, 44 and 87, I didn't argue. On what grounds would I object? I had almost no experience with Thai food.

But I grew to like Mix Bowl and began eating there on my own. It's at 1520 Indian Hill Boulevard, a half-mile south of Claremont, and within easy reach.

I was timid at first, sticking to pad Thai, the spaghetti and meatballs of Thai food.

Much of the menu was baffling but enticing. Many dishes have Thai names: cha-po, pad prik king sod, beef panang. I still couldn't tell you the difference between, say, ka na mu krob and ka na pla kem without the menu as a cheat sheet.

Then there's the salad named larb. It sounds like a chair from Ikea.

By 2006, it had occurred to me that since I didn't know what anything on the menu was, why be picky? I might as well try anything. And since I was enjoying most of it, why not try everything?

And so I set out to methodically order every single item on the menu: 10 appetizers, nine soups, 15 salads, 26 noodle dishes, 31 rice dishes, eight vegetarian dishes, six a la carte items, 11 seafood dishes, eight barbecue entrees, 19 beverages and one dessert.

What can I say? I needed a hobby.

I kept track on a takeout menu, circling the number of each dish after I'd tried it. Each visit would take one or two more off the list.

When friends joined me, my takeout menu would be passed around in case they wanted to order an uncircled item. If I had some, by my rules that was enough to cross it off the list.

Good thing, because I couldn't have finished some items on my own. No. 14, the papaya salad, was ordered by my friend Mason. Made of shredded papaya, green beans, shrimp, lime juice and chili, it was so blazingly hot I lasted only a few bites.

As a warning to myself, in case I ever accidentally ordered it again, I not only circled the item on my menu but jotted a single word: "no."

Mix Bowl Cafe is a popular place. Not only is the food

good, but the combination of low prices (nothing is above $10) and late hours (until 2 a.m.) proves irresistible, especially to college students, night owls and local cops.

"Sometimes at 1 a.m., people come from nowhere and suddenly it's busy," one of the owners, Thongbai Artsavachaitakul, told me recently.

Housed in a former Wendy's, the restaurant opened in 1998. The interior, with its bright lights and colorful neon, is almost obnoxiously bright and cheerful. Twin clocks give the time here and in Bangkok.

I rarely feel self-conscious when eating solo at Mix Bowl because there are usually other solo diners too.

Foodies might argue that Mix Bowl isn't even the best Thai restaurant in that block, not with Sanamluang Cafe nearby. But the prices, casual atmosphere and slightly cheesy aesthetic of Mix Bowl keep me hooked.

Speaking of cheesy, the most embarrassing dish to order was No. 66, American fried rice. It's topped with fried chicken, a fried hot dog and a fried egg.

Why don't they just come right out and call it Ugly American fried rice?

On the other end of the scale is hor-mok. This doesn't refer to the act of belittling ladies of the evening; rather, it's fish baked with curry and topped with coconut and steamed vegetables. It's delicious.

My friend Wendy, who shared those two items and several more across several meals, got into the spirit of the thing. She even ordered the instant coffee (No. 100), which was almost undrinkable, just so I could take a sip and cross it off.

One recent evening, we ate the final four items.

Like Harry Potter vanquishing Voldemort, the end of my quest was preordained and, thus, slightly disappointing. No confetti dropped from the ceiling, no sirens blared. My stomach was full, yet inside I felt empty.

Days later, I spoke by phone to Artsavachaitakul, the co-owner. Did you know Mix Bowl was originally named Big Bowl Cafe, until a restaurant in Chicago with the same name complained?

I began our conversation by mentioning that I'd eaten every item on the menu. She had no reaction. Later in our chat I brought it up again, at greater length. Again, no reaction.

Do people tell her this every day? She seemed to be waiting for me to get to the point.

But I ate 144 items! Every item on her menu! That *is* the point!

Sigh. No one who doesn't share a hobby ever understands it.

As for which items are my favorites, may I recommend numbers 2, 5, 10, 15, 37, 53, 56, 72, 84, 91 and 113?

For Music Fans, Virgin Sacrifice Was Heaven-Sent

January 11, 2009

Two years ago, Tower Records had a closeout sale, an event that seemed like the end of an era for music fans. I grieved by engaging in long sessions of crazed bargain-hunting. We all have our own way of coping.

Oh, what a glorious season of discount shopping. But the death of Tower seemed like a one-shot deal.

I forgot how history tends to repeat itself.

Thus, the past few weeks have been spent picking clean the corpse of Circuit City in Pomona, and then doing the same with Virgin Megastore at Ontario Mills, where their loss has been my gain.

I've been buying CDs and DVDs in alarming quantities at alarmingly low prices.

You can have your Mervyns, Linens N Things and Great Indoors closeout sales. My inner college student still wants rock albums.

Let me explain. For a lot of people – the ones not stealing their music off the internet or buying off Amazon or iTunes – Walmart and Best Buy are sufficient for their slight music needs. And that's fine.

Some of us are committed fans. Take a singer like Van Morrison. He's probably put out 40 albums, and at those chain stores, you'd be lucky to find one or two.

Thus, the allure of record stores. You already understand the allure of going-out-of-business sales.

Circuit City never had a big stock of music or movies, but at 25 percent off, and then 40, 50 and 60 percent off, scavenging was a fun, if ghoulish, experience.

I got the soundtracks for *A Charlie Brown Christmas*, *The Darjeeling Limited* and *Once* and, for $7.79, the new album by a band named TV on the Radio. *Rolling Stone* later placed that album atop its best of 2008 list. Buying it made me both hip and thrifty.

I also hoovered up TV on DVD: three seasons of *Curb Your Enthusiasm* ($20 each), two seasons of *Arrested Development* ($21 and $15) and the final season of *Seinfeld* ($16).

Unable to resist, I also got the first season of *Saturday Night Live*, normally $50, for $20. If I were Emily Litella, I would have assumed I'd heard wrong.

Virgin Megastore, though, was the big kahuna. The enormous store had been one of the Mills' anchors since 1996. While no Tower, Virgin's selection was impressive, but its prices were sky-high, which is why I rarely bought anything there.

Even the first weeks of its going-out-of-business sale, when discounts were 25 percent, weren't worth bothering with. But once the discounts reached 40 percent, I swung into action.

I picked up four albums by the Replacements and one by Aretha Franklin, as well as a boxed set of blues songs about the Depression. It'll make good listening for the new depression.

A week later, the discounts reached 50 percent. I returned for albums by Warren Zevon, Otis Redding, Sonny Rollins, John Coltrane, Pat Metheny and Charlie Haden, Traffic, Fountains of Wayne, the Fireman and the Go-Betweens.

Good thing I had Christmas cash. Besides, who needs frivolous luxuries like food and shelter?

Each visit to Virgin involved careful calculations of supply, demand, projected discounts to come and actual value to me.

The deluxe edition of R.E.M.'s *Murmur*: Worth it at 40 percent, or should I wait for 50 percent? There were a dozen copies. I waited, saving another $3.20.

Radiohead's early albums: Worth it at 50 percent off? Not to me, I held out for 60 and lost out. Shrug.

At 50 percent off, I missed out on the last copy of a Hitchcock DVD boxed set by waiting. So I bought a Frank Capra DVD set rather than risk losing it too.

As shelves emptied, sections of the store were cordoned off. Pickings became slimmer. Everything was for sale, even tables, display cases and the employee microwave.

Undeterred, I went back twice more for albums at 60 percent off: the Modern Jazz Quartet, Dengue Fever, Franco, another R.E.M., the Raconteurs and Steinski. I hear good things about Steinski, a remix pioneer, and the new R.E.M. is supposed to be a return to form (and about time).

For $5.70 each (rather than $18.99), why not? Those are 1975 prices.

By midweek, Virgin was still stocked in depth on *I Am Legend* and *300* on DVD at 70 percent off. The store was practically empty and is scheduled to close today.

My most memorable visit was on December 30, when prices were 50 percent off and the shelves still held surprises. Five of us music obsessives from the *Bulletin* newsroom went after work.

After gorging on cheap CDs, we ate bad food in the food court, pulled our purchases from our bags and showed them off, yakking about great deals and great music.

That evening felt nostalgic even while it was happening. Will such a gathering ever convene again? We were like kids passing around baseball cards or comic books (things no kids do anymore).

It's sobering to realize that going to a store and buying an album, an activity that was once commonplace, has become almost quaint, like collecting butterflies.

Longtime Inland Valley residents will remember when record stores were easily found: Licorice Pizza, Rudi Pock's, Music Galaxy, Discount Record Center, The Wherehouse, Music Plus and so many more.

Now the only full-service music retailer left from La Verne to Norco is Rhino Records, a wonderful store in Claremont that needs our support now more than ever.

And it will continue to get mine.

Just let me absorb some of this pile of music first.

An Afternoon at the Opera

March 11, 2009

Opera fans are trilling in excitement over LA Opera's plans for *The Ring of the Nibelung*, the four-part epic that, at 15 hours, makes the *Godfather* trilogy seem like a half-hour sitcom.

A fresh *Ring* opera will be staged every few months, with all of them performed in sequence in spring 2010. That kicks off the year-long Ring Festival L.A., which civic boosters predict will draw legions of bristly bearded Germanic opera obsessives from all over the world.

Well, they act like it's a good thing.

Personally, my primary experience with opera is via Bugs Bunny, but I'd long wanted to go to one, and this seemed like a good time.

And so, I bought a matinee ticket online for the first part, *Das Rheingold*. Lightning did not flash, thunder did not roil the heavens, but perhaps somewhere, the gods were pleased.

By the way, high culture may be intimidating, but it's cheaper than most concerts.

Yes, there are $200-and-up tickets to *Das Rheingold* – which continues tonight at 7:30 and concludes Sunday with a 2 p.m. matinee – but there are $20 tickets too.

I opted for a $38 seat, which is in the upper balcony. Unlike the $20 seat, the view isn't obstructed by a handrail. I'm thrifty, but I'm practical.

The only thing that gave me pause was the news that *Das Rheingold* lasts two hours and 45 minutes, with no intermission, just as intended by composer Richard Wagner. His bladder, like his themes, must have been expansive.

Sure, I blanched. Then it occurred to me that hordes of people the same weekend would be sitting through another entertainment that lasts two hours and 43 minutes: *Watchmen*. And many of them would be sipping 64-ounce sodas.

And so on Sunday morning, I took Metrolink into L.A., ate a late breakfast and made sure not to drink much of anything before arriving at the Dorothy Chandler Pavilion.

A sign inside the Chandler notes the length of the show and the lack of an intermission and advises, in the refined way one would expect of an opera hall, "Please plan accordingly."

On my way back from the restrooms, I overheard one woman confide, referring to her husband: "He's going to 'plan accordingly.'"

I didn't see anyone I knew, not surprisingly, but the opera crowd seemed to encompass a broad range of ages, income levels and ethnicities. Hardly anyone had comical facial hair, a far cry from the severe gents populating the Marx Brothers' *A Night at the Opera*.

My seat was on the fourth floor. As a woman in front of me whispered, as we all lined up: "This is the riff-raff section."

Climbing to Row Q, I found I was near the ceiling, in the next to last row. The seat almost induced vertigo. At least I wasn't stuck back in Row R. Suckers!

As for the opera itself, here's the short version:

A dwarf steals magic gold from beneath the Rhine River and fashions a ring with the power to rule the world. The ring, which corrupts the wearer, is passed from hand to hand over the course of the next three operas and eventually leads to the death of the gods.

There, I just saved you 15 hours and at least $80. And unless you held it funny, this column wasn't even obstructed by a handrail.

The LA Opera production is untraditional, using masks, surreal costumes and occasional puppetry. One character has four arms. At one point, the Rhine is passed over by – why not? – an airplane.

Some people hate this production for its oddity. Some love it for its inventiveness and lack of horned helmets.

I managed to stay awake, although it took effort.

The opera was partly to blame: The characters and scenes are mostly static, and what with the masks and all, it wasn't always clear who was singing. Looking down on all this from the great height of Row Q induced a certain aloofness.

What wasn't the opera's fault was that I was coming down with a cold and wearing two layers of shirts, both factors making me warm and slightly groggy. (I felt even worse Monday as I wrote this. For once, I have a valid excuse if my column doesn't make sense.)

I missed a few of the super-titles – the translations projected above the stage – when my eyes closed for too long.

But mostly I kept up with it. The story is pretty cool, and one moment could have been straight outta 2009. As the giants attempt to foreclose on his McCastle because he hadn't lived up to the construction contract, Wotan, the top god, complains: "This debt has made you cruel and greedy."

Valhalla, meet Fontana.

The opera finished early, in two hours and 30 minutes. Despite the time, and all the water imagery of the Rhine, I was able to saunter to the restroom.

And in a nice surprise, I bumped into someone I know: Jack Mercer, the retired Chaffey High band director.

"Wasn't that something?" Mercer enthused. The octogenarian was embarrassed he'd never seen the Ring cycle before but sounded raring to go for the next three parts.

When I told him this was my first opera, Mercer replied cheerfully: "I'm glad you're getting educated." Spoken like a true teacher.

Don't tell Mercer, but I'm not so sure I'll go back for *Die Walkure* (debuting April 4), *Siegfried* (Sept. 26) and *Gotterdammerung* (April 23, 2010) — especially after reading that each of them is even longer.

Gotterdammerung lasts (gulp) six hours, 30 minutes. Presumably it has an intermission or two, but even so, that's a long time to sit in the dark.

"Gotterdammerung," incidentally, means "Twilight of the Gods." It's expected to star Bank of America, General Motors and AIG.

Crowd in Pomona Shows a Lot of (Heart) for Obama

March 20, 2009

Having never seen a president before, I hustled to Pomona on Thursday morning, hoping to catch a glimpse.

At 9:10 a.m., I began my vigil on the northeast corner of Holt and East End avenues.

Hundreds of people soon thronged the four corners, all of us crossing our fingers that Obama's motorcade would come east on Holt and hang a right on East End for his tour of an Edison plant a block south.

Among the homemade signs people held:

"I (Heart) My Electric Car"

"Jail Bankers Not Immigrants"

"I Freakin' (Heart) You Obama"

Pomona (hearts) him, they really (heart) him!

A sidewalk entrepreneur in a Raiders cap walked along selling Obama T-shirts that were draped over his shoulder. The only sizes were XL and XXXL, $5 each.

"Do I look like an extra large to you?" a slender Laura Palomino challenged the seller. She bought two shirts anyway.

The stay-at-home mom from Chino was compelled to be there for a peek at Obama.

"Even if we don't get to see him, he'll be here. The air is full of excitement," Palomino said.

She marveled that Obama is aiming so high and, in her view, trying so hard and being so forthright. If she had made a sign, and she was kicking herself that she hadn't, it would have read, simply, "Hope."

Pilar Diaz did make a sign. At the last minute, in her car. The Upland woman remembered she had poster boards and markers stashed there, so she wrote out "Mr. Obama, President of the People."

Diaz emigrated here legally from Ecuador in 1971. Thanks to their jobs with the phone company, she and her husband put three children through college.

"America has been wonderful for us. We love this country," Diaz said.

"When I talk to my family in Ecuador, they're so hopeful. It's like they helped elect Obama too," Diaz said.

At 10:05 a.m., Palomino spoke to her aunt in Oregon by phone, describing the scene and adding: "And I was interviewed by Channel 5!"

I turned toward her, my cap logo visible.

"I mean the *Daily Bulletin*!" Palomino said.

At 10:30 a.m., right on time, Obama's motorcade was spotted to the west on Holt, coming this way – and turning south a block early, to approach the Edison facility the back way.

Shucks.

There was always the chance that when he left, the president would come up East End. More likely was that he'd leave the way he came.

I headed west on foot to Hershey Street, where Obama had

turned south. The landmark is the enormous yellow Minit Man Car Wash sign.

People were gathered here too. A woman used her digital camera to show me the photos she'd taken of the motorcade.

Hershey doesn't continue north of Holt, giving us an unbroken stretch of sidewalk to stand on.

Holt was blocked off to vehicle traffic for several blocks in either direction. Businesses were open, nominally, except no one could get to them.

I stood in front of Star Tire and Auto Center. Mechanics in pale blue shirts milled in the parking lot with nothing to do. Not that you'd want to be working on a transmission with the president a block away.

There were two false alarms. At 10:55 a.m., a convoy of vehicles, including two empty limousines, turned onto Hershey. At 11:15 a.m., several vehicles, including two empty limousines, left.

Motorcycle officers in the intersection stayed put.

Mike Suarez, president of the Inland Valley Democratic Club, came over. "I'm waiting here like everyone else," Suarez told me. "Spell my name right!"

At 11:31 a.m., a woman asked the nearest motorcycle officer, "Is the president still here?"

The officer replied with a smile, "Are you asking me a question I'm not supposed to answer?"

A sharpshooter was still visible on a rooftop, another good sign the president hadn't left.

At 11:45 a.m., the officers swung into action. Two limousines with small flags on the front corners rolled up Hershey. This seemed to be it.

A wild cheer went up. As the second limo turned onto

Holt, just 25 feet from us, President Obama could be seen clearly through the rear passenger window.

He leaned forward, smiling broadly.

He waved.

OMG, I saw the president!

People flipped out. They high-fived each other. Some hugged. Two girls even cried.

Steven Almanzam made a phone call: "I saw Obama, dawg! He waved at me!"

A stranger, Martha Arreguin, teasingly interjected: "He waved at *me*!"

Others joked about how Obama was clearly waving to them, not to anyone else.

"I made eye contact," Steven said to the friend on the other end of the call. "That's all that matters."

Steven, 17, a Pomona High student (there was no school Thursday), brought his three little brothers in hopes of seeing the president.

"When he passed by, my heart stopped a little bit," Steven told me, awed. "The wait was worth it."

He's right, dawg. It was.

Taking Measure of the Big Apple

May 27, 2009

Before my first-ever visit to New York City recently, I had worries.

What if it turned out I like NY-style pizza better than actual NY pizza? What if I like Claremont's 42nd Street Bagel better than 42nd Street or bagels?

So there was a lot of pressure. That's the problem with America's biggest city: There's so much hype, so many things you're told you have to see, so many areas in which New York asserts that it's the best.

Can the city itself measure up? Can you?

The answer to both questions was yes. I was prepared to love NYC, and I did.

If anything, New York was even better than I'd imagined. And I'd imagined a lot, the result of a lifetime of absorbing the city through songs, movies, writing and TV.

The experience was similar to my post-college excitement at being in California after growing up in the Midwest. Ventura Highway? I know that song. La Jolla? Manhattan Beach? "Surfin' USA." Cable cars? Rice-a-Roni, that San Francisco treat.

Now I was in New York. There's 30 Rock, from *30 Rock*. There's 59th Street, feelin' groovy. Miracle of miracles, there's 34th Street.

Everywhere you turn in Manhattan, another icon. Times Square. The Empire State Building. Macy's. The United Nations. The Chrysler Building. The Staten Island Ferry. Madison Square Garden. Penn Station. The Public Library lions.

At one point, Rockefeller Center and its Prometheus statue were to my left, Saks Fifth Avenue to my right and St. Patrick's Cathedral up ahead. Radio City Music Hall was around the corner. Wonder what was in the next block?

The highlight may have been Grand Central Station's concourse. Just last month I saw it in *Duplicity*. And here it was in front of me: expansive, soaring, beautiful and thronged with people.

The subway system itself is a marvel. I like L.A.'s subways, but our already inadequate trains seem even more laughable after New York's intricate network.

You can get almost anywhere in New York by subway. At least it seems that way to a first-time user. A $25, seven-day, unlimited-ride MetroCard was a bargain even though I was there only four days.

The subways are clean, graffiti-free and air-conditioned. No more straps, I was surprised to see, just overhead metal bars to hang onto.

A cross-section of New York is riding, from businessmen and the elderly to students and families. Interesting sights abounded. A young man in a backwards baseball cap next to me was reading Camus. A woman exited at a run with an enormous bag of kitty litter – slogan: "Immediate Odor Control" – slung over her shoulder. Emergency at home?

In the stations, there was sometimes free entertainment. A violinist played Vivaldi. A group of black old-timey musicians named the Ebony Hillbillies performed Stephen Foster's

"Hard Times." At another station, a seated man coaxed a pop standard from a musical saw. A little Appalachia in the Big Apple.

I will give L.A. credit for having more and better public art at its subway stations, but other than that, we've got a long way to go.

As for the food, I had a mile-high pastrami at Carnegie Deli, pizza from Grimaldi's in Brooklyn and a hot dog from Gray's Papaya. Not to mention cheesecake from Junior's, by far the best I've had.

The mid-May weather was sunny and pleasant. In fact, I was about ready to abandon Claremont for New York until remembering that it's probably unlivable for eight months of the year.

(I had the same second thoughts after vacationing in Portland, Oregon, during a rare dry spell.)

As for why I hadn't been to New York before: Intimidation.

I'm a small-town boy fascinated by cities. But like its skyscrapers, New York loomed so large in my imagination that I felt a kind of paralysis about going. Could I find my way around someplace so huge? Plus, you always hear how expensive it is.

Well, hotels aren't cheap, but everything else was more affordable than expected. And as a colleague points out, L.A. is more intimidating than New York: It's more spread out and you have to drive everywhere.

New York proved fairly easy to get around in. People, while not friendly, weren't unfriendly. In fact, a couple of people volunteered directions.

I didn't have a single bad experience. Well, except for walking behind an odoriferous woman on the subway platform. But that was only for a few seconds.

Before my flight home, I even gave serious thought to buying an "I ♥ NY" T-shirt. Ultimately, it seemed too corny. And where would I wear it? Upland?

But I don't mind declaring my feelings here: I really did love NY. And, making up for lost time, I've already made a list of stuff to see on my next visit.

Silence wasn't golden for Claremont's champ talker

July 3, 2009

As always, this Claremont resident is looking forward to the city's Fourth of July activities in Memorial Park, its sno-cone stand and the old-fashioned parade.

And yet the holiday won't feel quite the same without T. Willard Hunter, the man who turned a gift for gab and a love of country into a city tradition known as the Speakers Corner.

Just as Charlie Brown lamented that Christmas was too commercial, Hunter, who died Monday at age 93, felt the message of Independence Day had been lost amid hot dogs and fireworks.

And so in 1977 Hunter created the Speakers Corner, an area of the park with a lectern, microphone and stage. Patterned after London's Hyde Park speakers corner, the Claremont version became an annual event and a distinctive part of the city's approach to the holiday.

Anyone who signs up in advance gets 10 minutes to reflect, hold forth or spout off on any topic they choose – city politics, organic farming, the Iraq war, whatever.

Of course, no one is obligated to pay attention – it's not called the Listeners Corner – but people do wander over and linger a while. This year's event is scheduled from 10:45 a.m. to 3 p.m.

"Someone should stand in the corner of the park to say why we should celebrate the Fourth of July," Hunter explained in 2003. "Someone should give context to this."

Hunter loved to talk and he traveled the country doing so on topics he cared about, including Charles Lindbergh, Will Rogers and the founding fathers.

In 1982 Hunter set a world record for blabbery by yakking at Independence Hall in Philadelphia for 34 hours and 8 minutes straight.

It wouldn't surprise me to learn that he talked in his sleep. Or if he rises during his funeral to give the eulogy.

(For the record, services for Hunter will be at 10:30 a.m. Tuesday at Claremont United Church of Christ.)

I'd had no idea until this week that Hunter is also credited with founding L.A.'s annual Labor Day Walk.

Responding to a call from Mayor Tom Bradley for ways to mark the 1981 bicentennial of the arrival of the city's first settlers, Hunter hit on the idea of repeating their journey on foot.

The nine-mile walk from the San Gabriel Mission to Olvera Street has become a popular event. I guess that when it came to history, Hunter not only talked the talk, he walked the walk.

Hunter, by the way, was a flag-waving Democrat (not an oxymoron) and frequent letter writer to this and other newspapers.

He was happy to pay his taxes and – I hope you're sitting down for this – argued passionately that his taxes should be higher. When tax rebates were mailed out under George W. Bush's presidency to stimulate the economy, he sent the money back to be applied to the national debt.

In short, he was a heckuva guy, and I'm happy to have made

his acquaintance.

Hunter wasn't able to participate in the Speakers Corner last year, but traditionally he would talk about America and recite portions of classic speeches and our founding documents from memory. I recall him reciting "Casey at the Bat" too.

As Hunter once told me: "Everybody else gets 10 minutes. Since I started the thing, I get an hour."

Saturday's plan includes a reading of the Declaration of Independence by Hunter's friend John Maguire at 2:40 p.m. and an unspecified tribute at noon.

A moment of silence? That would seem wrong somehow.

Exploring moon mission excitement

July 19, 2009

Remember the moon? After years of ignoring it, people are talking about it again.

Trust me, there was a period when the moon was the center of the universe, when "moonwalk" was more than a dance move.

JFK died before I was born, but as a member of what might be called the NASA generation, I can tell you exactly where I was when Neil Armstrong stepped foot on the moon: at grandma's house,

On July 20, 1969 – 40 years ago Monday – I was 5 years old. The NASA missions are the only news events from early childhood I remember. I was impressionable – and they made a big impression.

My recollection is that our family watched news broadcasts on my Illinois grandparents' B&W console TV of the lunar module's descent and its touchdown, which took place at 3:18 p.m. Central Time.

There was a lot of waiting. Bedtime intervened. But sometime around 9:39 p.m., when Armstrong opened the hatch, I was awakened to come watch history being made.

As the grainy images were beamed 250,000 miles from a celestial body to a farmhouse in Humboldt, Illinois, Armstrong's boot touched the moon's surface at 9:56 p.m.

He uttered his "one small step for man, one giant leap for mankind" remark and we whooped in joy. And then I went back to bed.

That's how I remember it, anyway. Last time I asked, my parents didn't recall anything about the moon landing other than that it happened. Although that's more than the conspiracy theorists can say.

It's impossible to overstate how astonishing the moon landing was. It may seem even more astonishing in retrospect, now that laptops, cell phones and iPods are commonplace, to think that somehow we put a man on the moon with punch cards, slide rules and computers the size of elephants.

The Associated Press tried to capture the awe by going with a deliberately understated lead sentence for its story: "Man landed on the moon, this day, Sunday, July 20, 1969."

I prefer what the satirical newspaper *The Onion* did years later with a mock front page in 1969 style, topped by a six-column, three-deck headline that can only be printed in a family newspaper like this: "HOLY (expletive)/MAN WALKS ON (expletive) MOON."

No matter which words you use, the Apollo 11 mission rocked my childhood. How about yours?

My friend Monica, who was also 5, tells me that when the rocket launched from Cape Canaveral, Florida, she was so excited she went outside and trained her toy binoculars at the sky, thinking the rocket would be visible from Los Angeles.

You'd have to be older to have been cognizant of all the space-race hoopla. From a little boy's perspective, I remember that moon, space and rocket stuff was everywhere.

I watched *Space Ghost* on Saturday mornings, ate Quisp cereal with its sugary saucer shapes, played with my Major Matt Mason astronaut toys and enacted my own Saturn launches with a plastic two-stage rocket in our living room.

I must have begged for a jar of Tang, the awful powdered-orange beverage of the astronauts, but the allure of that wore off pretty fast.

All the NASA missions were of enormous interest to me: the spacewalks, the moon buggy, the splashdowns. After Apollo 17, in 1972, the last moon landing, I avidly followed the three Skylab space station voyages in 1973 and the unmanned Viking craft that landed on Mars in 1976. It transmitted the first images from the surface of another planet.

What we saw was a rocky, red, unpopulated landscape. After about a minute, when no little green men or space babes had materialized, everyone kind of shrugged and moved on. Even me.

After we'd won the space race with the Soviets, it was like the air went out of the airlessness thing. And the lunar missions began to seem repetitive, like variations on a trick we'd all seen.

Space probes and the Hubble telescope may have been more useful than manned missions. But the excitement, and momentum, evaporated.

Where are the lunar outposts, the missions to Mars, the space tourism, the domed cities, the hyper-drive?

And, speaking selfishly, where is my flying car? Where is my jetpack? Where is my steak dinner in pill form? Not that I'd want to wash it down with Tang.

The NASA generation feels cheated.

You'd think America would be clamoring to return to outer space. With one-third of Americans obese, space travel is their only hope for weightlessness.

I am curious how the Apollo missions are viewed by the younger people who didn't live through them, especially since they carry pocket-sized marvels as a matter of course.

Do the moon landings seem amazing still, or are they just another "what were they thinking" eye-roller from the '70s like macrame vests, flared pants and Richard Nixon?

To some the missions were always a waste of energy and money. I would disagree, obviously.

Today, even modest policy changes are treated like the end of the world and truly big undertakings appear to be beyond us. Against this national loss of ambition, the moon landings feel like a rebuke.

They remind us, uncomfortably, of a time when our dreams were big, and even one small step might be a giant leap we were willing to make.

'This Film' Puts Area P.I. Under Magnifying Glass

August 28, 2009

Becky Altringer is a female private eye who works the mean streets of La Verne.

Not quite Raymond Chandler territory, especially when you hear that Altringer, 46, named her firm, Ariel Investigations, after the Disney character in *The Little Mermaid*, with whom she identifies.

"She's always into everything – she gets into scrapes," Altringer explains.

But don't underestimate her. Altringer was featured in an acclaimed documentary, *This Film Is Not Yet Rated*, in which she and the director teamed up to expose the secretive way that ratings are applied to movies.

As a result, Altringer is a minor celebrity around town. A waitress at downtown's Caffe Allegro once asked, "Weren't you in that documentary?"

I had the same thought recently when I spotted her in another La Verne restaurant, A Taste of Asia.

She spotted me spotting her. We two trained observers eyed each other surreptitiously. She quietly asked owner Virada Khowong who I was. I did the same. We were introduced and an interview arranged.

"I thought you looked like a writer," Altringer told me then. "I don't know if that's good or bad."

Me either.

We met up Wednesday for lunch at A Taste of Asia, her favorite restaurant, with Kirby Dick, the director of *This Film Is Not Yet Rated*. Dick was nominated for an Academy Award for a previous documentary, *Twist of Faith*.

Khowong should have laid out a red carpet.

Dick was nice enough to drive out from Silver Lake, a tribute to his respect and affection for Altringer.

He says he had long wanted to make a documentary on the Motion Picture Association of America, which decides if a movie should be G, PG, PG-13, R or NC-17. The organization, he says, benefits from its wall of silence.

"People think it's a government organization," Dick says. "You say, 'It's a private organization run by the studios' and they say, 'Hmm.'"

Who are the movie raters? The MPAA would say they were parents, and that's it.

"We wanted to get the names of the ratings board members because they were kept secret for 40 years," Dick explains. "*Nightline* and other networks had tried to get the names and couldn't."

Dick decided to hire a private eye to help him and interviewed several before finding Altringer.

He liked her exuberance, which made her a natural character to appear on camera. Also, she was confident. Other investigators promised only to try.

"Becky said, 'We're going to get them,'" Dick recalled.

Actually, Altringer says she had doubts but kept them to herself. The pair spent almost a year, off and on, working the case. Portions of the movie were filmed in her La Verne home and office.

The MPAA was so secretive that the security guard wouldn't even confirm that its office was its office.

The breakthrough finally came when, as she staked out the offices, the security guard left his booth. Altringer peered in and saw a list of names and phone extensions posted on the wall.

Bingo.

With that head start, Altringer and Dick checked license plates of vehicles leaving the building, methodically dialed phone extensions after hours to listen to voicemail greetings and rummaged through suspected raters' trash cans to find MPAA documents.

So who were the raters deciding what was fit for children to watch? These "parents" had adult children or none at all, and no special expertise.

This Film argues persuasively that violence is rated more leniently than sex, that gay sex is taboo and that big-budget studio releases get more leeway than independent films.

A lot of people saw the documentary but not much changed in Hollywood. Dick points to the creepy, brutal Batman movie of last year, which skated by with a PG-13 instead of an R and probably gave nightmares to thousands of children.

In any case, Altringer's presence enlivened his movie.

"There wouldn't have been a hero without her. We absolutely needed Becky," Dick says.

"When people talk about the film," he adds, "the second thing out of their mouth is, 'That P.I. is so great. She doesn't fit the stereotype.' "

Altringer cracks that she's "pudgy and middle-aged" and a far cry from one of Charlie's Angels. Then there's her collection of Disney merchandise, which fills a room in her house. It's an escape, she explains, from a dark job in which she deals with a lot of bad people.

Moviegoers also were touched by her relationship with her partner, Cheryl Howell, with whom Altringer has been involved since 1990. They became heroes in the gay and lesbian community.

Also breaking the mold is Altringer's disarming personality. She's friendly, with an open face and seemingly guileless manner.

"She doesn't look like a P.I., so she can go places where other people would get caught," Dick says. "It's a great cover."

Altringer says that in general, "someone like me who's meek and makes fun" can get people to open up where an intimidating man in a suit might fail.

She plays dumb at times. But it's not always an act, she adds.

"Sometimes," she admits, "I *am* a big dork."

Can you imagine Philip Marlowe saying such a thing?

La Verne is where Howell had a home, so Altringer relocated from Azusa. She's had her own firm since 1998.

"I always liked spying on people," she told me when we first met. "And I always wanted to be in the movies. I never thought I'd get to do both."

Most of her time is spent on more mundane investigations such as insurance fraud, hit-and-run accidents and runaway children. With the recession, business is down. Next month, she's teaching a one-day seminar for prospective investigators.

Altringer is credited with "investigations" on Dick's latest movie, *Outrage*, but doesn't appear on camera.

The movie examines the anti-gay voting records of GOP leaders who may have personal reasons to support gay rights.

Altringer's congressman, David Dreier, is one of them. See it for yourself – the DVD version is due on Tuesday.

What's next? Altringer has an agent and is pursuing a deal for a reality-TV series she envisions as "Hollywood Becky, P.I."

I imagine that's a more commercial title than "La Verne Becky, P.I."

In the meantime, there are more investigations in the offing, some very close at hand.

When the Taste of Asia server delivers the salad and remarks on the "special housemade dressing," Dick brightens.

"It's a secret?" he asks slyly, placing his hand on Altringer's shoulder. "We'll have Becky find out what it is."

BREAKING UP IS HARD TO DO, EVEN WITH A MAGAZINE

September 13, 2009

Breakups are never easy. This turns out to be true even when you break up with a magazine.

In my case, it was *The New Yorker*. I first subscribed to *The New Yorker* in 1995 and faithfully renewed every year, sticking with it through two jobs and three changes of address.

That is, until recently, when, despite the circulation department's entreaties, I let my subscription expire.

I won't say it was traumatic, but even a relationship with a periodical, when it lasts 14 years, can become strangely serious.

Magazines and newspapers have that effect on some of us. Over time, they can become like a member of the household or a treasured friend.

They arrive with comforting regularity. Their conversational paths follow a familiar pattern. They have quirks and preoccupations and we accept them. Sometimes they get on our nerves,

In *The New Yorker*'s case, it was all of the above.

A holdover from the days of general interest magazines, the weekly is known for its in-depth articles and elegant style.

You can't skim or scan *The New Yorker* like you would *People.* There are no boldfaced names and few photos. It's text-heavy and most of the articles go on and on.

A recent issue included an evaluation of the Kindle electronic reader. The story was 6,300 words long. That's like reading eight or nine of my columns in a row. Which is not recommended, by the way.

One great thing about the magazine is that even articles on unlikely subjects might turn out to be fascinating.

I found myself engrossed in long articles on such oddball topics as light pollution, the demise of card catalogs at libraries and an unmusical man who, after a brain injury, developed an intense love of music, leading to estrangement from his family.

A piece about the Great Wall of China focused on an American obsessive who is trying to walk every mile of the wall, even the parts in rural China that have crumbled. The wall is so long that nobody has ever documented the whole thing. Who knew?

It's the details that make a *New Yorker* story – or bog it down.

A profile of bluegrass icon Ralph Stanley included a delightful description of his home's all-red living room, said by the writer to be the reddest room he'd ever seen.

On the other hand, an interminable piece about compact disc technology explained that one surface is shinier than the other and reflects a spectrum of color when held to the light. Yes, I've seen CDs before, thanks.

In newspapers, we have to get to the point much faster. (At least eight or nine times faster, in my case.)

That's why I especially liked The Talk of the Town, the magazine's section of NYC vignettes. They're short. And they often involve mundane events that benefit from the writers' detailed approach.

For instance, in 2003 there was a hilarious piece about a 79-year-old lawyer who was "one year, five months and four days" behind in reading the *New York Times*. He'd have been further behind if he didn't skip the Sports, Escapes and Circuits sections to save time.

"I realize I'm not going to catch up, but I like to believe I will," he told the magazine optimistically.

Close observation and a detached point of view can produce hilarity. Dry wit helps too. A first-person piece in 2008 on an expensive California spa chronicled its purification regimens, including enemas. The writer had one.

The procedure began, she wrote elegantly, with the nozzle's insertion into "the pertinent orifice."

The pertinent orifice! As a writer, I would kill for a phrase like that.

Besides general inspiration like that, the magazine at times was of direct help with my columns.

Perhaps because *The New Yorker* sells more copies in California than in New York, Southern California is a frequent setting.

I can think of at least six Inland Valley references over the years, set in Chino, Claremont (twice), Fontana (twice) and Pomona.

The magazine is famous for its cartoons, which are reliably amusing. One favorite, because I'm frequently cold, depicts three senior citizens standing in a pit of fire under the heading "Old People in Hell."

Their dialogue, in sequence: "You call this hot?", "I need a sweater" and "Brr."

The New Yorker was my constant companion. I'd take it to

lunch, dinner and council meetings. I marked my place with a loose subscription card.

So why did I end my subscription? Fatigue.

Each issue was consuming my week. Obsessed, I even read the notes on the contributors and the fine print on the contents page that gives the title of the cover art.

Also, there was the matter of the magazine's long-windedness. A trait that had once been endearing was now irritating.

I needed a break.

The New Yorker didn't want to accept this. It pelted me with gracefully written, yet increasingly panicked, renewal cards. But I held firm.

Oddly, the price never got better. It was always $34.95 per year. If they're not even going to try to win me back, well, they just made our breakup easier.

Originally I had thought I might subscribe to a new magazine, but for now, like any bachelor, I've been enjoying my freedom.

Still, I like to think we parted amicably. A couple of times, browsing in a bookstore, I've encountered the magazine and caught up. It was like old times.

Perhaps one day I'll subscribe again. For now, I hope *The New Yorker* and I can still be friends.

Cucamonga Justice at $100 a Month

October 18, 2009

Larry Thorne wasn't what you'd call a hanging judge. He meted out justice in rural Cucamonga from 1957 to 1980, which mostly meant dealing with strangers speeding through town on Route 66 or citizens who got too exuberant at an Alta Loma watering hole, Ernie's.

"It was a community of rambunctious people," Thorne recalls, a twinkle in his eye.

The Cucamonga Justice Court was in the heart of town at Archibald and Foothill. It was open for limited hours and handled minor disputes that weren't worth a trip to Municipal Court.

Thorne, now 79 and living in Costa Mesa, presided over a different era in jurisprudence. San Bernardino County had 26 justice courts when he was elected and just one or two when he left, as justice became more formalized.

Life was slower, and maybe a little sillier.

"Carl Massengale, our No. 1 citizen, was honored by having the sewer treatment plant named for him," Thorne says, amused, in an interview in his backyard. "He owned most of the buildings in town."

Some offenders hauled before Judge Thorne had been caught hunting without a license. Some had been nabbed driving 100 mph. Some had been drunk and disorderly in public.

Attorney John Mannerino describes the courtroom as professional but informal. No one argued a case, per se.

"He knew us, we knew him. He knew most of the offenders," Mannerino says.

"What I remember is the tenor in which Judge Thorne dealt with offenders. It was almost like being scolded: 'Fred, what am I going to do with you? Here you are again.'"

Times were so different that Thorne was also a practicing attorney, with law partner Harold Baylen, as well as a judge. The judgeship was only part time.

Not all judges were scrupulous about separating their two roles. "I knew one judge," Thorne says, "who used to tell a defendant, 'What you need is a good lawyer,' and hand him his card."

Speaking of cards – I mean besides Thorne himself – he remembers a circuit judge with the business card motto "Have Gavel, Will Travel," and another judge who, like his bailiff, stood 6-foot-6, which explains their joint motto, "13 Feet of Justice."

Cucamonga, as the community was known then, did see serious crime on occasion. Alta Loma housewife Lucille Miller killed her husband and her sensational murder trial in San Bernardino was memorialized by writer Joan Didion.

Thorne could preside over felony arraignments and preliminary hearings and take a plea for misdemeanors and felonies. He was no rube. Still, his docket tended to be filled with small claims and small crimes.

One bit of excitement came when a suspected rapist was held in the court's single cell. He escaped by telling the bailiff he needed to use the restroom, then ran away when she unlocked the door.

"She drew her gun, then said, 'I can't shoot him,' so she ran after him," Thorne recalls. After a long foot chase, she tackled him.

This same bailiff doubled as Thorne's court clerk. Sometimes she'd say: "Give me the gavel. I can take care of this whole thing better than you can."

Every Christmas the judge hosted a party at the courthouse for law enforcement. One year a neighbor called the sheriff's office to complain about the noise. Since deputies were the ones making the racket, he was advised to join the party.

That peace-loving neighbor probably wasn't musician Frank Zappa, whose slightly disreputable Studio Z recording studio was in the next block. Zappa was arrested in 1965 for producing a smutty audiotape and after 10 days in jail left town for good.

Whether Thorne was involved in that celebrated case is unclear. He remembers having Zappa in his courtroom, laughing at the tape and sentencing him.

But the *Daily Report*, after initially indicating Zappa would be arraigned in Cucamonga, said Judge Roland C. Rutledge in Ontario Municipal Court handled the preliminary hearing and sentencing.

Well, a little mystery helps keep history alive.

Thorne was somewhat unconventional. Born into a family of lawyers, the Oakland native took an independent path after earning his law degree from UC Berkeley in 1955, shunning large firms and instead driving to small towns around California and asking about legal prospects.

He landed in Upland working for Wiley, Wells and Mather, an almost mummified firm where everyone was in their 70s and which, he jokes, "practiced law, sort of" – actual cases being scarce.

A couple of years later, Thorne ran for judge against an incumbent he says always sided with prosecutors because he had no clue what he was doing.

Thorne campaigned door to door, telling voters it was time for a younger judge. He recalls the tally as 300 votes to 200, in his favor.

"I was the youngest judge in the state. I was 26, 27," Thorne says. "I got a job that lasted 22 1/2 years. Of course, it paid $100 a month."

He adds impishly: "I now get $8,500 a month in retirement benefits."

He was unseated in 1980, went back to practicing law full time, this time with partner Robert Beloud, and retired a decade ago. Living with his wife, Shirley, he's in fragile health with Parkinson's and other problems.

A year or two after his defeat, the justice court moved to Ontario and then was absorbed by the municipal court. That Ontario courthouse later closed and a multistory Superior Court was erected in Rancho Cucamonga.

Cucamonga must be a magnet for justice.

But Mannerino remains fond of the humble Cucamonga Justice Court, which resolved lower-level cases with dispatch and humanity.

"It was an informal meting out of justice, which was probably what was called for at that time," Mannerino says. "We could probably use a little of that today."

Thorne has his own take on the difference in eras.

"When I became a judge, there were 200 lawyers in San Bernardino County," Thorne reflects. "By the time I left, there were more than 200 in Cucamonga."

The price of progress, I guess.

A Night on the (Very Dull) Town in Ontario

November 1, 2009

This is a tale of alienation and anomie in the big city, Ontario.

I'd been curious about the movie *Black Dynamite*, a loving parody of 1970s blaxploitation flicks like *Shaft* and *Coffy*. Even though it got an 85 percent approval rating on Rotten Tomatoes, the movie earned under $200,000 its first week – a figure only an unfrozen Dr. Evil would find impressive – and it was clear I'd have to hurry to catch it.

And so last Tuesday I left the office early (is 5:15 p.m. early?) and hustled down the street to the AMC 30 Ontario Mills, the only local theater still showing *Black Dynamite*, for the 5:25 showing.

I got to the box office at 5:28. One person was ahead of me, a befuddled woman in her late 50s who was in no hurry.

She told the bored ticket seller through the glass that she didn't know what any of the movies were. Not a surprise: Out of a slate of 20 movies, perhaps only two would interest anyone of voting age.

She asked about *Paranormal Activity*.

"It's a documentary about a thriller," replied the ticket seller, offering perhaps the worst synopsis ever. He probably thinks *The Blair Witch Project* is nonfiction too.

The woman asked politely, "Are there any other documentaries playing?"

This had turned into a gathering of the dumbest people in the Inland Valley. (*Idiocracy* fans will instantly grasp the significance of a Fuddruckers across the parking lot.)

The ticket seller asked the woman to step aside so paying customers could buy their tickets. As I put my change away, the woman returned to the window and asked, "What movie is starting now?"

In Theater 6, my arrival doubled the size of the audience. A few others drifted in before the commercials ended – including, poor thing, the woman who wanted to see the first movie playing.

Black Dynamite begins with a fake ad for fictional Anaconda malt liquor – I had to wonder what the woman made of that – and proceeds to unfold as an unearthed early '70s B-movie, complete with wide lapels, big afros, power handshakes and black militants in berets.

Rather than a slapstick parody a la the Wayans brothers, *Black Dynamite* is subtly hilarious, employing wooden acting, purposeful mistakes and plot-advancing dialogue.

To wit: Black Dynamite goes to his brother's apartment to look for clues in his murder. But the door is wide open.

In a voiceover, Black Dynamite thinks: "Somebody broke into my dead brother Jimmy's apartment!"

Or in another scene, the camera moves back and forth between close-ups of Dynamite and a prostitute who is telling a woeful tale about heroin in the ghetto. A fake-looking glycerine tear is under her left eye. Next shot, it's gone. Next shot, it's back. Next shot, it's gone. Next shot, it's back.

Dynamite, incensed, stands suddenly and a boom microphone is briefly visible above his head as he issues a vow to bring the dealers to justice.

I'm laughing out loud during all this and the theater's seven other people, including the befuddled woman, hands in her lap, are dead quiet.

In fact, no matter how ridiculous the movie gets, including a fight on Kung Fu Island against Dr. Fu, and the introduction of a pimp named Chocolate Giddy-Up, no more than twice did anyone other than me laugh.

Did they think it was a straight action movie? The number of ironists in the Inland Valley must be small indeed.

Once outside the theater – and I was the only one who stayed through the credits – I faced the decision of where to eat. Head into the mall? Yeah, I could eat at Sbarro's, the favorite N.Y. pizza of Michael Scott on *The Office*.

No thanks. Retrieving my car, I mulled my options in the chain-restaurant hell of Ontario Mills.

I ended up at the Greek place on Milliken by the Arco. It was 7:30 p.m. and the restaurant would be closing at 8.

Closing at 8? This is what passes for nightlife in eastern Ontario, the city's unofficial downtown. Inside the restaurant, I was the sole customer. Maybe they should close at 7.

A fullback-sized man in a Merriman jersey came in and ordered one gyro, plain, and two mini gyros, also plain, to go. If it weren't for the pita bread, he'd have a takeout bag of meat.

As the time neared the witching hour of 8 p.m., my plate empty, the manager bringing in the outdoor furniture, I closed my book and headed for the door.

The wind had picked up. I clutched my jacket to keep it from whipping around me as I walked toward my car by the spindly parking lot tree.

Suddenly the wind – acting as the meteorological equivalent of one of Proust's madeleines – gave me a remembrance of things past.

A decade ago, a group of us frequently went to the Mills for a movie and a lame food court meal, in the days when there was little else to do here.

Now there's more to do, and it's rare that I spend an evening around the Mills. The wind was a strong (very strong) reminder of when I did.

Like the Santa Anas that turn the air dry and the landscape alien, this Ontario gale made me see the barren parking lot and blazing corporate logos in a new, if fluorescent, light.

What might sensibly have remained an inhospitable open plain by a freeway interchange instead is home to (sigh) Denny's, Del Taco and Arizona Leather. I suddenly saw a series of placeless places, buffeted by winds that tried but failed to sweep them from the landscape.

Maybe you get these what-am-I-doing-here feelings yourself sometimes, maybe not. On Milliken I passed Hooter's and hit the westbound freeway, gripping the wheel to keep the gusts of wind from blowing my car into the next lane.

In a weird way, however, my sense of displacement was oddly comforting. Because it was nothing new.

In the valley's most characterless commercial district, character is hard to discern. But that just makes the search more rewarding, because like Monterey's lone cypress, character stubbornly survives: the boba shop that sells Indonesian food, the truck stop across the freeway whose restaurant made the Food Channel.

Life here changes and yet it doesn't. In a slate of bland, empty movies at the multiplex, one oddball choice had slipped in under everyone's radar.

Seasons shift, years pass, but reassuringly, culture in the Inland Valley continues to follow its familiar pattern: usually arriving by accident, unnoticed by most, understood by few, here today, gone tomorrow.

But not always gone tomorrow. Friday's movie listings showed that *Black Dynamite* has been held over for a few more days. Dynamite.

Kidney Stone Leads to a Display of True Grit

November 11, 2009

So I had a kidney stone.

At first I didn't know it was a kidney stone, of course, having never had one. For all I knew it was the bacon club sandwich of a few hours earlier.

It was 4 a.m. and a blinding pain had awakened me.

The pain was in my left side. It instantly brought back memories of the day I had a pain in my right side, which led to an appendectomy.

So we could rule out appendicitis.

Something inside me wanted out, but for an excruciatingly long time, exactly what it was or where it wished to depart was an open question.

After sufficient time had elapsed that it was clear this was more than a bad bacon club sandwich, I drove myself to San Antonio Community Hospital around 8 a.m. I still felt sheepish.

You know how it is. You worry you're overreacting and wasting everyone's time.

"I have a pain in my left side," I told the emergency room receptionist. It sounded lame to me, too.

There was no one in the waiting room and I was brought back almost immediately. If you're ever thinking of having a medical emergency, 8 a.m. might be a good time.

A woman asked my level of pain on a scale of 0 to 10. On the desk was a handy chart describing each even number, accompanied by simplified cartoon faces with expressions ranging from smiling to screaming.

Under one of them, I think 8, was what I at first took to say "severed" but which actually was in Spanish and read "severo." Good, because if 8 is the pain you feel when some piece of you has been severed, I don't want to feel a 10.

I judged my pain to be a 6 – it was more like a 7, but I wasn't sure odd numbers were allowed – and was soon in the emergency room, on a bed and in a gown.

A nurse practitioner heard me describe the pain, which had migrated to my left lower back, and said a kidney stone was almost certainly the cause.

This was a relief in a way. It made perfect sense and dispelled the need for a lot of guesswork, like was one of my internal organs failing, was a tiny man inside me hacking me with a knife, etc.

Within minutes I was hooked up to a morphine drip and suddenly, to quote the Beatles song "Yesterday," all my troubles seemed so far away.

A CT scan revealed the kidney stone to be a mere 2 or 3 millimeters in diameter, like a piece of grit, or the exact opposite of the size of the federal deficit. The doctor said the pain occurs when the stone travels from the kidney to the bladder through a tiny tube.

My understanding is that there's a sign at the tube's entrance that says "Fluids Only," but tragically, the kidney stone can't read.

The stone would pass within 24 hours, the doctor said. No need to drink lots of water or do anything special. Just take it easy.

(A shout-out here to James, Julian, David, Lisa, Walter and Dr. Astudillo for the courteous service.)

Now, when it comes to medical things, I have to admit, I get queasy. And kidney stones, as a concept, were always vaguely frightening.

Take childbirth. Somehow women are able to produce a baby through an aperture that really isn't capable of such a feat. Need I (wince) say more?

Several women who've birthed both kidney stones and babies tell me the pain is comparable, or even that stones are worse.

"I had two babies and my husband had four stones," Nancy said with a laugh. "Kidney stones are God's punishment on men."

Shouldn't we at least get special breathing classes?

Among my fellow males, Tom said it was the worst pain he's ever had, and Pat, a comic book fan, said ruefully: "Now I know what Kryptonite does to Superman."

In my case, the stone was so small, the doctor said it might not even be felt on its way out. Whew.

And so that afternoon and evening I was at home, going about my business, distracted, in mild discomfort, but no longer in pain. It was a waiting game.

At 1 a.m., I was awakened from a sound sleep by what might be described as an insistent rapping upon the door.

A minute later, the stone was passed without incident. And soon, the stone's proud parent was resting comfortably.

Cigars all around!

PARADE, AND FORMER GRAND MARSHAL, RETURN

December 9, 2009

My choice as the grand marshal of the 2007 Pomona Christmas Parade was so momentous, the parade had to take 2008 off to recover.

Either that or my selection doomed the parade. In 2008, in any event, there was no event. The Jaycees, the longtime sponsors, were barely functioning and couldn't raise the dough.

But the parade returns Saturday for its 61st edition in its 62 years of life.

And for the first time since the 1970s, the parade will occur downtown, where it began in 1948, rather than on East Holt Avenue.

Holt is nice and wide, but my feeling is it's too wide for a good parade, besides its, um, aesthetic issues. For some, though, the parade has always been on Holt.

"We've had resistance from the status quo," admitted Larry Egan. He heads the Downtown Pomona Owners Association, the business improvement group sponsoring the parade.

The route through downtown will have its challenges because Second Street is a mere 24 feet wide, but Egan says the parade will make up in ambiance what it loses in maneuverability.

Downtown is looking forward to its close-up.

"There are people in this city who haven't been downtown since Buffum's was here," Egan said, referring to the department store that closed in 1991. "We want to show off how safe the downtown is, how vibrant it's becoming. This is a great public relations tool for us."

Beginning at 10 a.m., the parade will trundle west on Second Street from Gibbs Street to Park Avenue, head south on Park to Eighth Street and then east to the Civic Center, where more holiday festivities are planned until 4 p.m. That evening brings the monthly Art Walk, more downtown fun, at the nearly 40 galleries.

As of Monday, the parade had 105 entries, more than in 2007, and will feature more than 1,700 people: marching bands, service clubs, veterans, Boy and Girl Scouts, vintage cars, floats, martial arts studios, Mr. and Mrs. Claus, even an opera troupe.

To break any lingering jinx, you'll also find a certain newspaper columnist in the parade.

There was talk of making me grand marshal again, but apparently the parallels with 2007 were too frightening. No point in thumbing our noses at the parade gods.

Kibitzing, I suggested the Village Academy students and their teacher, whose video persuaded President Barack Obama to visit Pomona. They'll all be grand marshal.

But I'm in the parade. As of Monday, I'm entry No. 53.

"You're just ahead of Richard Martinez" – superintendent of Pomona Unified – "and just behind the Pomona Steelers Cheer Squad," Egan informed me. "But that could change."

If you see me, wave.

SMILES WERE THEIR UMBRELLAS IN PARADE

December 16, 2009

Not to say it was raining heavily on Saturday, but there were times when I thought I was in the Seattle Christmas Parade.

But no, despite the intermittent showers, it was Pomona, not Seattle. Maybe the downtown Starbucks fooled me.

The first Christmas Parade on downtown streets since the 1970s, and the first since my stint as grand marshal in 2007, was a wet affair – the 12 deluges of Christmas? – but spirits were only slightly dampened.

One couldn't help but be impressed by the marching bands and JROTC squads walking the parade route in the rain, looking determined. Not to mention the huddled masses in rain ponchos and umbrellas all along the route.

Pomona's a tough town. A little rain? Feh.

I got to the parade a half-hour early and waited under a tent in the staging area as the rain poured. Members of the Masonic Lodge were nearby, their plumed hats covered in plastic as protection. There were jokes that there might be more people in the parade than watching it.

As entry No. 53, I didn't see any need to hustle, and nobody was telling me where to go, so I focused on staying dry.

The rain let up as the parade began. I wandered off hoping

to find someone to tell me where my parade car was.

Someone did, frantically: "Your car's about to leave!"

My driver was asking a volunteer, "Should I just leave without him?" as I approached. I'm still curious how that would have worked: a white-haired retiree riding the parade route in a car with my name on the placards? People would have wondered how long ago my photo was taken.

Anyway, I got into Bob Haagenson's 1931 Oldsmobile sports coupe – a covered car, not a convertible, I was relieved to see – and we joined the parade somewhere around entry No. 12. (Organization is perhaps not Pomona's strong suit.)

We rode west on Second Street past antiques shops as a light rain fell. Arturo Jimenez, who's a city planning commissioner, shouted from the sidewalk, "If you'd have been grand marshal, it would've been sunshine!"

(Parade organizers, take note.)

On the other side of Garey Avenue, Larry Egan, executive director of the sponsoring Downtown Pomona Owners Association and the person who did the most to make the parade happen, noticed the rain had stopped. As had the line of parade vehicles.

"It's apropos it stopped raining when you drove by. Stay right here," Egan joked.

But the cars began moving again and the rain began falling again.

As we drove west along Second, the one-time pedestrian mall, Haagenson commented approvingly on the size of the mature trees in the street planters. He'd been a surveyor who, circa 1961, had helped determine where to place the planters and the utilities.

The previous weekend he'd driven in the Upland Christmas Parade. Although there had been concerns that downtown

Pomona's streets were too narrow for a parade compared to the usual route along Holt Avenue, Haagenson said downtown Upland's streets are even narrower.

Personally, I thought the route was a big improvement. With cozier confines, there was more interaction between parade entrants and parade watchers.

On the sidewalk, two women held up Olympic-style judging cards, one reading "10!," the other "Hot!" Some of my Arts Colony friends – A.S. Ashley, Cheryl Bookout, Juan Thorp – gave a cheer as I passed by.

At Main Street, John Lopez shouted "Go, Dave!" At Park Avenue, David Ybarra reminded me he's the one who walked up to my car in the 2007 parade with a copy of my column and a pen and requested my autograph.

The blogger known as the Goddess of Pomona stepped forward to snap a photo.

Yes, smiles were our umbrellas. So were actual umbrellas.

I made sure to wave at all the children, mostly because they can reliably be counted on to get excited and wave back. When you're a child, it's always a thrill to be noticed, isn't it?

All too soon we were at the end of the line on Eighth Street. I walked a few blocks to Park and Mission Boulevard to watch the parade with my friends Lisa and Jason McPheron.

Yes, I was able to have my parade and watch it too.

"If you see yourself in the parade," Jason advised me, "don't touch. The universe may explode."

I didn't see myself, but I saw more than half of the parade.

From her parade vehicle, gardening goddess Dawn Van Allen (no relation) shouted to me, "Why aren't you in a car?" I shouted back that I had been. She replied, "It must be a long parade!"

We were lucky only 98 entrants out of 118 showed up. It also turns out I had been lucky to get a car – thank you, Mr. Haagenson.

Virtually all the car clubs that were supposed to drive the dignitaries (and the columnist) had called to cancel the morning of the parade. No rain must touch our precious cars. They're not built for that!

As Egan recalled his thinking when he got the news, "It's too late to go to Enterprise. We'll have to use what we have."

And so most of the bigwigs drove their own cars. And waved.

Ever tried driving and waving at the same time? I'm glad I didn't have to try it. I might have skidded in the rain, plowed into one of those planters and snapped a tree.

The Year's Top 10 Strangest Stories

December 30, 2009

With my fingers crossed that nothing too odd happens today or Thursday, let me count down the Inland Valley's 10 strangest news stories of 2009.

10. **SAHL'S WELL**: Comic Mort Sahl, who was living in Claremont and teaching at Claremont McKenna, was reported missing by his wife in May after she hadn't seen him for three days. Sahl, 81, contacted Claremont police after he learned they were looking for him. He was "where he wanted to be voluntarily," a police spokesman said. Awkward.

9. **GOOD QUESTION**: Noticing an intoxicated stranger standing on his back porch, a Claremont homeowner asked, "What are you doing in my backyard?" Apparently considering that a legitimate question, the stranger mused aloud, "What *am* I doing in your backyard?" He climbed over the fence and fled.

8. **STAMP STUMPER**: An airmail letter from Maryland intended for an address on Park Avenue West in Burlington, Ontario, Canada, was delivered to a home on West D Street in Ontario, California. Yes, an entirely different country. So much for airmail. Next time, try first class. Or email.

7. **ANCHOR RESTAURANT**: Thieves made off with a giant metal anchor and chain that decorated Sushi Cruise, a unique boat-shaped restaurant (originally Tugboat Annie's) in Claremont. Despite losing its anchor, the building did not

slowly float away, which would have moved this weird news item farther up the list.

6. **KNOW YOUR SURROUNDINGS**: At a social event in Pomona, an agitated man emptied his pockets of drug paraphernalia and asked shocked guests for rolling papers or a pipe. Police were on hand and arrested him. Where was he? At a Neighborhood Watch meeting.

5. **SCHOOLED**: He's really a lawyer, but a Pomona school board member, Andrew Wong, tried to call himself a "teacher" on the ballot. The teachers union took him to court and a judge agreed Wong isn't a teacher. In a hopeful sign for the societal standing of lawyers, Wong won re-election anyway.

4. **DON'T TRY THIS AT HOME**: An apartment dweller in Claremont used his microwave oven as a dryer. Alas, the metal zipper on his damp jacket ignited a fire. The man unplugged the burning oven and hurled it outside, still aflame. A police spokesman cautioned the public: "There's a specific purpose for a microwave, and that's to cook food."

3. **MINUTIAE**: In a story so weird it drew national attention, the days at two Chino Valley Unified schools were mistakenly shortened. Rather than make up the minutes, amounting to one to two school days, state officials said the 34 days involved wouldn't count at all. A 34-day summer school session was scheduled. Then state officials said summer school wouldn't count either, so it was canceled. They're still demanding $7 million in penalties from the district. Apparently Sacramento doesn't have any real problems to focus on.

2. **TRAVELING**: It was a tough commute for the Lakers in October as they traveled from L.A. to Ontario for work, i.e., an exhibition game. Because of a multi-car accident and a brushfire, making the 57-mile trip took the team bus two

hours and 40 minutes. That's an average speed of 22 mph, akin to traveling in a school zone. Next year, the team should fly from LAX to ONT. Or bring an audiobook, maybe by coach Phil Jackson.

And the strangest Inland Valley news story of 2009:

1. **SAUCER-EYED**: A "cigar-shaped aircraft" with lights was spotted over Ontario the night of December 16 and alarmed the easily alarmed. Then again, with traffic down at ONT, perhaps airplanes are becoming harder to recognize. One reader on *dailybulletin.com* wrote: "The UFO was scanning for intelligent life, but finding none in Ontario, it flew off!"

2009 ITEMS

January 21, 2009

Scripps College has a new class this semester: Music 127, "The Cultural History of Rap." According to the description, the course will explore rap's roots and oral traditions, analyze its aesthetics, discuss its influences and explore its controversies.

This reminds me that while attending the University of Illinois in the mid-1980s, I took a secret course in rock 'n' roll. It was hidden in the catalog as Speech Communications 252. Its name, "The Rhetoric of Dissent," did not mention rock music.

The class' true purpose was passed by word of mouth. "That's the rock 'n' roll class," past students would say knowingly, pointing to Speech Comm 252 in the catalog.

Those of us who got in were almost giddy as we took our seats the first day, like we'd put one over on The Man. The whole thing felt underground, like a club show.

I can't help thinking that by being so forthright, Scripps took half the fun out of it.

March 4, 2009

Fourth-graders in Tom Munoz's class at Creek View Elementary in Ontario had some good questions for me Monday about writing and reporting.

They also wondered if I make $2 an hour, whether my job interview at the Bulletin took "days and days" and whether this 44-year-old is contemplating retirement.

And, cutting to the chase, one boy asked: "Did you used to have hair?"

After a grilling like that, it was a pleasure to go back to a job where I get to ask the questions.

April 29, 2009

A lot of strange questions come your columnist's way, but among the strangest was a query by email Monday by a man in Northern California. He asked for confirmation of his belief that Dick Cheney attended La Verne College.

The man said he's sure he had a classmate named Richard Cheney in the 1960-61 school year who transferred to La Verne as a sophomore.

"Although there were only 400 students at that time, we had very little contact," my correspondent wrote. "He spent the previous year at Yale and I spent the prior year at East Los Angeles J.C."

He said he and Cheney watched the Kennedy-Nixon election returns and Kennedy's inauguration on TV, and that on another night, he and a friend "stole a goose from a nearby orchard and put it in" Cheney and his roommate's room "over a long holiday weekend."

What a way to treat the future vice president.

The man was suspicious that the University of La Verne, which is La Verne College's present name, has no record of Cheney's attendance, nor does Cheney's biography mention La Verne.

As he put it: "I need some help to figure out if I am nuts or if in fact a real conspiracy exists."

Does it have to be one or the other?

Needless to say, I swung into action immediately, forwarding the email to the university spokesman and then breaking for lunch.

After checking into the matter, ULV spokesman Charles Bentley – who swears he's not part of a coverup – reports that the college has seen nine Cheneys, "none of them named Richard or Dick."

There were two Cheneys, brothers James and Donald, who attended in the early 1960s.

"I've talked to some people who attended school here then and remember the Cheney brothers," Bentley related dryly, "and also remember that neither one of them became vice president."

I forgot to ask Bentley to prepare a bar graph on the number of transfer students La Verne gets from Yale.

May 6, 2009

Jack Kemp, the former congressman and housing secretary, died Saturday at age 73. And I have a Jack Kemp story.

As Bob Dole's presidential running mate in 1996, Kemp made a campaign stop in Apple Valley a few days before the election. I was a reporter for the *Victor Valley Daily Press* and was assigned to cover the event.

After his speech, radio and TV reporters quizzed the former Buffalo Bills and San Diego Chargers quarterback. Then, displaying the dispassion so crucial to the news business, they crowded around chummily, handing him items to autograph, including a football.

Illustrating the campaign's desperation, yours truly was granted a 15-minute one-on-one with Kemp.

There's not much a local reporter can do in a meeting like that. Kemp dutifully stuck to his talking points and pretended he didn't know Dole was going to be crushed like pineapple. His answers were crisp and articulate. He was clearly as smart as his reputation.

That said, his idea of a rousing pledge was to declare that within days of taking office, Dole would "index capital gains."

An aide signaled to me over Kemp's shoulder that my

time was up. In the journalistic equivalent of a hail-Mary pass – something the former quarterback would have been familiar with – I asked one final question:

"What does a vice presidential candidate carry in his pockets?"

The aide, exasperated, rolled her eyes. Kemp, however, emptied his front pockets onto the table and described the meager pile: "I got an Apple Valley pin. I got about $6. I got a note from a woman in a classroom."

His other pockets, Kemp said without demonstrating, held his address book and his wallet.

"I can't believe I answered that question," Kemp murmured to a chuckling Representative Jerry Lewis, who was also at the table, as we shook hands goodbye.

Kemp was, at least to a point, a good sport.

July 1, 2009

I ventured to Ventura last week for a conference for newspaper columnists, a visit that gave me another crack at the question, raised here last fall, of how to pronounce Ventura: Ven-tura or Ven-chura?

As a woman from the Visitors and Convention Bureau led us to a reception at the Mission, I listened intently, hanging on her every word, or at least one particular word.

She said Ven-tura several times. That seemed to settle the matter. That is, until she began saying Ven-chura, also several times.

At the reception, two journalists for the *Ventura County Star* told me Ven-tura is the preferred pronunciation but that some locals say Ven-chura.

That number apparently includes one of those very journalists, who was heard saying Ven-chura a few times in subsequent days.

Taking everyone's cue, I'm going to continue saying Ven-tura. Except when I don't.

August 2, 2009

At a neighborhood watch meeting in Pomona last week, a very animated man made the rounds during the social hour, chatting and introducing himself. "He seemed to be getting more animated – heading toward the edges of the comfort zone – as things went on," reports the M-M-M-My Pomona blog.

Bear in mind, this was in a room holding not only residents of the tony Lincoln Park neighborhood and its block captains, but a police detective and two uniformed police officers, all there to discuss suspicious behavior.

Speaking of which, the excitable fellow asked a resident: "Have you got any papers or a pipe?" The shocked response: "This is a neighborhood watch meeting!"

The man replied cryptically: "Yes, that's how they do it here."

Becoming increasingly agitated, and pacing around, the man emptied the contents of his pockets onto a table, including his cell phone and drug paraphernalia.

Brilliant move.

"At that point," the blogger writes, "various people drew the detective's attention to the drug paraphernalia, and he in turn drew the uniformed officers' attention to the agitated fellow. The result was a gen-yoo-ine, Starsky-and-Hutch style takedown."

Wow! Yes, that's how they do it here, indeed.

September 16, 2009

There were 26 of us at a reading Sunday by poet B.H. Fairchild at the Claremont Public Library. Fairchild, prefacing a poem by explaining its references, asked if anyone knew who Billy Batson was.

In a sea of blank faces surrounded by gray or white hair, your 1960s-born columnist was the only one who raised his hand to reply that Batson was the alter ego of 1940s superhero Captain Marvel.

As Batson would say, "Holy moley!"

Forget the perennial question, "What is happening to our young people?" I say, "What is happening to our old people?"

September 18, 2009

No carbs for you!: The Fazoli's fast-casual Italian restaurant near Ontario Mills has closed after several years of operation. Its selling point, at least in the early days, was a woman who roamed the lobby and dining room with a basket of hot breadsticks, handing them out for free.

On one early visit, I politely declined a second breadstick on her second pass around. As I was to learn, this apparently was not done.

Perhaps a month later, I returned and waited to order. The breadstick woman was working the line, handing out her item to each person, when she came to me.

"That's right, you don't want a breadstick," she said, passing to the next customer before I could say a word.

The Breadstick Nazi?

October 7, 2009

It's fair to say that actor-activist Edward James Olmos' talk Friday in Rancho Cucamonga wowed the crowd. We've already covered his talk, so I'll keep this short.

I got to meet Olmos afterward and can report that even tired and gnawing hungrily on a chocolate bar, he exudes a quiet dignity.

One telling moment occurred as Olmos walked a few paces outdoors to the library for a reception. He broke stride to greet a trio of cleaning women, all Latinas, waiting near the door by their rolling trash cans.

"Hello, ladies," Olmos said. Each shyly answered "Hello," their faces respectful and starstruck.

October 28, 2009

News of the 25th anniversary of the 1984 surgery at Loma Linda University Medical Center that transplanted the heart of a baboon into Baby Fae answered one enduring mystery for this pop music fan.

Finally, I know what Paul Simon was referring to on his 1986 album *Graceland* when, in the shortlist of modern wonders in the song "The Boy in the Bubble," he includes "the baby with the baboon heart."

Now if only someone would explain Simon's "Me and Julio Down by the Schoolyard"!

November 6, 2009

High school students have to attend a local council meeting for their government class, proving their attendance by getting a form signed or initialed by a city official afterward.

One girl at Tuesday's Ontario meeting tried to wriggle out of the requirement. Before the meeting began, she approached Christian Nelson, a Southern California Edison employee who was chatting with me in the rear of the room. She asked him to sign her form.

Nelson quipped that even though he was wearing a suit and tie, that didn't make him a city official. He playfully suggested that a certain woman nearby could sign the form.

That was our Ontario reporter, Liset Márquez, who as Nelson knew could not sign the form either. (What a scamp!) Márquez pointed the girl to John Brown, the city attorney, who was entering the room.

Brown, who as the city's legal representative is not easily

taken advantage of, told the girl: "No, you have to stay through the whole meeting."

Undeterred, the girl approached City Clerk Mary Wirtes on the dais, who likewise said: "No, you have to stay through the whole meeting."

Thinking quickly, the girl returned to Márquez with a unique translation of Wirtes' comment.

"Turns out you *can* sign it for me!" the girl said brightly. Márquez, who'd heard what Wirtes said, declined. The girl took a seat, pouting.

When the meeting adjourned, she was among those rushing the dais for a signature.

Gosh, the poor thing had to sit through one of those marathon Ontario council meetings. It began at 6:30 p.m. – and ended at 7:05.

Gumby Creator Shaped Childhoods

January 13, 2010

I never met Gumby animator Art Clokey, who had ties to Claremont and who died Friday in Los Osos at age 88. But Gumby and I go way back.

Among my earliest memories is watching *The Gumby Show* on TV circa 1968, when I was 4. I had bendable rubber figures of the green Gumby and his orange horse, Pokey. I also recall receiving a coveted Gumby tie-in, a plastic yellow Jeep for the two pals to ride in.

Why Gumby didn't ride on his friend is probably a matter of politeness, as well as one of those quirks of animation, such as why Pluto can't talk but Goofy walks upright.

As for Gumby's show, I have only a hazy memory of fun and a feeling that, because of the Jeep, there was travel and interesting terrain. *The New York Times* obituary for Clokey says the show involved "a string of gently quixotic adventures," which sounds right.

I also watched *Davey and Goliath*, Clokey's other clay-animated program. It aired in my part of the country on Sundays, a dead zone for children's programming. The Bible-based series was slightly dull but better than no TV at all.

(It was widely parodied just as Gumby was. A former newsroom colleague, Alissa Sandford, enjoyed greeting me in Goliath's slow, dopey voice: "Hey, Daaaavey.")

A few years ago, the Museum of Television and Radio in L.A. offered a Gumby retrospective, and the segments screened were truly odd, one involving Gumby's parents (Gumbo and Gumba) who lived in a suburban tract home, another a bizarre fantasia involving Gumby and Pokey and an ever-shifting backdrop of moving clay.

Whether the segments were typical of the series is hard to say. Perhaps not. Then again, there must be a generation of junior high students who grew up on the Dadaist baby talk of *Teletubbies* and whose recollection of that series is no more complex than mine is of Gumby, namely, one of pleasant childhood association and zero retention of the particulars.

As for Clokey himself, did you know he spent his formative years in Claremont?

After a tragic childhood in which his parents divorced, his father died in a car accident and his stepfather refused to take him in, young Arthur Farrington was adopted at age 11 by Joseph W. Clokey, a Pomona College music teacher and composer.

Clokey opened the world of art and culture to his son, encouraging his pursuits and taking him on trips to Canada and Mexico.

Art attended the Webb School in Claremont and its annual fossil-hunting expeditions, led by teacher Raymond Alf, fostered a love of adventure. He studied geology at Pomona College and, following World War II and film studies at USC, created the Gumby character while living in Covina.

The slope of Gumby's head, by the way, was meant to reflect that of Clokey's birth father, who had a large wave of hair. Long may Gumby wave.

Is pageant's return welcome? You be the judge

January 27, 2010

When they asked me to help judge the Miss Pomona pageant, I wasted little time in saying yes.

How often in life are you asked to judge a pageant? Besides, with four other judges and only three contestants, this seemed like an easy night's work.

As the date approached, I began having certain reservations (more on that later). Also, I wondered if there might not be more to my vague duties – as did some of you.

"Are you doing anything to prepare?" reader Hugh McBride asked. "Will you have to sing, like Bert Parks?"

Unlikely, but I was ready for the unexpected when I showed up Saturday evening as scheduled at the Masonic Temple. About 100 people sampled a buffet in the main meeting hall and socialized before the ceremony.

Pomona's pageant, like its Christmas Parade, had gone dormant before boosters rallied to revive them. Their back-to-back successes are a welcome sign of community competence.

As predicted, there wasn't much for the judges to do.

For one thing, somebody else sang. (Whew.) Also, a committee had already done the heavy lifting, whittling the 22 applicants to eight, and then three.

One Miss Pomona applicant was rejected out of hand, committee member Tim Saunders told me, still baffled: "She was from Fontana."

I suppose it's a compliment if it's more prestigious to be Miss Pomona than Miss Fontana.

"We picked three girls that will do a good job of representing Pomona," said Saunders, a councilman. "They have good grades, a positive personality and their heart is in the city."

I asked event co-chair Mickey Gallivan, president of the Historical Society and mother of four daughters, why she thought a pageant was important.

The contestants have sometimes overcome tough odds, Gallivan told me, and yet they also manage to do good in the community and could serve as role models.

"When you interview the candidates, it's just tremendously inspiring," Gallivan said.

Indeed, the biographies of the three finalists are intimidating. Just reading their list of activities – volunteerism, mentoring, sports, school clubs – was exhausting, and that's on top of high grades, honors classes and after-school jobs.

The trio have lofty ambitions. Daisy Cortez and Bedsairy (Betsy) Santoyo both plan to be medical professionals, and Angela Hernandez wants to protect wolves, an endangered species.

I had to ask Gallivan, though, whether a pageant isn't sexist in this day and age.

"It's not based on beauty. When we choose the semifinalists, we've never seen them. It's based purely on the applications," she said.

"I don't see anything sexist about it other than that it's a tradition," she added, referring to the practice of cities being represented by a miss. "The questions we ask could be asked of anyone and could be answered by anyone."

True. But they weren't.

The ceremony soon began. The centerpiece was a short speech by each contestant. Hernandez spoke about unity, youth and city cleanup.

Santoyo noted Pomona has 56,000 residents under 19 but, gulp, the fourth-highest dropout rate in California.

Cortez emphasized the need for Neighborhood Watch programs to combat gangs and fix-up rather than demolition for historic buildings.

All worthy causes close to home. None of the pageant contestants mentioned world peace.

In her remarks from the stage, Gallivan surprised me by referring to our interview earlier. Saying David Allen had asked her why the event was important, she repeated her answer. Then she said David Allen had asked if the event was sexist and she explained why she didn't think it was.

Since we've known each other for years, our interview hadn't ended in the traditional way. Otherwise, she might have said: "And then David Allen asked me, 'Would you spell your first and last names?'"

My fellow judges were medical school president Philip Pumerantz, downtown business leader Carolyn Hemming, college outreach director Jonnie Owens and former school board member John Avila.

We sat at a table in front, but we didn't confer. We each filled out score sheets on the speakers' poise, presentation, content, assurance and potential. Nope, nothing about legs. Others tallied the scores and declared who was Miss Pomona: Betsy Santoyo.

Congratulations, Betsy.

Tiaras, sashes, scepters and flowers were distributed with the help of Mayor Elliott Rothman, but so were prop checks for scholarships: $2,000 for Santoyo and $1,000 each for Cortez and Hernandez. The five semifinalists got $500 each.

Miss Pomona and her "court," when available, will represent Pomona at civic functions, schools and new-business openings. It was a nice event, tasteful and unobjectionably handled.

Unless you object on principle to pageants, which I'm afraid I do.

Even in their current benign form, with swimsuits and evening gowns thankfully excised, crowning a Miss City is a little too retro for me.

Nor does the "tradition" argument sway me. I think civic pageants ought to be left in the 20th century. Let's just have a scholarship program, same criteria, but open to all.

I wasn't the only one in the room to harbor doubts.

"The idea that it's not sexist is a bunch of baloney," one young woman confided. "There's no Mr. Pomona."

A man countered that the princess ideal is ingrained in girls. Besides, he observed, girls may need money for college more than boys do, so what's the harm?

Perhaps none. Speaking of ingrained, though, I've got a deep-seated reason myself to be wary of a pageant like Pomona's, and of these three young women.

Overachievers always make me nervous. And a little guilty.

Fresh talk from the strawberry Donut Man

April 18, 2010

It's strawberry season, and the Donut Man rates this spring's crop as fair, delayed due to cold weather, damaged slightly by hail.

"It's good but not great. The flavor's pretty good," the Donut Man told me.

This agriculture report comes courtesy of Jim Nakano, perhaps the only doughnut maker in California who can speak knowledgeably about local produce.

His Glendora shop, Donut Man, serves up old-fashioneds, maple bars and other standards from its 915 E. Route 66 location, but the shop's claim to fame is its strawberry doughnut.

Filled with whole strawberries bursting from a split pastry, the doughnut arrives in a box with a plastic fork and practically constitutes a meal. Especially at the price: $2.80 (and worth every penny).

Foodies have elevated the item into an object of idolatry. Nakano and his creation have been featured on the Food Network and Huell Howser's *California's Gold* and in innumerable newspaper and magazine write-ups.

The latest – well, until this column – was in February, when *LA Weekly* included the Donut Man's strawberry doughnut in a cover story memorably titled "99 Things to

Eat in L.A. Before You Die." It was the only Inland Valley foodstuff so honored.

"A lot of food people have been very nice to us. Everything helps," Nakano told me Wednesday morning in his small shop, leaning against a counter next to stacked flats of fresh strawberries.

Nakano picks up strawberries six days a week from a grower who farms at Cal Poly Pomona and in Rowland Heights. Holding up a berry, he draws my attention to the light green leaves.

"Look at the leaves, they aren't wilted or anything. Most berries, when you get them in the store, they're a day or two old. I tell my grower he can pick mine riper," Nakano explained.

After the berries are washed and their tops removed, they are mixed with a light, translucent glaze of Nakano's design. A puffy, chewy jelly doughnut without the jelly is used as the shell. It's split in three-quarters and berries are spooned in.

"And we just stuff it," Nakano said as an employee heaps a second spoonful into the doughnut. "A 12-ounce cup, we figure, goes into each one."

Hmm. The USDA recommends two 8-ounce servings of fruit per day. Eat two strawberry doughnuts, and you're good (except for the calorie and fat part).

Nakano created the strawberry doughnut in 1974 at the urging of a strawberry grower in town who offered to supply him. The doughnut was a hit and remains Donut Man's biggest seller more than three decades later. (The tiger tail, a chocolate twist, is No. 2.)

Among the most devoted fans are a club of unicyclists from Harvey Mudd College.

In an April tradition that began in 1980, a small group of

students and alumni will pedal their one-wheeled bikes 8.7 miles from Claremont to Glendora, a journey that takes four hours, simply for a complimentary strawberry doughnut and beverage from an impressed Nakano.

The doughnut is only available in season, usually from February until July. Nakano shifts to a fresh peach doughnut in July for about six weeks.

The other six months, I'm afraid, you have to get your fruit in non-doughnut form. (I wonder if Nakano has ever considered vegetable doughnuts.)

Expanding his fruit selection, Nakano uses fresh blueberries and raspberries to make his own jelly for the jelly-filled doughnuts. He gave me a spoonful of his raspberry jelly.

It's homemade, all right.

"When you taste it, you get seeds. It's real strong," Nakano said.

Real ingredients, not imitation, are his hallmark. He's stubborn that way. Rather than compromise on quality, he raises his prices, and gets away with it.

Donut Man is open 24 hours. On weekends, he and his staff are baking 18 hours a day.

"For a hole-in-the-wall store, we do a phenomenal amount of business. I think 50 percent of my customers come from more than five miles away," Nakano said. "The busier a place is, the fresher it is, because you've really got to turn it out."

Born in East L.A., Nakano is a third-generation Japanese American, the son of a wholesale produce man. Interned in Poston, Arizona, during World War II, his family was among the 110,000 Japanese Americans sent to war relocation camps.

Nakano was in the camp from ages 2 to 5. His father fought on the American side in the war, as did five uncles, one of whom was killed in action.

One of those uncles was Mike Masaoka, who as head of the

Japanese American Citizens League urged cooperation with the internment.

It's a complicated legacy for his family. And explaining the compromises of the 1940s to people in the 21st century is difficult.

"People, especially younger people, say, 'Why didn't you protest?' They don't understand," Nakano said. "We couldn't protest. The media and the government were against us. They don't realize how the mood was in those days."

He speaks to service clubs and schools about the internment, which he considers a black mark against America.

"It happened twice. A lot of people don't know that. It happened to the American Indians, who were relocated, and it happened to us. It can't happen again," Nakano said.

His wife, Miyoko, inspired the doughnut stand. The family couldn't afford a house on Nakano's salary as a JC Penney manager. She liked doughnuts and suggested they go into business.

He liked Glendora and opened the stand in 1972 as a Foster's, later dropping the affiliation. He and his wife have one son, Justin, who lives in Rancho Cucamonga and works for the Chino Basin Watermaster.

"If you mention my son's name, he'll buy a bunch of copies," Nakano confided.

These are tough times in the newspaper business, so every copy helps, Justin.

Nakano, who turns 70 this year, is only vaguely contemplating retirement. These days he relies more on employees, especially Tanya Godwin and Kim Kuhn, whom he jokes can run the stand better than he can.

"Who knows, I'll keep it as long as I enjoy it. I still enjoy it," Nakano said. "I may be 80 and still doing it."

But let's return to the strawberry doughnut. Before I left, Nakano took up a perch on a steel counter and began snipping the tops off a tub of strawberries with a paring knife.

"We run through 70 to 80 flats a week. There are 12 pints in each flat," Nakano said.

If a half-pint of strawberries is in each doughnut, that means he's selling 1,800 per week.

I've been buying one or two per season for several years. Its pita-like form and overstuffed interior defy easy handling. You ignore the fork at the peril of your shirt and chin.

My current strategy is to eat half the strawberries with the fork, then pick up the more manageable doughnut and eat it from the wax paper liner.

First-timers are often baffled, Nakano confirmed.

"That's why we give them the fork," he said. He added: "When Huell Howser was here, he said the pros eat them by hand."

Then I still have amateur status. How does Nakano, who as inventor of the strawberry doughnut ought to know best, consume it?

"I don't remember the last time I actually ate a strawberry doughnut," Nakano admitted. "I eat the strawberries as I cut them."

Soup Nazi? No, more like Soup Niceguy

May 12, 2010

What was the highlight of my dinner with actors Linda Blair, Eric Roberts and Larry Thomas? It was when Thomas, better known as the Soup Nazi from *Seinfeld*, ladled me a bowlful of his namesake foodstuff.

It was Saturday afternoon, and we were dining at Taste of Asia in La Verne following a fundraiser at Bonita High involving the trio. Benefiting the *Exorcist* star's animal-rescue nonprofit, the event, previewed here last week, didn't go so hot, for which I hope no one blames me. I'm bedeviled enough.

Taste of Asia is the favorite restaurant of event organizer Becky Altringer, the La Verne private eye who was herself featured in a documentary on the movie ratings system, *This Film Is Not Yet Rated*.

Altringer and her partner, Cheryl Howell, eat there three times a week and are good friends with owner and chef Virada Khowong. They had been talking up the restaurant among the invited stars.

The Soup Nazi was particularly jazzed.

"He can't talk about anything else," Altringer told me earlier in the week.

There were 17 of us seated at a very long table. Arriving late, I was squeezed in next to Altringer at one end. Thomas was nearby, with girlfriend and Playboy model Max Wasa next to him, Roberts and Blair opposite.

A large bowl of egg flower soup arrived, the first of five soups coming. Altringer ladled some into small bowls for people near her, including Thomas.

For any non-*Seinfeld* fans reading this, the Soup Nazi was the nickname for a dictatorial chef on one famous episode who ran a soup-centered takeout restaurant and who chased out anyone who didn't comply with his rules by bellowing, "No soup for you!"

Unlike his character, Thomas was relaxed and charming. Huh! I guess that's why they call it acting.

"Just a little bit," Thomas requested of Altringer when she offered him egg flower soup. "I want to try all of them. Just one ladle."

Minutes later, a bowl of shrimp wonton soup arrived and was placed near Thomas. This time he did the honors for people near him.

In what was essentially the opposite of his famed line, the Soup Nazi asked me: "Would you like some soup?"

Let me think. Would I like to have soup served to me by the Soup Nazi, providing me with an anecdote I can tell for the rest of my life?

"Please," I replied, passing down my bowl. (I kept my seat rather than sidling left, eyes averted, to the nonexistent cash register, as on the show.)

Thomas ladled me soup, considerately finding a floating piece of carrot and adding it to my bowl before passing it back.

"Thank you," I told the Soup Nazi.

Nothing against the shrimp wonton, which was excellent by the way, but my only regret is that it wasn't lobster bisque, jambalaya or mulligatawny, the Soup Nazi's TV specialties.

Meanwhile, Roberts, who played a gangster in *Batman: The Dark Knight* and starred in *The Pope of Greenwich Village* and *Runaway Train*, was outgoing and friendly.

The owner of four dogs, Roberts had instantly agreed to take part in the event. The onetime Oscar nominee judged the contests in the Bonita High parking lot for best-dressed dog and the dog with the best personality.

The dinner conversation turned to dealing with fans.

Thomas said most people who meet him or who leave comments on his website have little to say besides using his "No soup for you!" catchphrase. Not exactly a conversation starter.

"People think it's funny. I don't mind it, but it's not funny," Thomas said.

However, he told Blair that despite the photos of the two of them side by side on his website to plug their La Verne appearance, no fan had left a comment referring to her famous vomiting scene in *The Exorcist*. "C'mon, the Soup Nazi and Linda Blair!" Thomas exclaimed. "I was waiting for somebody to say it: 'No pea soup for you!'" Blair let out an explosive laugh.

Roberts said the *Pope of Greenwich Village* scene in which one of his thumbs is cut off remains fresh in the public's mind.

"Every airport I've ever been in, people say, 'You got your thumb back!' And I've heard it 10,000 times that hour, but I go, ha ha ha ha," Roberts said, pretending to double up in laughter and pointing at the imaginary joker as if to say, "wow, good one."

While all this was going on, other diners in the small restaurant minded their own business. One elderly man asked waiter Sean Khowong who the animated man was. When he heard the answer, the man said: "Who's Eric Roberts?" (The fate of a character actor.)

Khowong ran through his credits. "I knew his voice was familiar," the man eventually said.

Blair went unrecognized too. A family waiting outside for a table didn't react when told Linda Blair was inside. They perked up upon hearing she was the star of *The Exorcist* and peered inside with interest. But inside, at the sight of Blair, no one's head swiveled – not even a mere 90 degrees.

"Only in La Verne would they be left alone," Altringer said appreciatively. No one had bid for dinner with Blair at the fundraiser, possibly because she set the minimum bid at $300. "I don't think she really wanted anyone to win," Altringer whispered.

I couldn't blame her. At the event but unable to make the dinner, by the way, was character actor Bill Cobbs, but as the Upland resident has already been to Taste of Asia, it was probably no big deal to him.

Cobbs has a long list of TV and movie credits. This didn't stop people at the Bonita High event from misreading his name on the sign and exclaiming, "I never, ever thought I would meet Bill Cosby!"

Guess what, you still haven't.

But back to dinner, where Khowong, who came out to chat, got a round of applause. She joined in until someone told the flustered chef that it was for her.

"Hail to the chef!" Roberts said.

Leftovers were boxed up for the actors, who took home a little La Verne for their fridge. Thomas, who sampled the red, yellow and green curries and took home the rest, may not have to buy a meal all week.

From a standing position on her way to the restroom, Blair was still eating forkfuls of sticky rice with mango and raving: "This is insane. It was so yummy."

On her way past, Blair told me, indicating my notepad: "Write 'The best food. Amazing.'"

She was certainly exercised about it.

The guests at what I like to think of as the Blair Dinner Project posed for individual and group photos with Khowong, her family and anyone else.

I declined. Too cheesy for a respectable journalist. But I was happy for Khowong.

She had cooked Saturday for more than three hours and had shopped Friday for ingredients to suit the requests relayed in advance by Altringer.

(As you'd expect from high-maintenance celebs, there were food issues: One wouldn't consume milk or scallions, one was vegan and one wouldn't eat any food items that touch.)

Was she anxious? "Oh, yeah!" Khowong told me, laughing: "I couldn't sleep, I was so nervous. You see them come in and ah, ah, ah" – she simulated biting her nails.

She plans to display autographed headshots from Blair, Roberts, Thomas, Wasa and Cobbs, lending her 2-year-old restaurant a burst of glamour.

You can already guess what the Soup Nazi wrote on his.

"Virada, no soup for you!!"

Luckily, she makes her own.

POSITIVELY FEVERISH ABOUT GETTING BACK TO WORK

June 18, 2010

Whew! No sooner did I return from vacation in the Show Me State, seemingly refreshed, than I got sick and missed most of a week of work.

Theories abounded. On my blog, reader Bob Terry diagnosed my condition as "the St. Louie creeping crud," while the *Bulletin*'s Scoop feature blamed "the St. Louis blues."

Less picturesquely, the doctor called it an upper respiratory infection, if I understood her correctly over my coughing.

Speaking of the Scoop, one reader remarked: "I'd hate to be David Allen. He misses work and they put it on the front page! Now everyone knows he was sick." Ah, life in a fishbowl.

What bothered me most – well, besides the sore throat, rundown feeling and congestion – was that I had diligently written three columns ahead before leaving on vacation, with the goal of not depriving anyone in my absence. Then, shortly after returning, I got sick – and missed two columns.

I guess you can't cheat fate. The *Final Destination* movies taught us that.

Well, anyway. To help me ease back into the swing of things, allow me to warm up some leftovers collected over the past couple of weeks.

* * * * *

One vacation surprise I neglected to mention was whose photo filled the front page of the *St. Louis Post-Dispatch* one day during my visit: Thelma Melendez de Santa Ana, the former Pomona Unified school superintendent.

She was visiting a classroom in her new role as assistant U.S. secretary of education. Pomona, like it or not, follows me everywhere.

* * * * *

At Rabi's Cafe in Upland, where owner Rabi Albaghdadi is known for her pugnacious sense of humor, a man in his 20s was overheard Saturday asking for a to-go container for the remainder of his sandwich.

"We don't let customers take their food home," Albaghdadi informed the stunned diner.

"I'm serious," she continued. "Because sometimes people complain later and we don't have any control over what happens after the food leaves here. You have to stay here and eat all your food – and then wait 30 minutes."

Despite wearing a T-shirt with a printed obscenity, the young man sat open-mouthed, unsure how to respond.

Albaghdadi settled the matter by laughing and fetching a takeout box. Heh heh.

"You heard that, huh?" she said, amused, as she passed my table. Yep.

* * * * *

John Svenson, the octogenarian sculptor from San Antonio Heights, is recuperating after an unusual accident in late May.

"I tripped over my pet duck and broke my nose," Svenson told me. He had the swollen beak to prove it. Svenson, not the duck.

(I tripped over Svenson, in a manner of speaking, in the Claremont Village outside Starbucks on June 6, but I didn't break anything.)

What happened? Svenson said he was bringing food outside to his duck when it got underfoot and he took a spill, face-first. The duck, as is its habit, began nibbling at his ears. The sculptor had to shoo it away so he could examine himself.

He was back at work in his home studio almost immediately with ice packs on his face. His son drove to see him from Wrightwood – and got a fright even before seeing the old man.

"The first thing he saw was this duck covered in blood," Svenson said. "He didn't know what to think."

I occasionally see Svenson in the Village, where he likes to observe the local wildlife. He reminded me of our encounter a couple of summers ago outside the ice cream shop, where belly dancers were putting on an eye-opening performance.

"I see the most amazing things," Svenson said from the Starbucks patio. Earlier he'd spotted an attractive woman whose two front teeth were fitted with diamonds.

"Have you ever seen anything like that?" Svenson asked.

No.

"All these people with their piercings in their lips and nose and – are you allowed to write about this kind of thing?" Svenson paused to ask.

Yes.

"I don't know how they sleep," Svenson continued. "You'd think they'd get all tangled up."

* * * * *

People saving a seat at a movie or a concert usually leave a jacket. But what if you don't have a jacket?

At the LCD Soundsystem concert at the Pomona Fox on June 5, a man saved a first-row balcony seat, on the aisle, in unique fashion: with cash.

A crumpled dollar bill was left on the seat to mark it as taken. Despite the temptation, no one touched the bill for the more than 45 minutes that elapsed until the man claimed his seat in person.

Impressive. I don't know how U.S. money is doing overseas, but in Pomona, people still respect the power of the dollar.

* * * * *

This sounds like fun: Chino Community Theater is performing "The Compleat Works of Willm Shkspr (abridged)," in which three actors perform the Bard's oeuvre in whirlwind fashion, including a 43-second "Hamlet." To be or – oops, we're out of time.

'JAWS' MOVIE LOOMED LARGE IN 1970S CHILDHOODS

June 20, 2010

If you were the right age in 1975, and maybe the right gender too, you'll remember one thing about school break: It was the summer of *Jaws*.

I was 11, which was the optimal age, and as a boy I was definitely the optimal gender. C'mon, this was a movie about a killer shark. And in the first scene, he eats a naked woman. Now that's moviemaking.

Jaws opened June 20, 1975 – yep, 35 years ago today.

When the shark movie washed up at our single-screen theater in landlocked Olney, Illinois, it was such a hit, it was held over an unprecedented three times. If you didn't want to see *Jaws*, well, for a full month that summer you were out of luck.

I saw the movie twice in that first run, once with my parents and once on my own. *Jaws* was probably the first movie I saw more than once.

"I envy you," Pat Jankiewicz told me over lunch on Thursday. Jankiewicz, who counts *Jaws* as his favorite movie, wasn't allowed to see it in 1975.

"As a fraidy cat, my mom wouldn't let me see a movie about a killer fish, even if it was the grade-school event of the summer," Jankiewicz lamented.

How big of an event? On the playground of his native Sterling Heights, Michigan, Jankiewicz told me, "they would turn on the kid who faked having seen the movie."

Why am I telling you about Pat Jankiewicz? Hold on a second. I hear something approaching in the distance.

Da-dum.

Da-dum.

Da-dum, da-dum.

Da-dum, da-dum, da-dum, da-dum – it's bearing down on us!

The shark? No, you fool: *The local angle!!*

Jankiewicz, you see, is a freelance journalist in Upland – there you go – and author of *Just When You Thought It Was Safe: A Jaws Companion*, an expert's guide to the movie and its (who knew?) three sequels.

For the book, published last year by BearManor Media, he interviewed dozens of people connected with the movie (none of them named Steven Spielberg, alas) to pick up insider information.

One of the elements that made *Jaws* so effective was how rarely the shark was glimpsed. This increased our sense of dread.

Genius? Yes, but accidental genius.

For instance, the shark isn't seen at all during the opening scene, an attack on a nude swimmer, which made the woman's death all the more disturbing and mysterious. Yet the original intention was to show the shark.

However, the movie's mechanical shark frequently malfunctioned. Plans to give it more screen time had to be scaled back.

In other words, the movie's much-admired sense of restraint was forced upon it.

"A lot of what made the movie work was completely by accident," Jankiewicz explained. "By cutting around the shark, they made a much better film."

Less became more.

"Keeping the camera at water level made the audience extremely nervous. You know the shark is in the water someplace," Jankiewicz said.

"You always feel the presence of the shark. The music became the shark, the camera became the shark. He becomes this omnipresent villain."

Another happy accident: One of the most-quoted lines, "You're going to need a bigger boat," uttered by a shaken Chief Brody to Captain Quint after seeing the shark's size, wasn't in the script. It was concocted by actor Roy Scheider.

The ending was another lucky break. In Peter Benchley's original novel, "the shark literally bumps noses with the hero and dies – of natural causes," Jankiewicz complained. "That's not an ending!"

Obviously the movie's big confrontation couldn't end so anticlimactically. It was the production designer who came up with the idea of how to end the film in more, shall we say, explosive fashion.

Much of the lore connected with the movie is less momentous. Among the odder bits of trivia:

During the opening shark attack, the scenes above the water were filmed in Martha's Vineyard and the scenes below were filmed in Catalina, because its water was clearer.

The actress, meanwhile, really was nude, except for a harness with ropes yanked by crew members to simulate the shark jerking her around.

Some dialogue by Chief Brody's son Michael was dubbed by, of all people, June Foray, best known as the voice of Bullwinkle's pal, Rocky the Flying Squirrel. Hokey smokes!

Jankiewicz, by the way, has been a friend of mine for a decade. A man who celebrated acceptance of his *Just When You Thought It Was Safe* manuscript by splurging for a meal at Long John Silver's, and who can recite from memory triple bills at Ontario's Granada Theater from the 1980s, Jankiewicz is among Upland's bigger characters.

Or at least, at 6-foot-8, its taller characters.

No one-trick pony, the shark scribe is finishing his second book, about the 1977-1982 *Incredible Hulk* TV series, to be titled *You Wouldn't Like Me When I'm Angry: A Hulk Companion*. Give Jankiewicz this, he's got a knack for titles.

As for *Jaws*, the original movie was followed by three sequels. They may not have much artistic value, but as Jankiewicz tells it, the sequels boast strange stories – both on the screen and behind it.

Spielberg pitched an idea for a *Jaws 2* set in World War II about the days-long shark attack on the USS Indianapolis recounted in the first movie by Captain Quint. Interesting, eh? But the studio rushed ahead on a more direct sequel in which a new shark menaces the same town.

However, the director chosen for *Jaws 2* was soon fired. Scheider, the actor who played Chief Brody, was forced by his contract to appear in the sequel and was so angry about it, he got in a fight with the replacement director and choked him.

I vaguely remember being disappointed by *Jaws 2*, in which the shark attacks a low-flying helicopter and Brody kills it by getting it to chomp on an underwater electrical cable. Now I'm thinking he should have choked the shark instead.

Jankiewicz has seen the two further sequels, *Jaws 3-D* and *Jaws: The Revenge*, and says they're stinkers.

The third movie takes place in a water park and in the

fourth, Jankiewicz explained, "the shark chases Chief Brody's widow all the way to the Bahamas."

He offered to loan me the video. I declined.

But back to the original. *Jaws* was a phenomenon, spawning merchandise, parodies and spoofs. It's often considered the first summer blockbuster.

Jankiewicz and I can tell you more about *Jaws*, of course. But we're going to need a bigger column.

Mystery woman goes back to the past

July 7, 2010

One recent Saturday morning, an odd vision strode purposefully across the lawn: a woman in an 1880s-style dress, carrying a parasol.

I was sitting at my home computer, which faces a window that gives a view of the street.

She was crossing the street toward my landlord's home next door. Unsure what business my landlords might have with the 19th century, I kept typing. You never know what you're going to see in Claremont.

Five minutes later, there was a knock at my front door.

It was the woman in 19th-century garb, parasol over her shoulder.

No, she wasn't here to borrow a cup of molasses. But she did have a strange request, and with my landlords out of town, she turned to me.

"I'm a big fan of the *Back to the Future* movies," she explained, "and this house is the perfect backdrop to a photo I want to take. A man with a DeLorean will be here soon. Would it be OK if we drove the car part way up the driveway for the photo?"

Um... sure.

(In some life situations, there is no ready-made answer.)

With this command decision issued, I showered, shaved and dressed. Sometime later came another knock.

"The DeLorean is here," the woman said. "I thought you might like to see it."

Why, yes. Yes, I would.

There in the shared driveway was a DeLorean, both winglike doors open and aloft, as if the car were about to take flight. License plate: TYMECAR.

I was introduced to the middle-aged owner, who wore a *Back to the Future* T-shirt. He said he was approached by the woman recently and made an appointment. DeLorean owners get a lot of strange requests, many relating to the 1980s or to *Back to the Future*, in which a time-traveling DeLorean is a key feature.

"There are actually five DeLoreans in Claremont," he told me. "But the other four are in storage. Mine is the only one you'll see around town. I use it as my everyday car."

Meanwhile, the woman told me that she makes vintage clothes, including the 1880s-style dress she was wearing, which she thought matched the 1880s house next door perfectly. She also does work for Hollywood, such as clothes for two seasons of *Dancing With the Stars*.

A friend accompanied her. She was tasked with using a borrowed video camera to take still photos. This was not a smooth process.

"Do either of you know how to use a video camera?" the woman asked me and the DeLorean owner.

Sorry, no. And so the woman in vintage dress stood by the car, trying to look surprised – eyebrows up, eyes wide, fingertips against her cheek – while holding the pose for a solid minute until her friend could take a photo. The process was repeated. And repeated.

I had to admit I didn't know what this was all about. Only last summer did I see the first *Back to the Future* movie – in a free outdoor screening in downtown Pomona – and, well, it was cute, but maybe you had to have been a teenager in 1985 to appreciate it today.

The woman was stunned by my ignorance. (You readers, by contrast, are used to it.)

She said she was role-playing the 1885 schoolteacher from the third movie, as played by Mary Steenburgen. She made a period dress, found a period house by driving around town and found a replica of the movies' time-traveling DeLorean, all for the sake of photos for her scrapbook.

Mission accomplished.

The woman's friend suggested she pose inside the car. "You could wear a wristwatch," she brainstormed. "You could lift your sunglasses up and look at your watch and look surprised."

"I can't wear a wristwatch," the woman replied. "That wouldn't be appropriate for the time period."

True. But wasn't she wearing tinted glasses? And wasn't that a small jeweled stud in her nostril?

Before much longer, the photo shoot was over and the DeLorean owner was driving away. He promised to contact me regarding his participation in the plethora of DeLorean-related events planned for the car's 30th anniversary next year. As is usual in my line of work, I will probably never hear from him.

"Thank you for making my dream come true," the woman in 19th-century clothing told me earnestly before leaving as she'd come, in her 21st-century compact car.

And that was that.

Newspaper columns arrive in all sorts of ways. Some are cut and dried. Some must be courted over a period of time. Some require intense research.

Occasionally one falls in my lap.

But never, until now, had a column driven up my driveway and knocked on my door.

With bridge gone, one fewer kick on Route 66

July 28, 2010

Depending on your point of view, driving Foothill Boulevard between Rancho Cucamonga and Upland was either nostalgic or terrifying.

Some of us liked driving under that low railroad bridge with the closed-in concrete walls. Others didn't.

On my blog, reader Ramona said she would "involuntarily inhale to make myself (and my car??) thinner so I don't hit the side."

Cyclists had it worse, worried they'd be flattened against the wall if a vehicle passed. Pedestrians had to walk in traffic because there was no sidewalk.

"Narrow Subway," signs on either side of the bridge warned mysteriously. Perhaps only Jared Fogle could traverse it comfortably.

On Sunday, the Depression-era bridge was removed, the prelude to widening that "subway."

Now, the concrete abutments remain but there is nothing overhead. To quote John Lennon: "Above us only sky."

After hundreds of trips under the bridge, I felt like I owed it to posterity to see the structure come down.

And so Sunday morning I visited the construction site, forgoing my routine of reading the newspapers to go watch actual news being made.

I was given a hardhat and yellow vest to assert that I belonged – even though I clearly didn't – and to keep flying rivets from cracking my skull.

A bridge has traversed that spot since 1914. The current one was installed in 1929, when the road was last widened, to what must have seemed at the time like an absurdly expansive four lanes.

(Perhaps back then, motorists involuntarily exhaled to make themselves and their jalopies seem fatter.)

Until mid-century, the bridge carried Pacific Electric trolleys, back when Southern California had a functioning rail network, and also carried citrus from local growers.

For most of us, the quaint steel bridge, and the rural character of the surroundings, were a reminder of less harried times and the road's Route 66 past.

Removal of the bridge has been planned for years, stymied by lack of dough. Now that the estimated $19 million is secured, the project is finally underway.

The benefits are many, Councilman Sam Spagnolo told me at the construction site. Safety for motorists. Better access for cyclists and pedestrians. Completion of the trail that uses the bridge as a link. Addition of a trailhead park near the stand of eucalyptus trees.

That park sounds like a nice amenity. It will allow direct access to the trail, feature a timeline of city history and include a portion of the bridge.

A section of original Route 66 pavement has been uncovered, from an earlier alignment of the road, and that will be incorporated too.

By and large, residents seem supportive. Councilwoman Diane Williams said she's heard only a couple of negative comments.

"The widening of Foothill is far more important to the community than this bridge," Williams told me. "But it's a neat bridge."

Council members and City Hall department heads visited the site frequently in the bridge's final days to take photos and also to pose for photos, some of which are sure to be used in re-election mailers this fall to illustrate can-do action.

One construction worker joked Sunday to Williams: "If we'd charged 50 cents per photo, you'd have the bridge paid for by now."

Workers spent 12 hours Saturday pounding the concrete and rebar out of the bridge's base. That shed 100 tons of the bridge's 265-ton weight, according to associate city engineer Curt Billings, and probably worked faster than a lap band.

The bridge was freed of the linkages on both sides of the abutment and jacked up a few inches. Sunday morning, kevlar cables were wrapped around the bridge at two points, attached to two enormous cranes.

At 11:38 a.m., the bridge made popping sounds as it began to rise. Bits of concrete crumbled and fell.

Once in the air, the bridge was swung so that it was parallel to the traffic lanes, then slowly lowered. At 11:44, the 165-ton structure hung suspended 8 feet above the pavement as workers scurried underneath to build blocks to rest the bridge upon.

Nervous work if you can get it.

Nearly 100 people watched from nearby Baker Avenue, some taking photos or video. They applauded when the bridge was hoisted.

"Awesome!" one man said.

"Look at that thing," another said, impressed. "It's bigger than my house."

"Finally, you guys did something right," came one backhanded compliment.

One bystander in a green tank top and maroon sweatpants asked my *Bulletin* colleague Jennifer Cappuccio Maher if her photos would be online. He said casually that he was going to steal them for his blog. I imagine its title is "View From a Slob."

But back to the bridge, which at 11:57 was lowered onto the temporary supports. Known for doing things in a big way, Rancho Cucamonga now had not a disabled car but an entire disabled bridge up on blocks.

Before code enforcement could cite it as a nuisance, a trailer was slid under the bridge and the whole thing moved a quarter-mile to the east to the future trailhead park.

Not everyone is thrilled by the bridge's removal. On my Facebook page, reader Tracey Cook Turner wrote: "What a shame. Rancho marches along with their 'Destroy History' plan."

As a sentimentalist, I'm a little sorry to see the bridge go, although hearing about the trailhead park softened my reaction.

The bridge has been living on borrowed time. I'm pleased it lasted into this century, long enough for a latecomer like me to experience it.

Like a lot of things, the bridge mattered not just for what it was – something old and roughly beautiful – but for what it represented. For most people, Rancho Cucamonga, as a city, stopped at the bridge, which seemed like a boundary, a transition point between rural and urban.

Yet the city's borders actually stretch another one-third mile west to Grove Avenue, encompassing old-time restaurants (Sycamore Inn, Magic Lamp, Vince's Spaghetti and Red Hill

Coffee Shop) that "feel" like they're in Upland.

Not for much longer. Once Foothill is expanded to three lanes in each direction from Vineyard to Grove, Rancho Cucamonga's portion of Foothill Boulevard will be seamless, equal in appearance from Grove all the way to Victoria Gardens and beyond.

Progress? I suppose.

The abutments will be removed starting in October for the widening of Foothill, which is expected to take more than a year.

Until fall, then, motorists will have the slightly disorienting experience of driving under a phantom bridge.

"Narrow Subway"? No, just "Narrow Way."

RC BRIDGE LORE: LESS THAN MEETS THE EYE

September 3, 2010

Regarding my recent column on the removal of the old rail bridge over Rancho Cucamonga's Foothill Boulevard, a caller named Ted phoned to bring my attention to a local legend.

That would be the story that Sammy Davis Jr. lost his eye in an accident at that bridge in 1954.

Well, there's a reason I didn't include this "fact" in my piece on the bridge: It's not true.

The singer was returning from an engagement in Las Vegas when he was seriously injured in an automobile accident on November 19, 1954, and lost his left eye.

Several resources, including a history piece in this newspaper in 2008, give the location of the accident as a fork in Route 66 at Cajon Boulevard and Kendall Drive in San Bernardino. Davis was treated at two San Bernardino hospitals.

In fact, his healing included converting while in San Bernardino Community Hospital to Judaism. But that's a feather in San Bernardino's cap, not ours.

Just as Cher didn't attend Montclair High (but rather Montclair Prep in Van Nuys) and Jim Morrison never lived in Claremont (but rather the Clairemont neighborhood of San Diego), I'm afraid Sammy-in-Cucamonga is another rumored celebrity connection to the Inland Valley that doesn't hold up.

But if construction workers in Rancho Cucamonga unearth an eyeball, obviously we'll take a closer look.

ONE MAN WITH TWO LIVES AND MANY FRIENDS

August 27, 2010

Frank Clark was known in Rancho Cucamonga as the jocular, mustached man behind the counter at Nancy's Cafe.

At the popular breakfast and lunch spot he owned with his wife, his favorite trick was to whisk a customer's plate away between forkfuls, feign surprise that the customer wasn't done eating, then wink and return it.

In early 2009, he and Nancy divorced. And Clark became known in a second community, Upland, where he lived on the streets of downtown.

Quite a comedown. But the newly homeless man found a new home, of sorts, even in the alleys, stoops and trash enclosures of downtown. Merchants knew him as Homeless Frank and gave him a surprising amount of care.

On July 20, that new life ended. Having already tumbled far, Clark fell in a more literal way, rolling off a curb into the path of an oncoming car. He was 58.

A *Daily Bulletin* story on the accident drew 60 comments online, some from people who knew him in very different circumstances.

An informal tribute took place August 2 at First United Methodist Church in downtown Upland.

The church, at Euclid Avenue and C Street, set aside a time for any neighbors and friends who wished to say goodbye or make comments. The tribute was called "Remembering Frank." Fliers were printed.

Organizers didn't know what to expect.

"We got out 30 chairs. And we got out 10 more, and 10 more. There were 95 people there," Molly Brouse told me.

A musician sang the Eagles' "Desperado," one of Clark's favorite songs. ("Your prison is walking through this world all alone," one line goes.) Numerous people offered their reflections, including employees of J.D. Allison's, Caffe Allegro, the Grove Theater and 7-Eleven.

Clark's family spoke on behalf of the husband and father they knew, a man who was a mystery to most of the Uplanders in the audience. "They only knew him as Frank the homeless man," ex-wife Nancy Westenhaver told me later, amazed. "He had a whole other life there."

Nancy and Frank were married 17 years. She knew he had had problems with substance abuse before their marriage – "he was a child of Woodstock," she said – but thought he had conquered his demons.

But in 2008 he began hanging out with a bad crowd and behaving erratically. He moved out of the house and in with a girlfriend. He and Nancy divorced, he and his girlfriend broke up and he turned up in Upland.

Some first noticed him when he showed up for Good Friday services at the Methodist Church in April 2009. He took communion.

The Rev. William deBos, who had invited him, spoke with him privately. Clark was overcome with emotion.

"He said, 'I can't stop crying,'" deBos remembered.

Clark returned for a church barbecue, a pancake breakfast (where he refused seconds) and for services. He was also a fixture downtown, saying hello to merchants as he wandered the streets after packing up his bedroll for the morning.

He was usually unwashed, which did not encourage intimacy, but a friendly relationship developed.

"He talked, he greeted people, he knew about cars," said Brouse, who owns Molly's Souper restaurant. "We all cared about Frank even before we knew who he was."

A roofer with an office downtown may have been the first to connect the homeless man to Nancy's Cafe.

Perhaps because he was so recently employed, Brouse and deBos both say Clark was different from the handful of other street people they encounter.

He rarely panhandled, other than perhaps after a few drinks made him bolder. He turned down Brouse's offers of meals, although he did accept meals from others.

When a woman was crying outside the Methodist Church one day, Clark sat quietly and wanted to know only that she was OK, then moved on.

"He had his issues with addiction, but it never broke his kind and gentle spirit," deBos said. "It was a reflection of who he probably was."

Police in the self-proclaimed City of Gracious Living tend to encourage homeless people to head a few blocks south to Ontario, deBos said. Officers asked him to tell Clark to get off the church's property.

"All the more reason for me to let him stay," deBos told me, a twinkle in his eye.

Some merchants, led by Brouse, are hoping to do more for downtown's homeless. Clark, and his death, have made street people suddenly snap into place as individuals, not just streetscape.

"I have this sense now that I should have done more. A lot of us feel the same way," Brouse told me.

DeBos said he was surprised by the effect Clark had and is unable to completely explain it.

"You don't want to make more of him than he was," deBos said, "but he had an impact."

Clark did not completely sever ties to his old life.

He occasionally took the bus to Nancy's Cafe. He would ask for precisely $20, which Westenhaver or her staff would give him, but would decline offers of food or other assistance.

One visit he went table to table, shaking hands with customers, as if he still managed the restaurant, until Westenhaver gently directed her aromatic ex to wait by the entrance.

On another, she saw needle tracks on his arm.

"I was attacked by a pack of wild coyotes," Clark explained, embarrassed. "I wouldn't do drugs."

He visited the cafe again days before his death. He didn't look good. He said he needed $20 because he was getting his own apartment.

He looked at his ex-wife as if they'd never met.

She prefers to remember the Frank Clark she married, the one who, after their cafe's closing time, gently carried her children to the car.

Even in his down-and-out life, people saw something in Frank Clark.

An artist from Oregon met him when visiting Upland. She took his photo and, back home, drew his portrait in pencil, intending it as a gift on her next visit. By then he was dead.

The portrait was given to Nancy Westenhaver. She hung it high on the entry wall of her restaurant, above a chalkboard with the daily specials and near a shelf of pig figurines, a Norman Rockwell magazine cover and a sassy tin sign.

Westenhaver took the portrait down one day recently to show me. It depicts a bearded man with soulful eyes whose cap bears the motto "King of the Hill."

In small letters at the bottom, the artist wrote a title: "Frank, King of Upland."

Westenhaver said customers might think the subject is a generic grizzled fisherman.

"People might wonder who it is and why it's there. They don't know the connection he had here," Westenhaver said.

"It's my restaurant," she added firmly. "I think it should be here."

He ended his life rootless, addicted and confused. But memorialized on the wall of the cafe, keeping an eye on customers as they enter and leave, Frank Clark once again has a home.

IT WAS HEADIER THAN DANDELION WINE

October 13, 2010

The chance to introduce author Ray Bradbury at his talk in Pomona last Friday was offered to me tentatively ("would you be interested?") and accepted enthusiastically ("heck yes!").

Ray Bradbury, after all, has been the answer to the question "who is your favorite author?" since I was 10 years old. Evidently my tastes haven't changed much.

Bradbury was coming to Western University to talk about his novel *Fahrenheit 451*, the choice for Pomona's Big Read, in which students and adults alike are encouraged to read a single book and take part in activities or discussions.

For me, Friday's thrills started early. A couple dozen of us got to meet Bradbury in the green room – actually, a staff lounge – beforehand.

The Great Man was eating cheese and drinking wine with his biographer, Sam Weller, who was there to facilitate the later discussion.

In a wheelchair, somewhat immobilized due to strokes and practically deaf, Bradbury at 90 isn't someone to strike up a casual conversation with, at least when you're a soft-spoken fellow like myself, but I shook his hand – and gave him a treat.

Having read Weller's book carefully, I knew Bradbury's favorite candy is a Clark bar. They're not easy to find, but a month ago I made a special trip to Galco's in Highland Park, bought one and put it in my fridge, just for this moment.

"Thank you!" Bradbury said, looking delighted. He held the Clark bar up and kissed it twice. A handler tucked it like a cigar into the breast pocket of Bradbury's jacket for later.

Soon enough, it was showtime. The auditorium seats 350 and, because it's a lecture hall, is raked steeply. When filled, it resembles a wall of people.

Gulp. I took a first-row seat next to my friend Karol Almanzar, a Western University librarian who had approached me about speaking, and anxiously revised my notes.

Reader John Forbing stopped by and gave me a boost, telling me that despite my self-deprecating comments in this space, he knew I would do a good job.

It probably also helped that the other 250 or so people in attendance were unseen in another room, watching on video feed, where I didn't have to face them.

After comments by university President Philip Pumerantz and Mayor Elliott Rothman, I took the handheld microphone to a confidence-building round of applause.

Taking a tip from Pumerantz, I did what he had done and stood up against the first row. Not only was this an in-your-face position, it meant I could rest my notes on the table – rather than hold them in hands that might tremble with nerves.

"Ray Bradbury is one of the reasons I became a writer," I declared. After a pause, I added: "If you can call what I do for the newspaper 'writing.'"

From there I talked about discovering Bradbury's work in an anthology as a child, scooping up all his books and feeling a connection to him because, like me, he was from Illinois.

I had no expectation of ever seeing him in person. He lived in Los Angeles, an immeasurable distance away.

But in 1994, just weeks after I'd moved to Southern California, he spoke at the library in Big Bear Lake, not far from where I was living.

It was at this point in my talk that Muriel Spill of the Pomona Public Library suddenly appeared at my elbow.

"We need you to move," Spill whispered. "The camera isn't picking you up. They can't see you in the other room."

She took my arm and led me away.

I knew they would come for me someday, but I assumed they'd be wearing white coats.

I stopped at the spot where the university president had stood and began arranging my notes on the table again.

Before I could say a word, Spill again took my arm and began leading me backward.

"Hey, that spot was good enough for Pumerantz," I protested.

"You're still not on camera there," Spill whispered.

She positioned me by the desk where Bradbury and Weller would sit.

"You know, you're really killing this anecdote," I joked to the retreating Spill.

Just teasing, Muriel. I had to say something. As a friend in the audience put it later, "It was like you were getting a guided tour of the front of the room."

Actually, the interruption grabbed everyone's attention, which probably helped me, in a weird way.

Anyway, back to 1994. I waited in line nervously to have Bradbury sign a book. Eccentrically, he wore a shirt, necktie and jacket, paired with sneakers and tennis shorts. Business on top, party on the bottom.

I mentally rehearsed things to say to him, discarding all of them as dopey. When my turn came, I mutely handed him my book, he signed it and we shook hands.

Of course, I did say "thank you." We Midwesterners may be reserved, but we're polite.

Since then I've seen Bradbury at a few book signings. And in 2006 I mentioned him in a column about L.A.'s Music Box stairway, a setting he's used in three stories.

The day that column appeared, the phone rang at my desk.

"David, this is Ray Bradbury," his unmistakable voice said. "I read your column today about the Music Box steps. It was a good column."

What could I say? I said "thank you."

My remarks ended something like this:

"Four years later, here I am, helping welcome my childhood hero to Pomona. This won't be the highlight of his life, but it's a highlight of mine.

"And I still didn't know what to say to Ray Bradbury. Only one thing comes to mind. For 36 years of reading pleasure and inspiration, and as one Illinois boy to another: 'Ray Bradbury, thank you.'"

I got a nice ovation and passed by Weller and Bradbury. Weller gave me an attaboy. I looked down at Bradbury, who was looking off into space.

My guess is that he hadn't heard a word I'd said. But that's all right. He already knows people like him.

During his talk, Bradbury spoke about his inspirations for *Fahrenheit 451* and about his love of libraries.

He never had the money to attend college, instead educating himself by visits to the Los Angeles Central Library. For decades he's spoken at libraries without charge to repay that debt.

"I graduated from the library when I was 28 years old," Bradbury said. "Libraries are why I'm here. They are more important than the universities, more important than colleges."

Those comments and the interest in this year's Big Read were a boost to the Pomona Public Library, which has seen its hours slashed in an effort to save enough money to keep its doors open.

Besides enjoying Bradbury's fiction, I've taken some of my cues in life from his introductions to his books and from his public talks, in which he expresses a positive philosophy based on pursuing your passion.

"Do what you love and love what you do," he told the Pomona audience. "Don't do anything for money."

I agree wholeheartedly – which must be how I ended up in newspapers.

It was poignant to see the once-vital Bradbury hobbled by age, answering audience questions relayed to him by Weller speaking into his ear.

And yet even as he begins to resemble the mummified Thousand Times Great Grandmere from his novel *From the Dust Returned*, he's still got his marbles, his memory and his wit, and he's still Ray Bradbury, telling us he's working on his next book.

Afterward, he signed books, including one for me, a silent transaction. It might be the last time I ever see him.

Peeking up from his breast pocket, I noticed, was a red wrapper.

I imagined him unwrapping that candy bar on the ride home, or perhaps at his desk the next afternoon.

If that Clark bar brings him a few moments of joy, then I'm satisfied. I will have repaid a portion of my debt to him.

Surplus of memories follow passing of Miller's Outpost founder

October 31, 2010

The recent passing of Dave Miller, the founder of clothing giant Miller's Outpost, reminds us of a homegrown success story, one that started in an Ontario storefront. What became a jeans retailer began as Miller's Surplus, a shop in downtown Ontario selling Army and Navy surplus goods from World War II.

Every red-blooded boy's fantasy, right?

"They had jackets, canteens and that kind of thing," recalled Jim Bowman, now a councilman, who grew up in Ontario. "It was an amazing store for a young boy to go into and admire."

As a Chaffey High student, Bowman saved his pay from his after-school job as a dishwasher to buy an Air Force flight jacket for $15. "It made me feel like somebody," Bowman said with a chuckle.

The military stuff was in the basement. Upstairs was Miller's other specialty: jeans. Specifically, Levi's.

Levi's weren't commonplace in the 1960s, remembered Rick Gage, another Ontario native. Miller's was the only place kids knew of that sold the stiff, dark blue pants that had a cult following.

"I'm sure every kid in Ontario in the '50s and '60s went to Miller's to buy their jeans," Gage said.

Miller died October 8 at age 86. It was in all the papers, including this one, although the news seemed to have passed a lot of people by.

Mayor Paul Leon told me Wednesday he was saddened to learn of Miller's death.

"He was my first campaign contributor. He gave me a check for $1,000," Leon said. "He told me he would call me to scold me if I ever went in the wrong direction."

Numerous phone calls followed, Leon admitted.

He described Miller fondly: "He was like an older Barney Rubble. Short, square, flat head, jaw that stuck out." Miller, however, didn't have Barney's permanent five o'clock shadow.

The Ontario Library's Kelly Zackmann turned up some details on the store's early days for me.

Two brothers, Dave and Lou, founded Ontario War Surplus in 1948. The name changed to Miller's Surplus and the address changed a couple of times before the store settled in at 200 S. Euclid Avenue, with a second store at 418 E. Holt Avenue in Pomona; others followed.

The Ontario Miller's was on the corner of Euclid and Transit in the 1916-vintage Frankish Building, not far from the Post Office. The store was there from 1959 until the early 1970s, when the brothers went their separate ways.

Lou operated fashion stores named Lou Miller's, which in 1974 totaled six, with locations in Montclair (9460 Central Avenue), San Bernardino, Riverside, Orange, Whittier and East L.A.

Dave had Miller's Outpost, which specialized in jeans and other fashions for young people. In 1972, when the chain debuted, he had the two original stores in Ontario and Pomona, plus new locations in Upland (Eighth and Mountain) and El Monte.

In a 1972 advertisement in the *Daily Report*, Miller's Outpost offered an odd array of merchandise.

Amidst men's sweater vests ($4.88) and women's flared corduroys ($8.88) were tackle boxes (56 cents), cans of power steering fluid (19 cents) and plastic tarps (varied sizes and prices).

Miller's Outpost became a shopping mall staple in California and other states, selling jeans, casual wear and accessories while ditching the power steering fluid.

When the chain hit 100 stores, Miller threw a party, according to Brian Hurst, a former warehouseman.

"He was a nice man and would make a point to mingle on occasion with us lowly stockroom employees," Hurst, now an Ontario police detective, told me.

Under Miller, his employees were allowed to buy one complete outfit each month at half-price, Hurst said. (Which is way better than half an outfit at full price.)

Miller sold the company in 1980, shortly after the 100-store milestone, to the Amcena Corp., which expanded it to more than 300 stores by decade's end.

Amcena renamed Miller's Outpost store-brand jeans Anchor Blue. Later the stores were likewise named Anchor Blue, considered a teen-friendlier name.

So much for Miller's Outpost.

The Anchor Blue chain declared bankruptcy in 2009 and, under new owners, has slimmed to 110 stores.

How can they turn things around? Maybe what they need is canteens and flight jackets.

POLICE SAY SCAMS AGAINST THE ELDERLY ARE AGE-OLD

November 3, 2010

A tale recounted here in September was about a Rancho Cucamonga grandmother savvy enough to be suspicious when someone claiming to be her grandson phoned to say he was in jail in New York and needed bail money.

Dorothy West wisely refrained from wiring money to the alleged grandson and his alleged lawyer. She managed to reach her real grandson, who wasn't in a Gotham hoosegow but rather at breakfast only miles from her house.

Entertaining, if a trifle scary. And it turns out this was hardly an isolated incident.

Four readers – Maureen Hastings, Marilyn Fryer, Maureen MacGregor and Jan Fields – said similar ploys had been tried on themselves, relatives or friends. In each case, a caller claimed to be a grandson in trouble in a far-flung locale.

(Apparently a granddaughter in trouble would sound fishy.)

Others who've heard this tale before are the detectives in the financial crimes unit of the Ontario Police Department.

"The granny scam, that's what we call it," Diane Galindo said.

Galindo, Farlan Clutters and Brian Hurst, the unit's three detectives, sat down with me for a review of common scams against the elderly.

While most seniors are sharp enough to avoid the "granny scam," some are fooled.

"I just spoke with a 93-year-old widow who fell for it a few weeks ago. She wired $3,800 to Spain to get her 'grandson' out of jail," Hurst told me.

"Later in the day, his 'lawyer' called asking for $4,000 more to pay the bail. Luckily, this time the teller at the bank thought something was amiss and called the elder's daughter."

Good for the teller. Unfortunately, the woman is out her original $3,800 and there's little that police can do, given that the call came from overseas.

Speaking of overseas, an age-old scam involves foreign lotteries.

"Correct me if I'm wrong," Hurst asked his colleagues, "but can an American citizen win a lottery in a foreign country?"

"No," Galindo and Clutters said in unison.

Lotteries or other prizes often figure into woeful tales that end up in the newspaper.

A senior will be approached on the street by someone claiming to have won a substantial sum but needing money to claim it. This unlucky winner persuades the senior to go to the bank and withdraw, say, $5,000, which will enable the person to claim the prize, which will be split with the senior.

Of course, there is no lottery or prize and the senior loses the $5,000. No lottery asks for a processing fee before you can collect winnings.

These stories, while poignant, always mystify me. I figure seniors have seen it all. They're often tight with a dollar, by training or necessity.

So why do people who might give a grandchild a $10 check for Christmas fork over thousands of dollars to a stranger on the street? And why can't this stranger be me?

Sometimes the motivation is greed, the detectives admit, an impulse that might be coupled with a kind of satisfaction that they were chosen.

"They're going to be rewarded. 'Finally, the good Lord is looking out for me,'" Galindo said.

(Since it's a scam and they're being taken, the theological implications are best not dwelt upon.)

A kindly face, paired with a sob story, can override natural cynicism or common sense.

"It's trust. It's how they were raised," Galindo explained. "Your handshake is as good as your word. In the Depression, if a friend or neighbor needed something, they would give up their last clothes."

It's not always complete strangers who manage to trick elders. It can be hired help.

Galindo recounted a case in which a widow hired a handyman who began borrowing money against his wages. Even though the woman was careful to document every "loan," the total reached $40,000.

The bank alerted police. The woman was outraged. It was her money, and this man needed it.

"She was all alone. They begin forming an attachment with these people," Galindo explained.

Police persevered. The man was pulling the same scam on four other victims and he ended up getting 10 years in prison.

But this was too late for the Ontario woman. Her bank account was empty and her utilities were shut off. She has since died.

Even relatives sometimes take advantage of seniors. Hurst told the story of a granddaughter who moved in with her Ontario grandmother as a caretaker and persuaded her to take out a reverse mortgage on her home to extract its value.

The granddaughter siphoned $260,000 before she was caught.

The three detectives urged closer attention to newcomers, like handymen, around an elder's home. Family or close friends should also keep an eye on the elder's financial affairs, down to knowing their bank account numbers.

OK, but if there's a chance a granddaughter is going to steal your money in the guise of helping, why should elders trust their own relatives?

Don't simply trust one person, Galindo said. There's safety in numbers,

"It has to be a group effort," Galindo said. "The whole family has to get involved."

She likened this oversight to the operation of a business, where it's unwise to have only one person taking care of the books and counting the cash.

The detectives also urged bank tellers to be watchful.

"It would behoove bank tellers to keep an eye on their customers, especially their elders," Hurst said. "If you see something at all suspicious, please call police."

Ontario police detectives frequently give talks at senior centers and senior apartments about elder scams. If you're interested, phone your local police department.

Like immigrants, seniors are vulnerable to scams and are often hesitant to come forward. In the case of seniors, that's usually due to embarrassment.

Seniors might not want to admit to police, or even to family, that they've been played for suckers. That's human nature.

They may not even want to admit it to themselves. Galindo knows of an Ontario man still convinced he won a $5 million Jamaican lottery and that his winnings and a new car are arriving any day now, despite delays. Self-delusion is easier than admitting he lost $400,000 – yikes! – to ripoff artists.

But swallowing your pride and phoning police is important, detectives said, because the more victims they can find, the better a case they can build.

What do their own parents think of the detectives' vigilance?

"My mom says I'm paranoid," Clutters said dryly. "I tell her to shred every credit card offer."

"My mom says I've been a cop too long," Galindo added. Hurst doesn't hear that: His father is a retired cop who has made sure to get his estate in order.

Clutters, an Ontario native who has been with the Police Department 30 years, won't be investigating scams much longer.

"I'm retiring in December. But this fraud stuff is going to go on for hundreds of years," Clutters mused. "It's been going on since we've had currency."

MEN NEEDING TRIM WON'T GET SMART

December 12, 2010

In his 48 years cutting hair, barber Don Smart has seen hairstyles come and go and boys hit middle age. Now, Smart is retiring, closing his shop and cutting his losses.

Smart operates Sportsman's Barber Shop, 628 E. Holt Avenue, in Pomona. His last day is today.

"I can remember when customers said, 'I'll wait for the young barber,'" the white-haired Smart reflected. "Now I'm the old barber."

I stopped in Thursday afternoon for a chat – not for a trim, obviously – after a tip from reader Joseph Rodriguez.

Smart had already disposed of all but two barber chairs, scraped the sign off the floor-to-ceiling storefront window and taken down the rifles that lent the shop its name.

So there wasn't a lot left to see. Still, one of the two remaining, and battered, chairs has an emblem dating it to 1960; the other one is from 1965.

A rack of magazines near the door holds those mainstays of barber shops, *Popular Mechanics* and *Popular Science*.

A TV on a shelf was tuned to a rerun of *Everybody Loves Chris*. Next to the TV was a sign with the prices:

"Men & Boys $8. Style cuts, long hair $11. Flat tops $9."

Estevan Romero was in for a final trim. He'd been a regular since 1979. He'd tried other barbers, Romero told Smart, "but they don't have your special touch."

Smart has been saying a lot of farewells.

"A lot of friends and memories," Smart told me. "I like the people. You get an education in this job. You can learn all sorts of things. If I want to know how to lay a brick, I can ask somebody. It might not be straight when I lay it, but I'd know how to do it."

Smart is a man with a dry sense of humor. But the barber told me the name Smart has been a lifelong setup line for others.

"Get stopped by a cop or make a mistake in school with that name and hear what they say," Smart deadpanned as another longtime customer, Frank Flores, chuckled.

Smart hails from Pennsylvania and headed west in 1961 after a hitch in the Navy. He learned barbering to have a trade, working five days a week at a shop in Arcadia.

Looking for a sixth day of work, he happened upon Sportsman's in 1969. Owner Orville B. Chastain took him on. Smart was soon there full time.

Chastain had opened the shop in 1965.

"The day it opened, it was a beautiful clear day and you could see the mountains," Smart said, pointing north out the large window. "He was going to call it Mountain View Barber Shop until the next day and he couldn't even see the mountains. That's when it became the Sportsman's Barber Shop."

Smart bought the shop in 1976 and, tired, sold it in 1979. He hadn't had a vacation in 11 years.

"I came back and the new owner asked if I'd watch the shop for two weeks while he went on vacation. Two weeks turned into another 31 years," Smart said. "That's how that goes. This time I'm going, period."

The owner's widow decided recently she wanted to let the

lease go. She offered the shop back to Smart for free. But he decided to hang up his shears.

"It's time to go. I'm 73. I've been cutting hair 48 years," he said. "I didn't see my sons play ball. I should maybe watch my grandson play ball."

The shopping center across from the Ebell Club was the original site of Pomona High School. In its heyday, the center's main draws were a Hughes Market, Thrifty Drug Store, Newsboy Books and H. Salt Fish and Chips. It's now home to a Cardenas market and 99 Cents Only.

The neighborhood has deteriorated, and police don't seem to do anything about the "derelicts" who bring the center down, Smart said. Meanwhile, cheap haircuts are easy to find around town. Plenty of reasons to retire.

A large deer head formerly mounted on one wall beat him to retirement. A customer donated it because his wife didn't want it in the house.

"It was here 10 years. One day he came in and asked for it back," Smart said. "I said, 'I thought your wife wouldn't let you have it.' He said he changed wives."

The man's gain was the shop's loss.

"Kids used to like that deer head," Smart said. "I used to tell them the other half was in the laundromat next door. Sometimes they'd go look."

At Roberta's, you're always in with the Inn crowd

December 29, 2010

Roberta Virgin remembers her first day as a waitress at La Verne's Village Inn in 1977. It didn't go well.

"I hated it," she told me. "I was crying, my feet hurt, I said I'd never go back."

But her mother, Barbara, who also waitressed there, told her to stick with it. She did.

In fact, Virgin spent 24 years as a waitress, the last five as manager, before buying the coffee shop. Now that's working your way up. She even put her name on it: Roberta's Village Inn.

A year ago, burned out after 32 years at the business, she sold the Village Inn to her chef, Francisco "Pancho" Ramirez.

A mild tremor ran through La Verne, where the Village Inn is an institution.

"We all wondered how the transition would turn out," customer Jerry Dacus confided. "It has turned out great. The same atmosphere pervades as it did before. Everyone in town loves Pancho the way they did Roberta."

One reason the transition went so well is that Virgin remains involved.

She's now working as a teller at OneWest Bank a block

away from the restaurant, allowing her to pop in for breakfast and lunch.

Tuesdays and Wednesdays, she fills in for Ramirez so that he can take the days off – "although he never does," she added.

When I showed up on a Thursday evening for an interview, she was setting out utensils and napkins on tables.

"I'm here a lot," Virgin admitted.

(OK, let's deal with her name so we can move on. She was born Roberta Culling. Virgin is her ex-husband's name. She's that rare woman to become a Virgin only after marriage. Ba-da-bump.)

The Village Inn, which occupies a D Street storefront in the heart of downtown, is said to have opened in 1969. The two-story building dates to the early 1900s and has housed a meat market, the library and a five-and-dime, according to La Verne historian Galen Beery, a Village Inn regular.

The menu is American comfort food, and the decor is appealingly low on kitsch. What brings the place to life are the familiar faces, either the ones on the payroll or the ones in the booths.

"Everyone here is family," Dacus, a retired minister, said after finishing dinner. "I've said hello to 25, 30 people since I've been sitting here."

(Now that we've met, maybe he'll say hello to me next time.)

Rick and Nadyne Lapi, who were also having dinner, say the transition in owners has been invisible.

"The food's great, the employees are great, the people who come here are great," Rick said. "It's very homey, very comfortable."

"It's like the Cheers of diners," Nadyne said.

"Employees come over and ask how you're doing," Rick said. "And they care how you're doing."

The Village Inn has always benefited from an exceptionally loyal clientele.

There was John Richards, a plumber, who used the diner as his office.

"If anyone was looking for him, they would come in here or call. He was here every day," Virgin said. Seats at the counter are often occupied by regulars who sit in the same sequence. A large bunch from the Hillcrest retirement home walks there for breakfast once a week. Another breakfast group meets to swap town gossip and reminisce about old-time La Verne as Beery, the historian, jots notes for posterity.

When the doors open for breakfast, customers out on the sidewalk disperse to their usual booths.

"They run to their favorite spot," said Ramirez, the chef-turned-owner. "The girls have their water or coffee waiting. It also lets the other customers know those spots are taken."

Regulars announce impending vacations so their absence won't cause concern. Virgin always closed up in August for 10 days for her one vacation of the year. "A lot of people would plan their vacation around our vacation so they didn't miss us," Virgin said.

On 9/11, she debated whether to close the restaurant for the day but didn't.

"People were so glad we were open, and so glad we didn't have TVs. It's kind of a comfort zone," Virgin said of the restaurant. "People would be lost without it."

Virgin is a guarded person, but she did share the story of a personal tragedy from 1981, a traffic accident that put her son, a passenger in her car, in a coma for three years until his death.

Virgin was paralyzed on her right side, had to learn to walk again and taught herself to write with her left hand. She was off work for nearly two years. But customers didn't forget.

"They collected money for me when I had my accident," Virgin said.

When she was ready to come back to work, there was an opening for a waitress and she was rehired.

Ramirez was hired in 2001 while also working as a chef at Sierra La Verne Country Club.

Three days a week, he spent 6 a.m. to 3 p.m. at Roberta's, then 3 to 11 p.m. at the country club. Three other days he was at one place or the other all day. He had only one day a week off.

"Plus he has five kids," Virgin said. "Three of them are triplets. He's a hard worker."

When the triplets were born, customers chipped in $1,000 for diapers and clothes.

When Virgin, tired of the headaches of running a restaurant, decided to get out, a couple of other potential owners expressed interest, but she went with Ramirez, while retaining an ownership stake.

The sale became final on January 1, 2010. Ramirez, who left the country club, now takes it easy by working six days a week at only one job.

Virgin and Ramirez have a sort of mother-son bond.

Ramirez named one of his triplets Christopher, after Virgin's son. Ramirez is 35. "My son would be 36 if he had lived. I think that's why he and I are so close," Virgin said.

Always a breakfast and lunch spot, the diner is now open for dinner three nights a week, allowing Ramirez to stretch his wings in the kitchen. But not much has changed at Roberta's Village Inn.

Not even the name. Virgin said Ramirez fretted that scraping "Roberta's" off the sign, and adding "Francisco's," would hurt business.

Ramirez disagreed, telling me there's more than that behind leaving Roberta's name alone.

"I respect her a lot," he said. "There's no reason to change it."

So, Roberta's Village Inn it remains. Not a bad legacy for a woman who wanted to quit after her first day.

Counting down 2010's strangest news stories

December 31, 2010

The economy may be in the dumps for a third straight year, but 2010 saw a spike in one welcome area: weird news.

From coffee-drinking dogs to pot-purveying barbers, the Inland Valley saw a standout year, humor-wise. I had a hard time culling my collection of odd news stories to a mere 10. They're presented in descending order, from 10 to 1. Joblessness persists, but thanks to the year's silliest newsmakers, jokelessness is not an issue.

10. Can citizens at least watch Dancing with the Stars?

They're not footloose in Diamond Bar, where nightclubs are banned and city leaders ruled in January that dancing won't be allowed in any new restaurants or bars, either. Dancing at two existing bars will be grandfathered in – and in the city young people nickname Diamond Bore, perhaps only grandfathers are dancing.

9. We always cry at fake weddings

Pomona's then-Councilman Tim Saunders invited 300 people to his wedding at the Fox Theater in August but didn't disclose to guests that, oops, he'd just learned he was still married to his first wife. Voters retired Saunders in November, which should give him time to sort things out.

8. I'm a wreck without my morning coffee and chew toy

In April, a City News feature profiled Rosey, a 16-year-old dachshund in Rancho Cucamonga that slurps Costco coffee with cream each morning. The elixir of youth for this canine equivalent of a 112-year-old? Arf!

7. Is my watch 13 minutes slow?

When the chimes in Pomona College's Bixby Plaza clocktower were started up again in November after 10 years of silence, students decided they should ring on the 47th minute of each hour, from 9:47 a.m. to 5:47 p.m. weekdays. This ties into a tongue-in-cheek tradition on campus to "prove" that the number 47 appears in nature more often than any other random figure.

At the inaugural bell-ringing, the first 47 guests – the ones who remembered the ceremony began at 5:47 p.m. – received a clock necklace.

6. 'Counting money. What are you doing?'

Testimony in then-Rancho Cucamonga Councilman Rex Gutierrez's corruption trial included the tidbit that he exchanged 350 phone calls in 22 months with millionaire developer Jeff Burum, for an average of a call every other day. The pair also spoke by phone seven times – each call lasting under 30 seconds – during a council meeting.

As the *IE Weekly*'s George Donovan put it: "Why can't these dudes just poke each other on Facebook the way normal folks do?"

5. What part of 'irony' don't they understand?

In November, an anti-illegal immigration activist from Upland was turned away from a cruise to Mexico because she didn't know she had to have a passport. The law went into effect in June 2009. As a reader on our website put it: "She should be proud she got what she was fighting for, secure borders."

4. Business in the front, party in the back

At Groom Time barber shop in Pomona, the owner was arrested in May after police said a search of his car parked behind the shop turned up marijuana packaged to sell.

It was the bust that launched a thousand jokes. "That smell ... was not aftershave," cracked the *L.A. Times*. *IE Weekly* speculated that the shop's magazine rack held *High Times*, not *Maxim*.

I'm wondering if, at Groom Time, the time is always 4:20.

3. Where a speech really is an address

Under Mayor John Pomierski, Upland's state of the city events are breaking the mold. In 2008, Pomierski delivered his speech in Ontario, where he claimed the state of Upland was strong despite its lack of meeting facilities.

In 2010, the speech was never spoken. Instead, it was printed and delivered to residents by mail to avoid the expense of a ceremony. Punch and cookies were not mailed separately.

2. OMG, they're supremely out of touch

In April, the U.S. Supreme Court took up an Ontario lawsuit involving text messaging and, during oral arguments, seemed unclear what text messages are.

Chief Justice John Roberts, who is known to write legal opinions in longhand, asked the difference "between email and a pager." Antonin Scalia didn't know about service providers – "you mean it doesn't go right to me?" – and wondered if racy texts were ever printed out on paper and shared.

And our No. 1 weird news story of the year:

Suddenly, at the lifestyle center, a shot rang out

A gun brought to an outdoors store in Victoria Gardens in May for use in the firing range discharged unexpectedly at the front desk.

Blam! The bullet traveled 40 yards across the cavernous Bass Pro Shops showroom and struck a woman shopper in the keister, although the spent round didn't penetrate the skin.

The shooting was immortalized in the *Daily Bulletin* under the plain-spoken headline "Woman hit in butt at Bass Pro Shops."

Among the lingering questions: Was the hunter disappointed the woman couldn't be displayed as a trophy?

And does "Bass" have one letter too many?

2010 ITEMS

January 3, 2010

Some of the greatest flights of rhetoric occur not in literature or oratory but on the *Bulletin*'s Opinion pages. And they all seemed aimed at the left.

State Senator Bob Dutton, R-Rancho Cucamonga, probably set the tone in May with his guest column jabbing at "hard-left-leaning liberal Democrats." The phrase "liberal Democrats" has grown tired from overuse, necessitating a further, multi-hyphenated pejorative.

In subsequent broadsides, Dutton honed the phrase to "hard-left liberal Democrats." He also blasted "soft-on-crime Democrats," who are all too willing to capitulate to "unelected liberal judges."

The October 6 Opinion page brought two more verbal sallies full of color and verve, perhaps penned by students of Dutton's biting style.

A letter by Robert Almandinger decried the president's association with "progressive wing-nut extremists." And a guest column by Assemblyman Curt Hagman, R-Chino Hills, took aim at a fresh target, "extreme coastal environmentalists."

(But is it their views or their proximity to the coast that is extreme? Either could be irksome to an inland resident.)

All these word choices surprise and delight, linguistically speaking. At least that's what the shade of William Safire tells me.

After a two-month lull – and just about when I was going to hit the delete button on this stale item – a brand-new locution appeared on the December 22 Opinion page. Letter writer Gary Justus blamed the nation's woes on "a bleeding-heart, liberal hard-core minority."

As a fellow writer, I can only applaud everyone's effort – and anticipate the pacesetting Dutton's next flourish.

January 8, 2010

The movie *Up in the Air* begins with soul singer Sharon Jones' version of Woody Guthrie's "This Land is Your Land," with one significant lyric substitution: "This land is your land/From Riverside, California, to Staten Island."

January 22, 2010

For years I've heard of a Dave Allen who is vice president of marketing and sales at the Speedway in Fontana, but our paths never crossed until last weekend, when he gave a presentation at the Upland Public Library.

I attended, on the theory that the library would be quieter than the racetrack. Also, parking would be cheaper.

Allen talked to a small group about racing. Afterward, I introduced myself. He said that occasionally people will talk to him thinking he's me until he catches on and corrects them.

I appreciate them overlooking the obvious fact that the Dave Allen they're speaking to has a full head of hair and a goatee. Commendably, my readers are not hung up on superficialities.

Like me, Dave Allen suffers from having two first names, with people who are introduced to him often walking away saying, "Nice meeting you, Allen."

The two Dave Allens shook hands in farewell. The universe, thankfully, did not explode.

January 29, 2010

If you really want to hear about my reaction to J.D. Salinger's death Wednesday, the first thing you'll probably want to know is how many times I read *The Catcher in the Rye* and how much different *Nine Stories* is from all that *David Copperfield* crap, but (sniff) I don't feel like going into it, if you want to know the truth.

February 17, 2010

Walter Frederick Morrison, inventor of the flying disc that became the Frisbee, died February 9 in Utah at age 90.

Morrison sold San Gabriel-based Wham-O the rights to his Pluto Platter in 1957. Before that, he demonstrated and sold his discs around Southern California, including at the L.A. County Fair in Pomona.

As he tossed the platter back and forth with a helper, Morrison enjoyed telling fairgoers that the product traveled on invisible wires that came free with each purchase.

In the 1970s, Morrison operated Walt'z Hardware on Foothill Boulevard at today's Town Center Drive in La Verne. He returned to his native Utah in 1983.

I saw Morrison's obituary Saturday morning. Shortly afterward, while walking by the expansive lawn outside Bridges Auditorium, I noticed a couple of students tossing a Frisbee around on a picture-perfect Southern California afternoon.

Long may Morrison's memory soar.

March 17, 2010

It was an old-time L.A. weekend. I had lunch with one friend at Philippe's (founded 1908) and dinner with another at Musso and Frank Grill (founded 1919).

One old-time highlight, though, was a complete surprise.

On Saturday, cutting through the Grand Central Market (founded 1917) on foot, a friend and I emerged on Hill Street to see the Angels Flight funicular railway (founded 1901) back in operation!

Angels Flight, which closed in 1969 and reopened in 1996, had been closed again since a fatal 2001 accident. As money was raised for safety improvements and tests were made, numerous deadlines to reopen came and went.

But on Saturday, the old Sinai and Olivet cars were in motion up and down Bunker Hill and a uniformed man was standing by the open gate. I couldn't believe my luck.

Dazed, we climbed aboard for the short trip up. The wooden car had the pleasant click-clack sound I remembered. As one car ascends, the other car descends.

Halfway up, we passed the little terraced park immortalized in the movie *(500) Days of Summer*. The Joseph Gordon-Levitt character, who loved gazing at the vintage architecture spread out below him from a bench in the park, would be thrilled to see Angels Flight going again. Even if it did block his view.

At the top, we paid our quarters to the man in the ticket booth as photographer Gary Leonard, who's almost as much of a downtown icon as Angels Flight, captured the scene.

Apparently we had blundered into actual news: Angels Flight's reopening.

The strange thing was, we really did want to go up Bunker Hill, to the Museum of Contemporary Art, and I'd been calculating the best way to get there when I suggested taking the scenic route through the market. Must be my nose for news.

The next day's *L.A. Times* had photos too, reporting that "a group of mystery book aficionados got to ride the Angels Flight railway Saturday in advance of its public reopening Monday."

I guess I was part of a soft opening – and I wasn't even carrying a mystery book.

March 19, 2010

Dave Rife, the CEO of White Castle, was on CBS' *Undercover Boss* pretending to be a new hire in his own burger chain and, reported reader Mary Pineda, "his undercover name was David Allen." My undercover name is, of course, Dave Rife.

April 2, 2010

It's the end of an era at Pomona Cemetery, where Richard Rogers will be laid to rest Saturday on the same grounds he tended for half a century.

Rogers, 75, the cemetery's foreman, was looking for work in August 1961 after being laid off from the city of Pomona's parks department during a budget crisis. (Some things never change.) The 27-year-old was quickly hired by the cemetery as a gravedigger.

"He started when they dug graves by hand. He got the nickname of Digger," said Melody Baxter, the cemetery's general manager.

The cemetery switched to backhoes later in the 1960s, for which Rogers and his back were no doubt grateful. He became grounds supervisor in 1970 and later was named foreman.

Rogers was part of a tight-knit crew at the stately cemetery on South Towne Avenue, where the first burial was conducted in 1876.

"He said you really learn to appreciate life when you work in a cemetery," Baxter said.

"He was just a super nice person," said Sanford Newton, president of the cemetery board.

Despite heart trouble in later years, and advancing age, Rogers kept working, albeit in an administrative capacity and for half-days. He was employed at Pomona Cemetery for nearly 49 years.

"I don't know if anyone was more dedicated to his job than he was," Baxter said. "His life revolved around the cemetery."

He was stricken Monday while on the job. An ambulance came. Efforts to resuscitate him failed. Rogers didn't die at the cemetery, but he didn't make it much farther. On Saturday he'll return for good.

A Navy man, Rogers will be buried at 11 a.m. with military honors.

"I'm glad he'll be here instead of at Riverside National," Baxter said. "That way he can keep an eye on things."

May 9, 2010

On Thursday evening, hours after the stock market swooned, a newsroom colleague found this fortune in her fortune cookie: "Your best investment is in yourself."

May 19, 2010

High Expectations Dept.: A woman working in her yard in Pomona on Monday evening recognized me walking to my car, which was parked on her street, after a cheap pre-council meeting dinner at Tijuana's Tacos. We chatted for a minute.

She said, eyeing my battered, 12-year-old Corolla: "I thought that was you when you pulled up. But I wasn't sure. I figured you drove a Lexus."

July 23, 2010

One thing you've got to say about Rex Gutierrez, he doesn't put on airs. In the debut issue of his monthly newspaper, *the Vineyard Press*, the Rancho Cucamonga councilman writes a first-person piece, titled "One man's trash...," about picking up recyclables at city high schools while recently unemployed.

"Once I hit the jackpot," Gutierrez reveals. "I happened across the fields after an AYSO soccer tournament. I hadn't the bags to contain all my blessings. Since my sweat pants had elastic bands at the ankles, I stuffed 40 bottles and cans down my pants, all the way to the bottom."

Gutierrez continues: "This is the part where my wife asks, 'Have you no pride?' If anyone saw a lumpy little fat man wobbling through the field, it was me. But I don't care. I'm saving the planet!"

OK, thanks for oversharing!

This isn't Gutierrez's first public profession of combing through trash. He told our RC Now blog in 2008 that in an unofficial dump site he discovered a $25 gift certificate for a Victoria Gardens restaurant. He celebrated his find by taking City Manager Jack Lam to lunch (presumably after a change of clothing).

But let's look at the bigger picture. I have to say, I'm profoundly troubled by the prospect of a councilman with his own newspaper column. He's legislating *and* he's taking notes?

How am I going to get any scoops in Rancho Cucamonga under that deal?

July 25, 2010

A recent item here was about a customer at an Upland cafe whose request for a takeout box was met with a deadpan comment from the owner that boxes are not given and that he had to stay and finish his food.

Owner Rabi Albaghdadi later told me that the morning of that column, customers kept asking her for to-go boxes, and she didn't know why.

When one man sat down and immediately asked for a to-go box – before he'd even ordered – she asked him what the gag was and much of the dining room joined him in laughter.

(This will teach Albaghdadi never to go into work without having read the newspaper.)

The capper, Albaghdadi said, was when a 7-year-old girl

entered the restaurant and, having been prompted by a relative outside, asked sweetly, "Can I have a to-go box?"

August 20, 2010

If you want to buy a ticket to an event at Ontario's Citizens Business Bank Arena, you may have to time travel into the past. According to the venue's website: "Tickets may be purchased at Robinsons May, Tower Records, The Wherehouse, Ritmo Latino and other participating locations."

Must be boilerplate language. Most of these chains closed before the arena even opened.

I would suggest the arena update its website. For instance, it could say that "participating locations" include Fedco, Zody's and White Front.

October 27, 2010

So what did I do on my week off? For one thing, I reread *Fahrenheit 451*, then led a book talk Saturday at the Pomona Public Library as part of its Big Read slate of activities. The talk was attended by seven people, only one of whom wasn't a librarian. (Thank you, Ray Contreras.) Well, it made for a cozy event.

Other than that, my activities included a concert in Pomona, an opera in L.A., errands, laundry and organizing. I also visited four restaurants. Among them was the Homestyle Cafe.

As some of you may recall, the Homestyle Cafe was forced out of Guasti because of a pending redevelopment project – motorists on the 10 Freeway or near ONT can see how well that's worked out – and ended up in Chino.

Its signature item remains the pancake, which is a foot across and nearly an inch thick.

Feeling it was my duty, I ordered the pancake combo,

which is two cakes, two eggs and two sausage links. I polished off the auxiliary items but could only finish half of one pancake.

The staff is prepared for such an eventuality. For a take-home container, they give you a cardboard pizza box. The pancakes keep much better than in foam, and it's kind of a novelty.

"The customers get such a kick out of it," manager Tommy Hornbake told me.

This was on Wednesday. On Thursday I finished that leftover half-pancake, adorned with butter and syrup from separate plastic containers included in my pizza box. That left one entire pancake.

Friday, for a light breakfast, I had a quarter of the pancake. Picking up the pace, on Saturday I had one-third. Sunday I ate the rest.

Five meals in one? I guess so.

So what did I do on my staycation? Mostly, I ate two pancakes.

December 5, 2010

In Claremont, a man by the name of Grady Righthand has been arrested on suspicion of battery after clocking the host of a college party.

At about 1 a.m. November 21, the host asked Righthand if he'd enjoyed himself, to which Righthand is said to have replied, "I'm going to kill you."

With that, according to Tony Krickl in the *Claremont Courier*'s Police Blotter, "Mr. Righthand clenched his fist and punched the victim in the nose with his right hand before walking away."

Police later cited this Righthand man, who did not explain his actions.

Personally, I don't want them explained. I merely want to admire the delicate lace holding this tale together. If

Righthand were a lefty, the whole item would have been ruined.

Along the same lines: Does Righthand know what his left hand is doing?

December 26, 2010

Riding Metrolink east from L.A. earlier this month after a Sunday in the big city, some of us became entranced by a fellow passenger performing magic tricks.

He wasn't wearing a tuxedo, instead being clad in street clothes, a cap and black sneakers paired with white socks. He could just as easily have been hustling for change somewhere. But instead he was doing a trick with a nickel, which a fellow passenger initialed with a marker and handed over.

"Are you ready to see the impossible?" the magician asked from his seat across the aisle.

The nickel went into his pocket and seconds later was found within a pouch within a small matchbox within a larger matchbox, each of the three objects wrapped twice in a rubber band.

"This is all observable," the man said, keeping up a smooth line of magicianly patter, albeit with a more streetwise edge than is typical.

He next pulled out a pack of cards.

"This is the best four-ace trick in the world," the man began. "Prepare to be blown away."

He was laying out cards in the carpeted aisle as I stepped past, the train nearing my stop. People were leaning from their seats to watch and two small children were sitting in the aisle, rapt.

Just a little magic on Metrolink.

About David Allen

David Allen has been digging up stories in the Inland Empire for three decades. After starting his career at newspapers in Northern California, he moved south to work in Victorville for the *Daily Press* and then to Ontario for the *Inland Valley Daily Bulletin*, his home since 1997. His popular column covers people, places, government, history and more with a light and humane touch.

Besides the *Daily Bulletin*, his work appears in print and online in *The Press-Enterprise*, *The Sun* and other Southern California News Group newspapers. His work has been collected in four earlier books, all published by Pelekinesis: *Getting Started: 1997 to 2000*, *On Track: 2001 to 2005*, *Pomona A to Z* and *100 Years of the Los Angeles County Fair, 25 Years of Stories*.

A native of Illinois, he didn't grow up in the Inland Empire, but he's lived here longer than he lived in the Midwest, so what does that tell you?

112 Harvard Ave #65
Claremont, CA 91711 USA

pelekinesis@gmail.com
www.pelekinesis.com

Pelekinesis titles are available through Ingram, Gardners, directly from the publisher's website, and at your favorite local bookstore.

www.ingramcontent.com/pod-product-compliance
Lightning Source LLC
Chambersburg PA
CBHW020322170426
43200CB00006B/239